MW00343953

CELEBRITY GODS

Celebrity Gods

New Religions, Media,
and Authority in Occupied Japan

Benjamin Dorman

University of Hawai'i Press
HONOLULU

17 16 15 14 13 12   6 5 4 3 2 1

Library of Congress Cataloging-in-Publication Data
Dorman, Benjamin.
Celebrity gods : new religions, media, and authority in occupied Japan /
Benjamin Dorman.

   p. cm.—(Nanzan library of Asian religion and culture)

  Includes bibliographical references and index.
  ISBN 978-0-8248-3621-4 (hardcover : alk. paper)
   1. Mass media in religion—Japan—History—20th century. 2. Religion and
state—Japan—History—20th century. 3. Japan—Religion—20th century. 4.
Mass media—Japan—Religious aspects. I. Title. II. Series: Nanzan library of
Asian religion and culture.
   BV652.97.J3D67 2012
   201'.7095209044—dc23

                         2011022202

Acknowledgment is made to the following organizations for permission to
reprint images: page 91, Photograph 208-PU-58E, © Still Picture Research Room
(National Archives at College Park, MD, USA); pages 138, 141, and 152, © *Asahi
Shinbun* (Tokyo); pages 146, 172, and 193, © *Mainichi Shinbun* (Tokyo); page
164, © *Hokkoku Shinbun* (Kanazawa); page 200, © *Bungei Shunjū* (Tokyo).

Contents

Acknowledgments

THIS BOOK began with a discussion in 1997 at the Nanzan Institute of Religion and Culture with Robert Kisala, who suggested an investigation of the Occupation period. Through him I was able to spend time at the University of Tokyo under the guidance of Shimazono Susumu, who was generous with his time and advice. He introduced me to Tsushima Michihito of Kansei Gakuin University and Fujii Takeshi of Tokyo Gakugei University, experts in Jiu and Tenshō Kōtai Jingū Kyō respectively. They allowed me access to their materials and facilitated contacts with the groups. Nakano Tsuyoshi of Sōka University gave me a copy of his index of SCAP records relating to religion, which proved to be an invaluable guide at the beginning of the project.

I am indebted to the staff of the Japanese Political History Materials Room, National Diet Library, Tokyo, the archivists at the National Records and Archives Administration II building in College Park, Maryland, and those working at the Gordon W. Prange Collection at The University of Maryland.

At the Australian National University, I benefited greatly from the advice and constant support of John Powers. I was also lucky to have John Caiger, a great educator and mentor, on my side, and Tessa Morris-Suzuki provided excellent suggestions in times of need.

This research was supported by scholarships from the Japanese Government (Monkashō) and the Australian National University. I was able to carry out additional work through a Foreign Correspondents' Club of Japan Scholarship and a 20th Century Japan Research Award from the University of Maryland's Center for Historical Studies.

Jiu members Katsuki Tokujirō and Yamada Senta, despite their advanced ages at the times I interviewed them, provided valuable insights about Nagaoka Nagako (Jikōson). Members of Tenshō Kōtai Jingū Kyō consented to an interview at their headquarters in Tabuse, Yamaguchi, and Kitamura Kiyokazu, the granddaughter of Kitamura

Sayo, generously shared important materials. Wilton Dillon agreed to two extended interviews about his experiences as an Occupation press officer. Kawakami Tsuneo, formerly of the *Nihon Keizai Shinbun*, and Nishide Takeshi, formerly of Kyōdō News Service, offered vital perspectives on religion and the media in contemporary Japan.

Ian Reader has been particuarly encouraging throughout various stages of this work. I would also like to thank Clark Chilson, Erica Baffelli, Nishimura Akira, Victor S. Hori, Ōtani Eiichi, John Breen, Barbara Ambros, Levi McLaughlin, Daniel Metraux, Scott Schnell, Helen Hardacre, Jackie Stone, and John Jorgensen. Naturally, I assume responsibility for any errors within the book.

While all my colleagues of the Nanzan Institute for Religion and Culture and Nanzan University have been very supportive, Paul Swanson and James Heisig deserve special mention. Their unique attributes—scholarly rigor and technical expertise, combined with good humor and flashes of brilliance—have been a gift.

Finally, thanks go to my family, and especially my wife, Tomoko.

Introduction

IN 1934, the journalist and critic Ōya Sōichi (1900–1970) wrote an article that depicted leaders of new religions that were active at that time as "star gods" (*kamisama sutā*).[1] Ōya's caustic wit runs throughout the piece, which focuses on groups like Ōmoto and Hito no Michi. Despite their popularity, he claimed, these new religions were mere flashes in the pan of modern Japanese society. They looked to their predecessors, the new religions of the Meiji period, to gain their inspiration while promising the public something new. Their leaders enjoyed mass adulation at the time, and were soon to experience widespread opprobrium. Within a short time these two groups were harshly suppressed by the authorities.

Throughout his long career, Ōya displayed an uncanny knack for producing catchy phrases that summed up his cynicism while neatly capturing moods that resonated with his readers. Ōya eventually became one of Japan's most famous journalists, and his name is associated with an eponymous and prestigious literary award, the Ōya Sōichi Prize for Nonfiction (*Ōya Sōichi Nonfikushon Shō*). In 1995 the prize was awarded to Egawa Shōko. Egawa was the independent journalist whose exposés on the religious group Aum Shinrikyō highlighted its nefarious activities well before the sarin gas attack on the Tokyo subway system perpetrated by members of the group earlier that year. Considering Ōya's long-standing interest in religion, she was a highly suitable choice as recipient of the award.

Ōya's prewar work on "star gods" was not his first or last foray into reporting on new religions. He contributed the following observation to the major newspaper *Asahi Shinbun* on 10 October 1948 when Japan was still under the Allied Occupation (1945–1952):

> Although the public has forgotten about Jikōson, who caused a stir immediately after the termination of the war, a "dancing religion" has appeared in the city and is the subject of much discussion. Postwar society is a veritable hotbed in which pseudo religions flourish. They feed on the ignorance of the public who, in the postwar chaos, lack the power to judge right from wrong. The causes for this lie in the breakdown of feudalistic

traditions, the purge of the bureaucracy, and fears of another world war. Singing and dancing is a feature of this new group. The fact that some intelligentsia has joined the religion is of concern. Dealing with these types of groups is a major problem facing the authorities.

Jikōson (born Nagaoka Nagako, 1903–1984) was a woman who led a small religion called Jiu, whereas the "dancing religion" (*odoru shūkyō*) referred to Tenshō Kōtai Jingū Kyō, a group led by another woman named Kitamura Sayo (1900–1967). Kitamura was labeled "the dancing god" (*odoru kamisama*) by the press, although most of her supporters referred to her as Ōgamisama, "great god." Their groups were the first of many new religions to be covered by the Japanese print media during the Occupation into the early 1950s. While these women are no longer household names in Japan, for a brief period they were known nationally and widely portrayed through a variety of print media. Most of the media coverage was highly critical. These two leaders are the "celebrity gods" of this book.

This book examines the cases of these two women and the media representation—through print media in general, including newspapers, magazines, and books—that coincided and contributed to their brief period of celebrity and notoriety during a crucial time in Japan's religious and social history, the Allied Occupation and the postwar period up until the early 1950s. In order to explain their cases, which involve complex interactions between new religions, media workers, Japanese government and Occupation authorities, religious authorities, intellectuals, and ordinary people, I take a historical approach in explaining the relationships between these various parties.

In considering the leaders and followers of the groups themselves, and the impact of press reporting, it does not focus on issues concerning audience reception, such as how readers of the media reacted to the representations. Furthermore, it does not focus in detail on individual journalists' ideological motivations for reporting religious leaders in particular ways, but rather considers the trends of reporting that existed, and the social circumstances that influenced those trends. It is primarily concerned with media representation and its impact, and also with the development of themes from the Meiji period within media that have affected new religions at different periods in Japan. While media reporting can have a powerful influence on how a group is perceived, the reactions of the groups to press reports also play a significant role in their eventual trajectories. The behavior and attitudes of the groups themselves, and the decisions they make with regard to their interactions with "outside society" impact on media representations.

Finally, the purpose of this book is not to present an argument about unfair media treatment of minority religious groups resulting in a tale about social inequities that goes back to the Meiji period. Nor is it to expose the stories of little-known groups whose behavior was widely reported as being deviant and socially abnormal for a time. It is primarily to explore the historical reasons concerning why certain representations of new religions developed, and how and why images were produced, reproduced, altered, and perpetuated in the print media. Examining these issues from a historical perspective can provide clues concerning contemporary circumstances and events, such as the case of the new religion Aum Shinrikyō in the 1990s.

NEW RELIGIONS AND SCHOLARSHIP

Jiu and Tenshō Kōtai Jingū Kyō are generally described as new religions (*shinshūkyō*) in Japanese scholarship. The beginnings of Japanese new religions are usually located around the middle of the nineteenth century when popular religious groups began to appear as the feudal system of the Tokugawa period began to disintegrate. The groups were essentially "new" in an institutional or organizational sense compared to the established religions of Buddhism, Shinto, and Christianity. In many cases, the doctrines of the new religions of this period were mixed with Buddhist, Shinto, folk, and in some cases Christian beliefs. While there are a number of issues and debates associated with the actual term "new religions," this book will not dwell on them.[2] Hayashi Makoto indicates that there are significant "blanks" in the sociological study of new religions in Japan from the 1910s to the 1960s. He concludes that the "study of modern new religions as a whole has passionately discussed the 'beginning' and the 'end' of the history of new religions" but has left a major gap.[3] This book aims at addressing this lacuna for part of this period.

Scholars who study new religions in Japan have noted the conflicted relationships these groups have with the authorities, the public, and the media in their quest to promote themselves and their aims. Some have observed that from the Meiji period (1868–1912) onward, media reporting on new religions in Japan has been predominantly negative.[4] While the reasons for this are complex, patterns and trends relating to profit, ideologies, and social control can be distinguished from historical cases.

Groups that either caused or were represented as being the cause of social conflict often stimulated the public's interest in newspapers and magazines.

In the case of the new religion Renmonkyō in the Meiji period, which will be discussed further, a popular newspaper called *Yorozu Chōhō* increased its circulation partly through rumor and salacious tales concerning the group. But the explanation of profit seeking is only part of the story behind the intensity of the negative reports. Developing ideas of ideology, gender, and identity in the Meiji period played a significant role in the Renmonkyō case. The group's leader, a woman, was rumored to have engaged in "immoral" practices, an unacceptable image compared to "traditional" roles of women. Furthermore, she and her followers were accused of promoting "superstitions" and spurious healing techniques at a time when the state was emphasizing loyalty to emperor and nation, adherence to Confucian, patriarchal morality, and Western, scientific "rationality." Bureaucrats and the media employed terminology derived from Confucian discourses on religion and morality whereby practices that were perceived to be inconsistent with the state or "rational" Confucian interests were proscribed. They used terms such as *jakyō*[5] (the English equivalent used in Western media is the pejorative term "cult") that reflected broader social and official attitudes, and the *Yorozu Chōhō* used such negative terms to describe Renmonkyō. Newspapers at that time saw part of their role as educating the public and protecting the interests of the nation.

In the Meiji period, press criticisms of government actions, or lack thereof, toward "dangerous" new religions could be used to show the public that the press was acting to protect the purity of Shinto at the same time as showing how the bureaucracy was failing in its duty to protect the ideals of emperor and nation. New religions were eventually classified as "pseudo religions" (*ruiji shūkyō*) in government documents, and this was also picked up by the press to indicate groups that attempted to claim legitimate status as recognized religions, yet were highly questionable in doctrine and methods. By the 1920s, another new religion, Ōmoto, had achieved spectacular growth in a short time, just as Renmonkyō had some thirty years before. By this stage, other terms such as "newly arisen religions" (*shinkō shūkyō*), which carried a highly negative meaning, appeared in the 1930s and became a common journalistic catchphrase applied to new religions.

These issues, including the motivation of the press, had an influence in the cases of Jiu and Tenshō Kōtai Jingū Kyō in the immediate postwar period. However, compared to groups such as Ōmoto, Sōka Gakkai, or Aum Shinrikyō, Japanese and Western scholars have paid relatively little attention to these two small groups. While it may seem that their impact on Japan's religious and social history is minor, investigating these cases helps in understanding the issues other new religions faced at the time and can also provide clues with regard to the relationship of new religions, media, and authority in general.

After Japan's surrender in 1945, the Occupation authorities, collectively known as SCAP, introduced unprecedented freedom of religion.[6] Under SCAP's new regime, Japanese government authorities could no longer interfere in the affairs of religious groups. SCAP's liberal religious policies encouraged an efflorescence of new religions, which included some that were completely new, others that had existed since the Meiji period, and a number that had been suppressed by the Japanese authorities before the Occupation began. H. Neill McFarland titled his 1967 work on Japanese postwar new religions in a phrase that originally came from the media—"the rush hour of the gods" (*kamigami no rasshu awā*)—although other journalistic phrases such as "sprouting like bamboo shoots after the rain" (*ugo no takenoko no yō ni*) were also popular at the time.[7]

JIU AND TENSHŌ KŌTAI JINGŪ KYŌ

Jiu began in the early 1940s and was a Shinto-based group that had loose ties to Ōmoto, which had been comprehensively suppressed by the authorities in 1935. Jiu had a problematic relationship with the Japanese authorities before the end of the war because its doctrines conflicted with the orthodoxy of state-imposed Shinto. In January 1945 police arrested Jikōson but released her soon after due to lack of evidence. After the Occupation began, Jiu's problems with the Japanese police continued. The group was somewhat inept at public relations, or at least at negotiating compromises with those who were not part of its inner circle. Jikōson was inaccessible to most ordinary people and her followers worked to protect her from what they perceived as negative forces. The group's fortunes changed significantly after some famous followers of Jikōson—Go Seigen (1914–), a champion of the strategic board game of go, and Futabayama (1912–1968), a sumo champion and national hero—began to promote her teachings and millennial predictions.

Go and Futabayama embodied what sociologist Chris Rojek describes as "achieved celebrity," which derives from the perceived accomplishments of the individual in open competition. In contrast, Jikōson's eventual notoriety was "attributed celebrity," which is not related to someone's particular talents or skills but is "largely the result of the concentrated representation of an individual as noteworthy or exceptional by cultural intermediaries."[8]

Journalists played a major role in the case of Jiu as cultural intermediaries—those who develop and manipulate the public presentation of celebrity personalities in ways that can elicit positive or negative reactions from the audience. The participation of Go and Futabayama in the group triggered an explosion of press interest, predominantly from major newspapers and their local subsidiaries. Jiu and Jikōson suddenly became the focus of national attention. The group moved to the town of Kanazawa where it attempted to gain popular support. Naturally this drew the press to the town. Jikōson made various predictions about calamities that would befall the country, and Go and Futabayama marched through the streets with banners, calling for townspeople to take up Jikōson's teachings. The police, however, were concerned that Jikōson's millennial predictions might have a negative effect on social stability. Key members of the group, including Jikōson and Futabayama, were arrested under the lights of press cameras and taken to the police station. The charges included possession of weapons (ceremonial swords) and illegal hoarding of food, but the main purpose of these public arrests was to prevent Jiu from continuing its activities. Most of the press condemned Jikōson as a mad woman, whereas they portrayed Futabayama as a hapless buffoon who had been duped.

Although Jikōson and Jiu's attitudes were not the only factors that led to this situation, they were certainly crucial. Thus, a combination of bad press and official intervention by the police effectively curtailed Jiu's activities, the celebrity followers renounced Jikōson, and the group gradually disappeared from the public eye.

Tenshō Kōtai Jingū Kyō developed from the visions of Kitamura Sayo, a farmer's wife from a small town in Yamaguchi prefecture, who openly attacked the existing social structures, including the government, all other religions, and almost anyone who opposed her views after the surrender. Kitamura claimed that the "absolute god of the universe" resided in her stomach, and she began to attract attention in her hometown and surrounding areas before the surrender. But it was only in the postwar environment of freedom of religion that she began to attract significant media attention.

Unlike the case of Jiu, where national papers seized on the story, a local newspaper in her prefecture of Yamaguchi first reported on Kitamura. As her influence began to grow Kitamura started to travel across the country to spread her millennial predictions of disaster and salvation under a "kingdom of god." By mid-1947 the major newspapers had begun to take notice, although most of the reporting referenced the incidents surrounding Jiu, which were still circulating in media texts. As time passed, however, Tenshō Kōtai Jingū Kyō developed its own identity within the media. The group's practice of *muga no mai* (often translated as "dance of ecstasy"), in which participants swayed about in a seemingly random fashion, was mocked by many journalists, and Tenshō Kōtai Jingū Kyō was attacked in many media reports. Despite significant and sustained criticism in the press, Kitamura and her group displayed quite remarkable growth in the first few years of the Occupation. She attempted to turn the media criticism to her advantage, and called the media attention she received "god's strategy."

Kitamura's confrontational and dynamic style of leadership, together with her relative openness, contributed to significantly different relationships with the press. If she felt any disappointment over the negative press she eventually received she barely showed it, at least in public. She appeared to revel in the attention the press gave her and welcomed journalists who wanted to investigate her. In her public sermons and other activities in Tokyo and other cities and areas, she harangued passersby, she demanded her photograph be printed, and she disrupted proceedings at events to which she had not been invited. Inspired by her example, some of her followers took a strident stand on occasion. Under her guidance, the group managed to grow and eventually establish branches overseas but media attention dwindled significantly after Kitamura's death in 1967.

The reactions of the leaders and followers to the press coverage they received were significantly different. Jikōson avoided contact with the public and while Jiu's insularity was a significant factor in generating press suspicions, the involvement of Go and Futabayama also contributed to Jiu's problems. The famous followers left the group and it gradually disappeared from the public eye. On the other hand, Kitamura Sayo proved to be a master of self-promotion, and *Seisho*, the written record of her teachings, boldly states that bad rumors others spread can be used as a means of proselytization.[9] Kitamura's confrontational and dynamic style of leadership, together with her relative openness, contributed to the significantly different relationships Tenshō Kōtai Jingū Kyō had with the press compared to Jiu.

Both leaders advocated radical, albeit quite different, millennial teachings that presented grave predictions of disaster followed by their own versions of restructuring or renewing society. Catherine Wessinger has pointed out that the concept of "millennium" in scholarly discourse has changed from its original meaning of a period lasting one thousand years to become a synonym for belief in a collective terrestrial salvation.[10] Michael Barkun argues that the combination of disaster and the millennium, the first suggesting death and desolation while the second offers salvation and fulfillment, are themes that intertwine again and again in different societies.[11] While Tenshō Kōtai Jingū Kyō and Jiu advocated their own understandings of millennial world renewal (*yonaoshi*), such ideas of disaster and renewal have long been recognized in Japan. Although *yonaoshi* ideas varied in the details, they generally involved a sense that people were living in a time of crisis that would be resolved by some kind of divine intervention, resulting in a utopian world that promised better conditions for those who had faith. Forms of world renewal played a part in a number of different social protests in the early modern period, such as peasant uprisings and some new religions. For example, Yasumaru Yoshio has considered the cases of Fujikō, Maruyamakyō, and Ōmoto and their ideas of *yonaoshi* and investigated how their founders deviated from emperor ideology.[12]

AUM SHINRIKYŌ AND ITS AFTERMATH

While this book takes a historical approach in examining the interrelationships between new religions and media since the Meiji period and specifically during the Allied Occupation, any consideration of the relationship between media and religion must take into account the case of Aum Shinrikyō of the 1980s and 1990s. Although Aum-related incidents occurred some fifty years after the Occupation began and the media and social landscape was vastly different, the Aum affair provides a useful reference point to reflect on the historical cases raised in this book.

On 20 March 1995, members of Aum Shinrikyō perpetrated the most serious case of domestic terrorism in postwar Japan. The poisonous sarin gas they released in a series of coordinated attacks on the Tokyo subway system killed twelve people and injured thousands of others. Televised images of the aftermath of the horrific incident that showed victims lying prone on the subway floors or stumbling around in a daze gasping for air were broadcast around the world.

The "Aum incident" marked a turning point for Japan in terms of religion, media, and society. Just as the cases in Western countries of the People's Temple, the Branch Davidians, and the Order of the Solar Temple marked critical junctures in public understandings of religious movements, the name Aum Shinrikyō has become synonymous with a number of issues including religious violence, "cult behavior," social deviance, relations with religious groups and the state, media responsibility, and academic responsibility. It has had a deep effect on Japanese society. It is not surprising that in the years since the Aum affair the image of religion in Japan in general has become more negative, particularly among young people.[13]

Helen Hardacre has discussed the case of Aum in terms of print and broadcast media. In this analysis, Hardacre points out that after the sarin attack scholars and the general public alike depended heavily on media representations and information received through print and broadcast media. In discussing "manipulative techniques" and "sinister pictures" of religion these media used in the case, she calls for more scholarly understanding concerning "the processes by which the media produce meanings and attempt to control and market them, appreciating simultaneously that the 'semiotic excess' created by media technology, especially on television, means that readers and viewers play central roles in the creation of the meanings attributed to the news."[14]

This is not an issue that only affects Japan, and over the past few decades there has been more scholarly attention concerning the role that media play in shaping understandings of religion in general. Stuart Wright contends that scholars who have studied mass media coverage of new or nontraditional religions in other countries have been concerned with "the role of the media in constructing narratives that accentuate a particularly sinister picture of new religious groups, as if these innovations are intrinsically pathological or harmful to both their own members and society."[15] Underlying these concerns is the serious problem that faces religious groups that do not resort to violence or abhorrent behavior yet are effectively tarred with the same brush in certain media as groups that do. In general, the image of religion worsened in the wake of the Aum case.

Aum's extremely violent tendencies appeared early in its life and escalated as the group became more isolated from society. Furthermore, the social circumstances of Japan during the Allied Occupation were vastly different to the 1980s and 1990s leading up to the sarin gas incident. But the key issue of public understandings of religion based on media representation, and Hardacre's call for more scholarly understanding regarding media production, control, and marketing of "meaning" is significant. Rather than trying to place "new religions" on one side and "the media" on the other, this study calls for a closer examination of the factors that surround incidents involving new religions and the media representation that affects not only the groups concerned but media consumers in general.

AUM AND THE MEDIA

One way of considering Aum Shinrikyō is to investigate its relationship with the media that reported its activities and the dominant themes of representation that developed. Aum was one of a number of groups that appeared in the 1970s and 1980s which appropriated ideas that were outside of mainstream thought. It nevertheless attracted the interest of young people and benefited from a general mass media interest in groups that were active in this milieu. Aum grew at a time when there was increasing dissatisfaction particularly among young people with the Japanese education system and the work ethic, and a sense that spiritual satisfaction may exist outside the traditional structures of religion. Esoteric practices related to Tibetan Buddhism, psychic powers promoted by entertainers such as Uri Geller, prophecies by Nostradamus, New Age ideas imported from the West—these elements of spirituality and philosophy were introduced to people through various media.

Aum first came to public attention through a confrontation with the weekly magazine *Sandē Mainichi* in the late 1980s. The magazine ran interviews with families who claimed that Aum had "stolen their children," which were charges that had previously been leveled at the Unification Church (Tōitsu Kyōkai) and Jesus Ark (Iesu no Hakobune) in the 1970s and 1980s. The confrontation pitted traditional parental concerns with the constitutionally guaranteed right to freedom of religion. Aum Shinrikyō reacted against the *Sandē Mainichi* and launched a campaign to embarrass the editor, Maki Tarō. While television, radio, and other tabloids criticized Aum for its stance, the group's strategy of going on the offensive gave its leaders the opportunity to appear on television and present their case. Helen Hardacre notes that Aum leaders in media interviews effectively managed to counter the charges leveled at the group by simply denying them. Not only did the group use the confrontation as an opportunity for self-promotion, "the media lost all authority in live interviews with Aum leaders."[16] Nevertheless, the group was committing crimes by this stage, and launched a failed election bid in 1990.

A significant aspect of Aum's media strategy involved Asahara Shōkō, its leader. According to Ian Reader, in order to counter his negative image and that of the group in other media, Asahara launched a "charm offensive" and met various well-known personalities, such as Beat Takeshi, and various scholars.[17] Aum's own media published interviews that indicated they were apparently impressed by Asahara. Similarly, the Dalai Lama was reported as speaking positively about Asahara's efforts to promote Buddhism in Japan. The group's publications presented Asahara and senior leaders as being spiritually advanced beings, performing feats of levitation and pursuing ascetic practices. While it is not surprising that its own media would attempt to present a positive face, Aum Shinrikyō's public relations division attempted to improve its public image and appear to be open to scrutiny by facing its critics and opponents in the mainstream media.

On 28 September 1991 representatives of the group, including Asahara, appeared on *Asa made nama terebi*, a live four-hour-long television program on the major Asahi network. The main theme of the program addressed the question of why young people appeared to be turning to religion. It included a panel of academics and critics, and featured a debate between Aum representatives and those of its rival, Kōfuku no Kagaku.[18] Each party had the opportunity to present their philosophies and social contributions.

The Aum representatives came prepared, and they showed a well-constructed visual presentation that advertised the group's cultural exchanges with countries such as Laos, and included shots of Asahara meeting various dignitaries, such as the Dalai Lama and Buddhist leaders from Sri Lanka. Watanabe Manabu holds that Aum Shinrikyō representatives fared better than those from Kōfuku no Kagaku.[19] Another important factor, according to Nishide Takeshi, one of the few Japanese journalists with extensive experience in reporting religion, was that Asahara himself appeared on the program and left many commentators with a somewhat favorable impression. Kōfuku no Kagaku's leader, Ōkawa Ryūhō, did not appear and this had a negative effect on the group's image.[20] After the program aired, some academics made favorable comments on Aum Shinrikyō. This successful performance on television gave Aum Shinrikyō and Asahara a degree of authority in the public sphere within some circles relative to its major rival. Aum managed to assert itself as an authoritative voice among the new religious groups that young people were turning to, partly because of its claims to tradition. It also managed to stave off concerns among some that it was an unsavory religion.

Thus, there were relatively positive appraisals of Asahara after Aum applied its media strategy, and they were certainly more favorable compared to those after Aum's crimes and his personal involvement in them came to light. Asahara became, according to Ian Reader, "a figure of immense notoriety, portrayed in the media not simply as the main villain of the affair but as a personification of evil, a fraud and manipulator who beguiled idealistic young people into following him and into carrying out fanatical deeds on his behalf."[21] Reader continues, making the salient point that these images became a convenient way of explaining Asahara and the affair because after the gas attack, in the media's eyes, "[Asahara] was always evil, hence the affair was a manifestation of evil. He was always a fraud, hence Aum Shinrikyō was not a real religion." This image of the fraudulent religious leader remains powerful, and the facts that have been revealed so far about Asahara's deeds serve to justify the image.

SOCIAL MOVEMENTS AND MEDIA

Focusing on "the media" on the one hand and "religion" on the other tends to draw a sharp line between media that report religious groups or represent them in certain ways and the groups themselves. This is particularly so when considering a striking incident such as the Aum Shinrikyō case. According to Stewart M. Hoover, while early considerations of media and religion viewed them as separate entities that could be considered as acting independently, in reality "[a] good deal of what goes on in the multiple relationships between religion and the media involves layered interconnections between religious symbols, interests, and meanings and the modern media sphere within which much of contemporary culture is made and known."[22] This suggests that interactions between religious groups and their leaders and the media are crucial in the formation of narratives and images. These images will change over time depending on the circumstances. Hoover's perspective acknowledges the role that religious groups have in affecting the media, and vice versa.

Borrowing from the work of William Gamson and Gadi Wolfsfeld, new religions can be considered as social movements that present "a sustained and self-conscious challenge to authorities or cultural codes by a field of actors."[23] They argue that the relationship between the media and social movements is greatly imbalanced given their respective needs. From the media's perspective, stories about a social movement may provide photo opportunities, even drama, action, and conflict, which are the essential ingredients for promoting circulation.

Ultimately the media have far greater power because social movements are more dependent on the media. For example, social movements are generally concerned with engaging in public discourse or spreading their message, and the media can act as a promotional tool. The media have access to an audience that the group may not normally access through its own efforts, such as proselytizing in public or relying on word of mouth to spread the teachings. Also, a social movement may attempt to use the news media to validate its position. Once a movement is reported in the media, influential individuals or groups may then recognize it, be attracted to its message, and possibly lend support. Furthermore, media coverage may validate a movement in terms of public perception. If a group is reported in the media, there is a chance that the publicity will provide it the opportunity to be taken more seriously. Finally, media coverage presents an opportunity to broaden the scope of conflict.[24] A public conflict could allow the movement to gain some sympathy, as it were, or to improve its public standing. While this may be one way for new religions to challenge "the authorities and cultural codes," in reality Japanese new religions have rarely gained public support through the media in this way. Rather, the publicity has the potential to backfire against the movement if there is a broad perception that the messages the group espouses run counter to cultural norms.

One exception is the case of the new religion Kōfuku no Kagaku, which embarked on a high-profile propagation campaign at the beginning of 1991.[25] Although the group made skillful use of the mass media in advertising its name, after an event in July criticism, primarily in the print media, began to build against the group. *Friday*, a weekly magazine published by the Kōdansha company, ran a critical article on the group's founder, Ōkawa Ryūhō. In response, Kōfuku no Kagaku members bombarded the Kōdansha office with complaints by fax and telephone, the group mounted legal challenges, and a National Association of Kōdansha *Friday* Victims, which included prominent celebrities, organized public rallies.

Although, as Trevor Astley indicates, these actions indicated a shift of Kōfuku no Kagaku's focus from study to "aggressive activism,"[26] the group did gain public support for its campaign to change the ethical standards of the Japanese press. In the autumn of 1994 Kōfuku no Kagaku instigated a campaign to stop publishers violating a law forbidding the display of pubic hair (referred to in Japan as *hea nūdo*, "hair nudes"). Demonstrations were held in Osaka and Tokyo, with a reported 70,000 participants, and in November 1994 the Media Ethics Research Group (Masukomi Rinri Kenkyūkai) was set up to tackle the problem of loose ethics in the mass media. However, the public support in this case for Kōfuku no Kagaku was due to this ethical stance rather than its reactions to the criticisms against Kōdansha. In fact, from this point on, Kōfuku no Kagaku developed a reputation as a confrontational organization. After the Aum affair, the group was all but ignored by the mass media, and it was only when it began fielding candidates for the general elections of 2009 that the group began to appear in the news again.

KYŌSO AS MODELS

Scholars sometimes look at the cases of the founders of groups of new religions, including examining personal histories, to uncover the motivations of the activities of the groups they lead. Investigating the veneration of the founders or leaders of new religions has long been an important theme in sociological studies of religion in Japan.[27] The study of *kyōso*, a term that can refer to the founders or leaders of groups, was particularly strong during the 1970s and 1980s when new religions including Aum Shinrikyō, Agonshū, and GLA (God Light Association) appeared to be attracting young adherents.

In her examination of Ōmoto's Deguchi Onisaburō, Nancy Stalker points to the importance of charismatic leadership in new religions, particularly in their initial stages of growth. She reiterates the need for such leaders to have the ability to develop three specific areas. First, they need to command loyalty from followers and display a talent for prophecy or healing, and assume spiritual authority through revelations. Second, the leaders would need to be able to empathize with many people and establish a large following. Third, as described through the work of theorists such as Max Weber and Jean Comaroff, there is a revolutionary component of religious charisma that involves challenging established religious and secular authorities at various levels.[28] Stalker presents the idea of charismatic entrepreneurship, which is "a combination of spiritual authority, innovative use of technology and the mass media, and flexible accommodation of social concerns not addressed by the state or mainstream religions."[29] She argues that Deguchi Onisaburō's entrepreneurial flair was critical to the success of Ōmoto in many ventures. In showing how Onisaburō epitomized charismatic entrepreneurship, Stalker holds that Ōmoto effectively provided an important model and legacy for new religions that followed in the postwar period, including Jiu and Tenshō Kōtai Jingū Kyō. She also demonstrates how Onisaburō cultivated and developed his own image in order to maximize his exposure through a variety of media and public appearances.

The notion of charismatic entrepreneurship is appealing because it encapsulates characteristics that Onisaburō had in abundance: superb, if idiosyncratic, leadership skills; remarkable resilience; the ability to recover quickly from setbacks; an eye for new opportunities; and a willingness to change in the face of extreme pressure. Furthermore, the idea of applying business-model ideas to new religions that are seeking to make some impact in society can also be useful. One obvious area is the use of media to promote their activities, which Stalker presents in the case of Ōmoto. New religions make use of their own media to spread their message, and Japanese new religions have long produced media including newspapers, film, and *manga* to promote their leaders' visions. The leaders are often presented as exemplary figures and this plays a vital role in connecting members of a religious group to a shared identity and shared vision.

But the idea of considering Ōmoto and Deguchi Onisaburō as models requires some caution. There were a number of groups such as Seichō no Ie, Sekai Kyūsei Kyō, Mahikari, and Jiu whose founders had some connections with Ōmoto. The idea of Ōmoto's legacy might be reasonably applied in the sense that some ideas were shared between these groups. But Jiu had highly individualistic traits and methods that suggest problems with the new-religions-as-models notion. As Shimazono Susumu has shown, there are no archetypal founders or leaders.[30] Part of the appeal of new religions and their founders lies in individualistic claims to legitimacy and charismatic authority. Just as scholars may be tempted to demonstrate how groups are "modeled" on other groups from the past, journalists have sought to explain new groups in similar ways based on historical cases.

The claims made in various media regarding new religions and their leaders from the Meiji period through to the Occupation period shared a number of traits. Most of the print media coverage of the activities of Jiu and Tenshō Kōtai Jingū Kyō was highly critical. Religions were generally perceived by journalists in the postwar period as incompatible with the ideas of democracy, in addition to being "irrational." However, while both established religions and new religions were criticized, new religions were singled out particularly for promoting superstitions, folk remedies, and magic healing practices that were potentially hazardous to society. Jiu and Tenshō Kōtai Jingū Kyō were touted in the media as the first postwar "models" of problematic new religions. In describing them, journalists looked back to new religions of the past, such as Renmonkyō and Ōmoto.

The patterns of negative reporting about new religions developed from the Meiji period and eventually reflected the changing political and social conditions of the periods that followed. Media representations were products of multiple voices—journalists, government authorities, leaders of traditional religious institutions, psychologists, social critics, scholars of religion—each promoting a particular social vision or worldview concerning the new religions, which were often described variously as superstitious and irrational, "pseudo religions" or "evil cults." Individuals often attempted to influence the representations in a way that privileged their own social vision or worldview of new religions. While the following list is not exhaustive, new religions were often described as sharing some or all of these characteristics: (1) they advocated doctrines which were somehow suspect and dangerous to the public; (2) they engaged in medical quackery and illicit sexual practices; (3) they were involved in fraud of a material or financial nature; (4) their founders were mentally unstable; and (5) the people who followed the groups were either uneducated or they lacked the ability to judge right from wrong.

These representations were disseminated through the media and they influenced public opinion and general debates about new religions in society. After the Allied Occupation revoked the power of the Japanese state authorities to determine the validity of religious groups, the ideas about new religions continued to be reflected in the postwar print media, and they had a significant effect on the way that Jiu and Tenshō Kōtai Jingū Kyō were portrayed. Print media descriptions of the two groups during the postwar period reflected, and to a certain extent built upon, negative journalistic views about new religions that had been developing since the Meiji period. Journalists and other media commentators invariably returned to these issues in describing new religions, often citing the "models" from the past. One significant difference, however, was that religion was no longer controlled by the state. In the new era of imposed democracy, the media still drew on the past in describing new religions.

A key element of the "models of new religions" for media workers was the representation of the leaders and founders. As figureheads who were able to influence and attract followers from different walks of life, they were the focus of media attention. The representations often depended upon previous "models" of founders and leaders, and these models had an influence on the leaders and founders who followed them. In order to explain the term "celebrity gods" and how it applies to Kitamura Sayo and Jikōson, we now turn to contemporary ideas of celebrity, and the relationship between celebrity and religion.

CELEBRITY AND REPRESENTATION

The study of celebrity in Western scholarship includes considerations over the ephemeral nature of fame and the famous, and questions over "celebrity culture" and representation. Although Daniel Boorstin's conception of a celebrity, defined in his classic work *The Image* as "a person who is well-known for their well-knownness"[31] is probably the most widely known, it is not universally accepted. Graeme Turner argues that Boorstin's dismissal of a celebrity as "human pseudo event," someone who has become famous through the trivia of personality, developed from an elitist distaste for popular mass cultural practices.[32] Recent scholarly work has tended to emphasize that celebrity is not "a property of specific individuals. Rather, it is constituted discursively, by the way in which the individual is represented."[33] P. David Marshall views celebrity as a phenomenon that is a form of cultural power through which meanings are negotiated and organized.[34]

While certainly not being the only approaches on the subject, Boorstin and Marshall refer to the ubiquitous nature of fame, which is often described as "celebrity culture." In attempting to describe this, scholars have sought to locate the historical roots of celebrity. Graeme Turner shows that the standard view is that the spread of the mass media, particularly the visual media, is attached to the growth of celebrity.[35] Richard Schickel suggests that celebrity began with film contracts in Hollywood in the early years of the twentieth century,[36] whereas Neil Gabler argues in his biography of gossip journalist Walter Winchell that the culture of celebrity began with representations of celebrities' private lives in modern newspapers.[37] On the other hand, Leo Braudy claims in his monumental work that fame has a history in Western societies that can be traced back to early Roman times.[38] Tom Payne delves into examples of classical literature to argue that the process of exalting famous people and then tearing them down, which can be seen in the contemporary cases of Madonna and Britney Spears, for example, is part of human nature.[39] Rather than attempting to define a version of celebrity culture native to Japan and its historical beginnings, this study is concerned with media representations related to celebrity that affect new religions.

Media representation, Chris Rojek argues, "is at the heart of both the question of the mysterious tenacity of celebrity power and the peculiar fragility of celebrity presence."[40] He defines the phenomenon of celebrity as "the attribution of glamorous or notorious status to an individual within the public sphere." This position recognizes that "glamour" and "notoriety" are usually thought of in polarized terms.[41] Glamour, or positive attributes of fame, might be associated with, for example, a well-known model, whereas notoriety would be linked to a mass murderer. Apart from any moral considerations, Rojek suggests that those who become "glamorous" and those who become "notorious" are linked together by the impact they have on the public consciousness and culture. A common story that permeates media in all cultures is that of once great figures, for example movie stars or other performers, and even politicians and other public figures, who "fall from grace"; formerly positive representations are replaced by negative ones.

The "fragility of celebrity presence" recalls Max Weber's idea that the important aspect of charismatic authority is not the individual traits of charismatic leaders so much as the interaction and physical proximity between the leaders and followers. A charismatic leader's position is legitimized as long as the followers recognize their qualities.[42] As such, charismatic authority is precarious and dependent on perceptions of followers and their connection to the leader.

The connections between religion and celebrity have been raised in a number of studies. Media scholar P. David Marshall argues that "charismatic leaders of religious cults may have been the early purveyors of celebrity culture, where ideas moved through these individuals and their prophets who relayed stories of their unusual power and influence over the many."[43] Chris Rojek discusses celebrity and religion in general terms in relation to shamanism, Durkheim's idea of collective effervescence, and celebrity rituals of ascent and descent.[44] John Frow, on the other hand, investigates the apotheosis of Elvis Presley among fans, thus focusing attention on the individual celebrity.[45] In Stephen Prothero's examination of the trajectory of the image of Jesus in the United States from the 1920s to the current day, he argues that the image transformed from "character to personality," from "personality to celebrity," and finally to a "national icon."[46] Questions concerning religion and celebrity raise the issue of the phrase "celebrity gods."

CELEBRITY GODS

"Celebrity gods" appears in Malcolm Boyd's *Christ and Celebrity Gods: The Church in Mass Culture*, which was a theological examination of what he terms "the celebrity cult, outside and inside the Church." As a Christian minister who had worked in the entertainment industry, Boyd described the dangers of people slavishly following celebrities. Fame in the wrong hands was a potentially troublesome social condition that required a theological cure. In Boyd's eyes, the celebrity gods of the day were entertainers of the time, such as Liberace, Marilyn Monroe, and Elvis Presley. But they also included "church celebrities" like Norman Vincent Peale whose "system of techniques, of publicity, of preaching and writing seems to have accommodated biblical and theological considerations to the uninformed desires of the public."[47] He argued that celebrities are "symbols of various motifs of life" and that ordinary people "share vicariously in their obviously tragic-comic lives."[48] Although they write from different perspectives, Malcolm Boyd shares with Daniel Boorstin a distain of celebrity worship as inauthentic, and they both consider the phenomenon of celebrity as ephemeral yet potentially dangerous to the public.

"Celebrity gods" tends to be used in popular media to describe superstars such as Michael Jackson, who was the posthumous subject of an article published in the online version of *USA Today* titled "Why do we have celebrity gods?" In this article, religious studies scholar Gary Laderman states that in the United States "celebrity culture can produce icons who become immortal [and can be] incorporated intimately into the lives of some fans and serve as pivotal, ultimate points of reference."[49] Michael Jackson also made an appearance in an article published by ReligionLink, an online source for the Religion Newswriters Association, on 4 January 2010 entitled "Celebrity gods: The religion of stardom," which argued the following:

> The secular culture has canonized any number of "saints," from politicians like Abraham Lincoln to explicitly religious figures like Mother Teresa. But the bestowal upon an entertainment icon or pop culture celebrity, usually after his or her death, of a public reverence that rivals that of a religious figure appears to be a modern phenomenon.

In attempting to answer questions about the "cult of celebrity" and whether it is a religious phenomenon, the article suggests that "celebrity gods" are deceased figures from the entertainment world whose lives are far beyond the reach of ordinary people. In drawing on the case of Michael Jackson, these figures somehow achieve apotheosis irrespective of the notoriety they may have gained while alive. Laderman again appears in this article, arguing that Jackson achieved this status: "Like other saints, he will be forgiven by his public, and I expect, an inspiration and role model, in some ways, for those who want to make music, become famous, or leave a mark in this world."[50] This question of the public redemption of celebrities is extremely important, and it plays a role in the story of Jikōson's famous follower, the sumo wrestler Futabayama.

The idea that a religious leader could be labelled a "god" (*kamisama*) in the Japanese context is not unusual. Jikōson and Kitamura Sayo were viewed as living gods (*ikigami*) by their followers and supporters. The media used terms such as "dancing god" or "god on the run" to refer to these individuals, but in most cases the intention was to subvert the idea that the special status they had somehow achieved would be a positive force for society.

For the purposes of this book, "celebrity gods" is used specifically to indicate two aspects relating to the images of these leaders and their representations. The first, which reflects Weber's ideas of charismatic authority, concerns the ability of these religious leaders to attract attention to themselves and act in ways that made them appear special. In doing so, they also sustained supporters through their interactions with them. The second aspect involves a broader argument concerning media representation, referring to the ways in which media external to the founders and leaders of new religions represented them. These *kyōso* are discussed in relation to representations of religious figures of the past, and in terms of the impact they have on contemporary society and the future. As such, representations often concentrate on a version of the past, present, and future, and often include a discussion of potential consequences. While there were isolated and minor examples of relatively positive reporting on Kitamura Sayo, for the most part it was highly negative; on the other hand, Jikōson was portrayed as a notorious figure in media reports.

STRUCTURE OF THE BOOK

This book proceeds with two basic arguments—the first historical, the second sociological. With regards to the first, print media descriptions of Jiu and Tenshō Kōtai Jingū Kyō during the Occupation and postwar periods reflected primarily negative representations of new religions that had developed in the national media since the Meiji period. The main change in reporting involved the changing social and political conditions of the period of the Allied Occupation. The second argument considers the question of "celebrity gods" and the extent to which the new religions were active participants in the creation of their public image as it was represented in the media. "The media" refers primarily to print media sources, such as major newspapers or their local subsidiaries, and books that were published at the time. There are four main reasons why these media are considered in detail, as opposed to other media. First, the journalists who were linked with these groups, including Ōya Sōichi, presented their work in print media form. Second, the groups and their leaders reacted to what these journalists wrote in newspapers and magazines. Third, the Occupation authorities, and particularly SCAP's Religions Division officers, relied on articles (or translations of articles) that appeared in the Japanese print media concerning new religions. Finally, by focusing on print media representations of these two groups, it is possible to trace the images of the predecessors of these individuals as they appeared in print.

Chapters 1 and 2 deal with the prewar cases of Shimamura Mitsu and Deguchi Onisaburō, the leaders of Renmonkyō and Ōmoto respectively. Renmonkyō was a mid-Meiji period new religion, and Shimamura began her career as a faith healer. As her reputation grew, she developed a substantial following and some trenchant critics within the media. Renmonkyō developed around the same time as the growth of Japan's modern newspapers. Deguchi, on the other hand, was a flamboyant and apparently multitalented individual whose sometimes dazzling leadership attracted trouble from the authorities and censure from the press. Both these individuals and the groups they led were later referred to in the postwar press as models for new religions that appeared in the postwar period, particularly Jiu and Tenshō Kōtai Jingū Kyō. These chapters focus less on the charismatic aspects of these leaders and more on the development of the media and the interactions between new religions, authorities, and society in the different periods. The rise of Renmonkyō coincided with the formation of the media's dual roles of "watchdog" and "servant" at a time when issues of orthodoxy and heterodoxy were crucial in the development of ideas concerning the emerging nation. A quarter of a century after this, Onisaburō took over the leadership of Ōmoto, and effectively thumbed his nose at the authorities by engaging in public displays that challenged the status quo, including riding a white horse in public (something only the emperor was allowed to do). Nancy Stalker has already ably demonstrated his propensity for self-promotion through public exhibitions and the use of new image and media technologies, which enhanced his charisma and gained new audiences.[51] Therefore, this chapter focuses on media criticisms and representations of Ōmoto and Onisaburō.

Chapter 3 traces the prewar beginnings of Jikōson and Kitamura Sayo and deals with the growth of their groups under their leadership. External media representation did not begin at this point but the chapter highlights key events in their lives, including interactions with the authorities and the public that eventually took on significance during the immediate postwar period when the publicity surrounding them was at a peak.

Chapter 4 is concerned with the major legal changes that occurred with regard to religion and the press. It considers the dilemmas and tensions that occurred in immediate postwar Japanese society, which suddenly changed from a period of strict government control and entered a new era of unfamiliar and uneasy democracy. With the newly introduced freedom of religion and freedom of expression, Occupation authorities and their Japanese counterparts experienced a number of conflicts that affected the "religious world" due to fundamental differences in attitudes. On the other hand, the press was allowed significant liberties compared to the strict prewar controls they experienced while being subjected to censorship by the Occupation authorities.

Chapter 5 concentrates on the case of Jiu in the postwar period leading up to the "Kanazawa incident," which effectively left the group branded as a public threat. Although Jikōson was influenced by

Ōmoto in some ways, Onisaburō's grand expressions and "exhibitionist tendencies," to use Nancy Stalker's phrase, were a far cry from Jikōson's efforts to attract supporters to her cause. She gathered a group of fiercely protective individuals to take part in her vision of world renewal yet these activities, combined with her conflicted relationship with the press, contributed to the creation of her image as a notorious "celebrity god." Jiu's story is not only remarkable for its attempts to co-opt celebrities into its cause, it is also noteworthy because of its interactions between the authorities and the critical press.

Chapter 6 examines the postwar career of Tenshō Kōtai Jingū Kyō's Kitamura and her efforts at self-promotion. She had a very different relationship to the press than Jikōson and was very proactive in developing and maintaining contacts with the Occupation authorities. These interactions, combined with her own idiosyncratic efforts at getting her message across to the world, had an impact on her promotion as the next prominent "celebrity god" in media representations after Jikōson.

Finally, Chapter 7 considers the aftermath of the cases within the context of the Occupation period leading up to the promulgation of the Religious Corporations Law in 1951. The focus of media attention moved beyond the consideration of individual founders and leaders of new religions and broadened to cover debates about the impact of various issues, including the place of religion in a newly democratized society.

I

Renmonkyō
and the Meiji Press

ON 22 JANUARY 1947, poet and children's story writer Satō Hachirō (1903–1973) wrote an article in his regular column in the newly established *Tōkyō Taimuzu* on the subject of the new religion Jiu, which had just become embroiled in what the media were calling the "Kanazawa incident." Police involvement, arrests, and a shadowy figurehead featured in media reports about Jiu. Rather than focusing on the incident itself, Satō traced a clear line that seemed to connect Jiu to new religions since the Meiji period. Satō wrote: "Since the Meiji period, how many new religions do you think have suddenly appeared and then disappeared, or somehow struggled on? (If you've got some time on your hands, you should start counting away.) It's hard to believe but yet another one has just reared its head." He makes a call to the past when other religious groups became the center of public attention and caused trouble for society. In expressing scorn and incredulity about ephemeral new religions, Satō attempted to educate his readers on how these groups behave and how rational people (by implication, Satō and his readers) should react to them. He was effectively saying that new religions indicated trouble for society, and the roots of the trouble could be located in the past.

During the Meiji period, mass-produced newspapers and other print organs became part of the process of "creating a public," according to James Huffman.[1] Cheaply produced papers fed the public a mixed diet of political and social commentary, combined with scandals and moral lessons. The growth of this industry coincided with the broad development of some of the larger new religions, such as Tenrikyō, Maruyamakyō, and Renmonkyō. Satō does not specifically mention Renmonkyō or other new religions of the Meiji period. Yet the concentrated press campaign related to Renmonkyō combined with the reaction from established religious organizations and actions by government authorities in some ways mirrored what happened to new religions that followed.

According to Janine Sawada, the Renmonkyō case shows "how public moralists of the late nineteenth century used the new religious movements of the time to demarcate their vision of a Japanese religious orthodoxy."[2] The media's reaction to Renmonkyō became an important part of the formation of orthodoxy in its labeling of the group as an immoral and evil social influence. Confucian discourses on religion and morality played a significant role in the language used. As imperial China's state ideology and the official faith, Confucianism relegated its rivals to the status of heterodoxy (Ch. *yiduan*; Jpn. *itan*), and other faiths had to obtain permission by registering with the state. Nevertheless, powerful organizations, mainly syncretic Buddhist or Daoist groups, did arise from time to time to challenge the status quo. These were labeled "cults" (Ch. *xiejiao*; Jpn. *jakyō*), which originally indicated rituals that were considered to be outside the prescribed state rites. They were instrumental in fomenting popular rebellions and change.[3] *Jakyō* was also combined with *inshi* (literally "shrine of lewdness," a Confucian moralistic judgment implying sexual immorality and female promiscuity) to form *inshi jakyō* ("immoral heresy;" sometimes translated as "evil cult").

In Japan *inshi jakyō* was used in the Tokugawa period to refer to Christianity, Fujikō, and the Nichiren Fuju Fuse sect. James Ketelaar notes that *jakyō* (which he translates as "heresy") was "a common word used by everyone in the internecine struggles between Shinto, Confucian, Buddhist, Protestant, and Catholic writers. Again, this separation or distinction between teachings served to define each, in turn, in relation to 'others'."[4] While the media representations of Renmonkyō and its founder played a crucial role in the growing definitions of religious orthodoxy during the Meiji period, they also contributed to standards of normative behavior for good citizens of society.

SUPERSTITIONS AND SOCIAL EVILS

Japan's social and religious policies underwent dramatic change in 1868. Ideologues who formed the first Meiji government sought to introduce emperor-centered Shinto as the national faith. The Tokugawa-era ban on Christianity continued and the government ordered the separation of Shinto and Buddhism in order to remove Buddhist power within shrines and to elevate Shinto above all other faiths. In effect, the authorities attempted to define the boundaries of acceptable interaction between the public and religious institutions. Strong debate ensued for some years over what constituted "religion," and part of the construction of this category involved distinguishing phenomena that were excluded from it, specifically "superstition."[5] The intense persecution of Buddhism (*haibutsu kishaku*), and the introduction of regulations designed to deal with wandering Shugendō ascetics, exorcists, mediums, and diviners were part of the social negotiations.[6] Other measures included the introduction in 1871 of a system of shrine affiliation in order to harness popular feelings against Buddhism (this was dropped in 1873), and an education program, the Great Promulgation Campaign, which was launched to teach the people the new policies.

The Great Promulgation Campaign faltered, and Shinto administrators, who were initially granted the power to promulgate the teachings of the Meiji regime, could not control internal disputes or deal with external factors, such as the debates on religion.[7] The state became less interested in contributing to the cause of developing Shinto through financial support. The campaign to eradicate Buddhism ceased in 1872, and some Buddhist groups managed to convince the government to establish an Office of Temples in the Ministry of Civil Affairs. This gave them the opportunity to gain recognition and status through the auspices of a government office, which was a significant change from the first years of persecution.

Despite this, the ideology that became associated with state-directed Shinto, including reverence for the emperor and support for his servants (the bureaucracy and government officials), was promoted through the education system. From the beginning of the Meiji period, the state not only appropriated Shinto creation myths that placed the imperial line as direct descendants of Amaterasu Ōmikami, the sun goddess, it also attempted to link them in a wider ideology that emphasized the importance of modern, scientific rationality. The government adopted Western medical practices in 1871 and introduced a notice in 1874 prohibiting the use of magical incantations that would interfere with medical therapy. Eventually, ideas linking modern science with imperial myths became part of the education system. In 1882 the government dealt with the problematic issue of Shinto by creating two categories of state-centered Shinto and Sect Shinto. The thirteen Sect Shinto groups separated from the Shinto Office, and they became officially recognized as independent religions. The government came to the conclusion that state-centered Shinto was fundamentally nonreligious. In 1884, the government declared that Buddhism and Shinto had equal status, and it adopted a system of indirect supervision of Shinto and Buddhist orders.

Clearly, the efforts to establish state-centered Shinto were not unified, consistent, or particularly successful. After attempting to establish the primacy of state-centered Shinto, the government shifted to "a policy of benign neglect toward existing religions."[8] Buddhism was granted equal status to Shinto sects, and the government acquiesced to the demands of Western powers and some Buddhist organizations for religious freedom with the promulgation of the Meiji Constitution of 1889 and the inclusion of Article 28.[9] However, this freedom came with substantial qualifications, and it meant that the duties of people as subjects took precedence over individual beliefs. This provision ostensibly made it difficult for the government to assert the supremacy of one religion over others, while the emperor was acknowledged as holding unassailable powers under Articles 3 and 4.[10] However, the government, in making a nominal guarantee of religious freedom, also at the same time labeled Shinto a cult of national morality and patriotism, which allowed it to provide special privileges to Shinto.

The Meiji regime reinterpreted Shinto and the practice of emperor worship as constituting patriotic rather than religious acts. Soon after the promulgation of the constitution, shrine-related activities fell under the category of patriotic acts, and groups affiliated with Sect Shinto were not allowed to lead public worship at shrines. This reinforced the impression that the government was holding true to the principle of separation of church and state. This did not, however, mean that the government abandoned its attempts to assert Shinto's dominance over other religions. During the early 1890s the government put forward several proposals in order to achieve this, including the introduction of compulsory shrine worship and a mandatory requirement that citizens set up Shinto altars in their homes. However, Buddhist and Christian groups stridently opposed this imposition, and the proposals ultimately failed.

In 1890 the Imperial Rescript on Education instructed Japanese subjects to cultivate loyalty and filial piety toward the imperial household. Japan was portrayed as a unique polity based on the historical bonds of its benevolent rulers and loyal subjects. Japanese bureaucrats devised a statement that contained the ethical injunctions they considered the basis of Japanese society. Certified copies of the rescript were distributed to schools throughout the country and ceremoniously read at all important school events. Students were required to study and memorize its text for their moral education classes. But when Uchimura Kanzō, a Christian theologian and teacher, challenged the government's policy, he was banished from the teaching profession for his stance.[11] Under the system introduced by the government, new groups that appeared either became a sub-sect of one of the thirteen groups or existed as semi-religious organizations (*shūkyō ruiji dantai*) or as suspect, quasi-religious organizations (*giji shūkyō dantai*). Groups in the latter category particularly were regarded with suspicion and contempt by the authorities. The language that had only recently been applied to Buddhism was used to distinguish genuine religion from heresy, superstition, or fraudulent faith. While the term *jakyō* had been applied to Buddhism in the first years of Meiji, Buddhists in turn used this kind of critique against "superstitions" to redefine their own position. Buddhist philosopher Inoue Enryō was a central figure in the reformation of Buddhism as a legitimate "religion," and he worked to purge Buddhism of "superstitions" that had previously been central to its practice and invent aspects that would elevate its status.[12]

THREATS TO MORALITY

Yasumaru Yoshio has argued that from the early modern period, conventional morality (*tsūzoku dōtoku*) played an important part in the ethical self-reform of the Japanese people.[13] The religious cosmology of popular religions like Maruyamakyō and Fujikō, Yasumaru argues, was rooted in conventional morality. This was exemplified by virtues such as diligence, humility, and filial piety. Nevertheless, other groups such as Tenrikyō, Kurozumikyō, and Renmonkyō presented a challenge to the state and society on a number of levels. Many people were attracted to these groups because they promised practical worldly benefits (*genze riyaku*) and advocated spiritual healing practices that they claimed would cure widespread and devastating diseases like cholera, which was rampant in the mid-Meiji years. Initially the authorities remained relatively tolerant to new religions because official medical practices were not much more successful than spiritual healing.[14] Nevertheless, the authorities were concerned about the numbers of adherents they attracted. New religions were independent of established religions and were difficult to quantify and control; politicians viewed them with suspicion because of their capacity to attract adherents from various social groups.[15] This capacity to attract adherents from different social strata became a powerful theme in press reports that continues today. Their success indicated that they could potentially attract large numbers of people, and that they could also influence people to resist social policy.

Although new religions initially started with followings from rural communities and included merchants and artisans, distinctions such as gender and class became less important. As Helen Hardacre indicates, new religions tended to believe that people faced the same problems of sickness, poverty, and other troubles, regardless of gender distinctions. Reducing social problems in this way meant that they developed "a principle of equality among believers, weak status distinctions between leaders and followers, and a reduced emphasis on the pollution notions that in the established religious associations barred women from full participation."[16] Yet the orthodox social view was that women who were outside the home were considered to be sexually dangerous. Thus, female proselytizers of new religions openly challenged the orthodox gender ideology of Japan, which was founded on the notion of patriarchal authority, in law and often in practice.[17] Eventually this question of gender became an important factor in the case of Renmonkyō, and another theme that influenced media reports on groups that followed.

If new religions became affiliated with officially recognized groups, the authorities tolerated them to a certain extent and exploited their popularity by using them as instruments to carry out state goals, such as promoting tax payment and enforcing compulsory education. Some groups gain legitimacy by participating in the state's campaigns while others could not deal with the idea of doctrinal compromise.

The founder of Kurozumikyō, Kurozumi Munetada, who had been a low-ranking Shinto priest, managed to portray himself as a legitimate Shinto leader. Initially the founder of Konkōkyō, Kawate Bunjirō, could not accept the fact that some of his initial doctrines would have to be removed in order to accommodate the demands of the Shinto leaders. Eventually, however, both groups "mediated the relation between the state and the rural populace, introducing themselves as extensions of state authority and the state as distant authorizer of their own world view."[18] By the 1880s they had grown into national religious bodies, and eventually requested recognition as individual sects of Shinto. However, Tenrikyō's founder, Nakayama Miki, resisted pressure to conform to state demands and was arrested a total of eighteen times by the authorities for her efforts. After her death in 1887, her followers sought state recognition, which was finally achieved in 1908. By the beginning of the twentieth century, most of the new religions that had arisen in the late-

Tokugawa period had adopted emperor worship in their practices, and they incorporated nationalistic and patriotic themes in their teachings.

RENMONKYŌ'S ROOTS

Renmonkyō's founder, Shimamura Mitsu (1831–1904), began her path as a religious leader around the beginning of the Meiji period after a faith healer cured her of illness. Based in the town of Kokura in northern Kyushu, she became the healer's disciple until his death in 1877. She began to attract adherents by her faith healing and use of "holy water" (*shinsui*), which was promoted as a cure for all kinds of illness, particularly cholera. Renmonkyō successfully promoted various techniques for curing cholera, and this was a major factor in its growth. There were at least six major outbreaks of cholera between 1879 and 1895, and Renmonkyō managed to expand its numbers after each outbreak. However, it did not manage to capitalize on the final outbreak due to the extensive criticism it eventually faced.[19]

Shimamura extolled the benefits of the *Lotus Sutra*, and she combined aspects of Nichiren Buddhism with her own teachings. Although she was a gifted charismatic, her practice of vigils or "seclusion" conflicted with local morality, and she was incarcerated by the police on suspicions arising from her propagation activities.[20] After her release in 1878, she resumed her activities but was again jailed for several months after someone died under her care. Gaining her freedom again, she realized the chances of expansion were slim in Kokura, and in 1882 she left for Tokyo with a few followers. A particularly severe cholera epidemic struck that year, and her group attracted a number of new adherents in a short time through promoting its cure. Despite the official acceptance of Western medical practices, the reality was that for most people, pharmaceutical products and medical treatment were extremely expensive. Furthermore, there was a shortage of hospitals and doctors, and the government struggled to find resources to treat poorer people.[21] While Renmonkyō found great success promoting "holy water," local authorities prohibited its distribution. Shimamura and her chief disciple were fined and jailed for ten days.[22] It became clear to the group that its path to survival was official recognition from the government through affiliating with a sectarian Shinto group.

Although it actively promoted Buddhist ideas, Renmonkyō adopted aspects of Shinto in order to achieve official acceptance. In July 1882 it affiliated with a state-recognized Shinto sect, Taiseikyō, and Shimamura was ordained as an assistant religious instructor. In the ensuing years Renmonkyō began to assert itself as a significant religious organization and by 1894 the numbers of churches and believers expanded.[23] The growth in the group's status is clear not only from its property holdings. Shimamura herself received a continuing series of appointments within Taiseikyō, and she reached the top rank of chief-master by 1890. This was a remarkable achievement among sectarian Shinto groups. However, the group's success clashed with the growing consensus over social arrangements and the idealized expectations of the modern state as perceived by the media.

CONFLICTS WITHIN THE MEIJI PRESS

Around the time Renmonkyō was experiencing its greatest growth, the Meiji press was developing into a burgeoning industry. James Huffman argues that while education, political movements, and economic transformation were all important elements in the creation of a modern citizenry, the Meiji newspaper press was essential. The media was seen as one means of educating the "common people" in order to modernize the nation. It was understood that commoners could use the press to voice their concerns, and that while newspaper publishers were from a different social class, they could not ignore the needs of the buying public. Yet while editors appeared to stand by the common people, they also welcomed the support of elite, powerful officials and the wealthy.[24]

Leading politicians encouraged the publication of newspapers in the early years of Meiji in order to provide publicity for their reforms. Before 1868 writers were subjected to a great number of controls and prohibitions designed to suppress ideas that would undermine the Tokugawa regime. The new regime had its critics as well, and those who had been silenced through incarceration emerged somewhat disillusioned. On the other hand, government officials took a great interest in developing newspapers. Although writers were allowed significant freedoms for the first few months of Meiji, in August 1868 the government introduced a press-prohibition policy (*hakkō kinshi*), which meant that only officially licensed newspapers could publish provided the authorities deemed them to be suitable for promoting the national well-being and supporting traditional moral standards. In 1871 a series of official instructions were issued to create newspapers that would "foster people's knowledge" and "destroy the spirit of bigotry and narrow prejudice" which blocked progress. Government patronage stimulated the rapid growth of newspapers; by 1877, according to some reports, Japan had 225 newspapers. A decade later there were more than 470 newspapers. The government kept a tight rein on public discussions, and in the first sixteen years of the Meiji period it issued eighty-three different press decrees and regulations.

Satō Takumi writes of Japan's media history in terms of how two separate trends that developed in Western Europe and the United States respectively influenced the early Meiji press. In the class-based societies of England and Germany, there was a strong attachment to political newspapers that promoted ideology and specific parties, whereas in the consumer-oriented society of the United States, ostensibly objective financial newspapers were appearing. In the rapidly modernizing Japan, European-style political newspapers were dominant for a very short period prior to the introduction of US-style financial newspapers.[25] Although the earliest Meiji newspapers were set up as platforms for ruling politicians to promote government policy, the press also established a tradition of criticism and suspicion of government actions.

While politicians encouraged the establishment of newspapers as voices of the people, many papers did not shy away from criticism of the ruling regime. Newspaper essays were instrumental in encouraging popular movements and rebellions, such as various popular rights movements of the 1870s and 1880s.[26] By 1875 the government had enacted repressive laws to deal with papers that sided with the political opposition. In 1876 the Home Ministry was granted the right to suspend or ban any paper that violated public order or injured public morals. Although a new press law was introduced in 1883, there was a more positive shift in the early 1890s when the Diet allowed pre-censorship in times of emergency. In 1897 the government's right to suspend and ban newspapers became more limited. This meant that press policies were liberated slightly in the last fifteen years of the Meiji period.[27]

"WATCHDOGS" AND "SERVANTS"

The shifting stance of the media in relation to state authority indicates what Susan Pharr argues can be termed as dual traditions regarding the media's role from 1868 to 1945: the "servant tradition," which sees the media working toward forging consensus on political and social values, and the "watchdog" tradition, whereby the media works on behalf of society to protect the public interest from official abuses.[28] James Huffman argues that journalists generally perceived the role of the press as defenders of the public interest.[29] Similarly, John Pierson holds that during the Meiji period journalists were seen as government critics who were true to their profession only when they were "registering dissent, decrying abuse, and awakening people to alternative, and generally more liberal, policies and programs for modernization."[30] Two catchphrases—"neutrality and fairness" (*chūritsu kōsei*) and "without prejudice or bias" (*fuhen futō*)—that developed in the media during the period ostensibly encapsulated press objectivity and their freedom from political interference.

On the other hand, many journalists were also blatantly nationalistic, indicating aspects of the "servant" tradition. Most newspapers made substantial efforts to promote state myths and journalists participated in "the state's battle to manipulate traditional values about authority and to expand the cult of the emperor."[31] While journalists criticized government ineptitude, they made "a sharp distinction between their beloved nation and its emperor on the one hand, and the all-too-human politicians and officials on the other."[32] In this sense, criticism could be leveled at government authorities by the press, and their claims of protecting the interests of the nation would resonate with the public. In this way, the potential repercussions from government authorities over press criticisms could be buffered by the claim that they were acting in the interests of the nation.

Yorozu Chōhō was an example of a popular newspaper that negotiated both the "watchdog" and "servant" traditions. *Yorozu Chōhō* participated energetically in the production of discourses of social morality and nationalism during the 1890s. As Janine Sawada notes, "one of *Yorozu*'s most distinctive contributions to this process was its concentrated use of religion as a gauge of Japanese civic propriety."[33]

SCANDALS AND SALES

To a certain extent, *Yorozu Chōhō* was representative of a new paradigm in the newspaper industry of the Meiji period. It started a new genre of print media publications that aimed to appeal to a broad range of mostly working-class people. It began in November 1892, and was essentially a tabloid paper. Around the 1890s, when "yellow journalism," a term synonymous with scandal-mongering and sensationalism, was developing through the circulation battles between Joseph Pulitzer and William Randolph Hearst in the United States, Japan saw the introduction of "red newspapers," which grew after *Yorozu Chōhō* experimented with red paper in 1897 and 1898 to see if the public would take to the gimmick. The term became synonymous with sensationalist newspapers of the times.

Tamaki Akira holds that in the early years of Meiji newspapers, reporting concentrated mainly on providing as realistic a picture of the subjects "just as they were" without trying to present them as being different from the readers. Yet this changed with the advent of popular newspapers such as *Yorozu Chōhō*. With the advent of "social interest stories" that were often centered on police crime reports, *Yorozu Chōhō* and other papers tried to present a model of "how people should be." By attempting to define normative social behavior, Tamaki claims that *Yorozu Chōhō* was the first paper in modern Japan to introduce scandals to the public, including the Renmonkyō campaign. Papers like *Yorozu* developed a form of condemnatory reporting (*danzai hōdō*) that preceded the kinds of reporting that can be seen in the weekly magazines (*shūkanshi*) of postwar Japan.[34] This process attempted to place journalists and media workers as authoritative, reliable sources of information who could guide the public (and lax government authorities) down a path they believed would help the nation. Tamaki's argument reflects Benedict Anderson's idea of nations as "imagined communities," which are partly based on a "deep, horizontal comradeship" whereby the members never know most of their fellows yet share an image of their communion.[35] In his assessment of *Yorozu Chōhō*, Tamaki shares Anderson's view that the growth of the print media is "the key to the generation of wholly new ideas of simultaneity."[36]

As opposed to more intellectual broadsheets, *Yorozu Chōhō* set its sights firmly on the masses. A low-cost paper with a four-page limit and short, snappy, easily digestible articles, it staked a claim in the "watchdog" tradition by claiming independence from political parties, large business interests, and the wealthy classes. Other papers made similar claims at the time. In one case in 1893, a scandal involving a wealthy family, *Yorozu Chōhō* pitched the story as a battle between the establishment and the poor, and was suspended four times by the government. The paper won widespread public support for its stance and it subsequently became a huge commercial success. The paper claimed it would pursue and report "truth" fearlessly for the sake of the common people. As such, the paper wanted to be seen as leading public opinion and demanding changes which it deemed necessary, thus playing the role of "watchdog." "We do not have any lovers," the paper's founder, Kuroiwa Ruikō (1862–1920) claimed, "no government, no political parties, no politicians, no commercial interests. We go our independent way. We simply are honest and sincere."[37] Kuroiwa had cut his editorial teeth at the *Miyako Shinbun* with his bold policies of adapting foreign novels, printing short reviews, and writing sharply worded editorials. After a disagreement with the company president, he branched out on his own with a number of colleagues.[38]

Despite its self-conscious anti-establishment stance, *Yorozu Chōhō* clearly wanted to play a part in creating a modern nation. It achieved phenomenal sales in 1894 with its coverage of the Sino-Japanese War (1894–1895). In August 1894, its sales figures doubled that of its nearest rival, *Tōkyō Asahi Shinbun*. In fact, it maintained the highest circulation figures among newspapers for a number of years.[39] The paper boldly declared on 18 October 1894 that the press were responsible for the war, and reported in the same month how citizens were pledging private contributions to uphold the "heroic Yamato spirit."[40] However, by maintaining a critical stance toward the authorities, the paper could avoid the charge of acting merely as a mouthpiece of government policy. In 1901 Kuroiwa wrote that a newspaper's role was to point out clearly for the public the difference between right and wrong and between purity and corruption. In short, he held, a newspaper had the power "to save people from confusion."[41] Thus, as Yamamoto Taketoshi points out, the "scandal journalism" championed by *Yorozu Chōhō* concentrated on applying pressure onto the authorities rather than ordinary people (*minshū*).[42] The stance articulated by *Yorozu Chōhō*'s founder provides an insight as to why Renmonkyō proved to be an excellent target. Kuroiwa's assertion about a newspaper's capacity to "save" people could be read as a sign of empathy for the public's plight. But while he may have "wanted to think as the general public felt, to feel anger with them and solve problems with them,"[43] he was also a shrewd business man who sought to maximize his profits.

YOROZU CHŌHŌ AS MORAL COMPASS

Although *Yorozu Chōhō* began publishing its own stories on Renmonkyō in 1894, it was not the first print media organ to level attacks at the group. In 1891 the *Yomiuri Shinbun* published a serialized novel written by a popular author based on a fictitious new religion that closely resembled Renmonkyō. The novel, *Kōhaku dokumanjū* (Red and white poison dumplings), was partly based on rumors that were circulating about Renmonkyō, which inferred that the group engaged in suspicious practices and was a danger to society. This lent substantial weight to *Yorozu Chōhō*'s reports, which began on 12 February 1894. From that point, *Yorozu Chōhō* became a self-appointed moral compass for society. Claiming that it would act in the public interest by exposing the "true" nature of the group, the paper set off on a determined campaign to discredit Renmonkyō.[44]

This initial report asserted that the new freedom of religion spawned a number of these groups, and that among them Renmonkyō was definitely the worst as it poisoned society with the effects of its evil teachings. It compared the activities at Renmonkyō's shrine to those of a brothel, concluding that the religion was nothing more than a "high-class harlot." In raising this suggestion that freedom of religion contributed to the rise of pernicious groups masquerading as religions, the newspaper challenged the government's authority and policies. Thus, in playing the role of "watchdog" the newspaper sent a clear message that the government authorities had been deficient in their public duty because they had allowed morally questionable groups like Renmonkyō to affiliate with the authorized Shinto sect Taiseikyō. In effect, the paper tried to assert its authority as a faithful reporter, pointing out the potential dangers that may occur if the authorities did not exercise proper control.

The theme of criticisms of inadequate legal provisions and suggestions of bureaucratic ineptitude that caused or contributed to a surge of suspect religions resurfaced in the print media during the 1930s and the Occupation period. It was also powerfully employed during the debates over revising the Religious Corporations Law in 1995 in the wake of the Aum affair. After its first report in early February 1894, *Yorozu Chōhō* subsequently produced a ninety-four-part series of articles on Renmonkyō that began in March and ended in October. A special editorial series that ran from April to May 1894 focused on the broad theme of Renmonkyō's defilement of Shinto. Holding that it exerted an evil influence on society, the paper stated that Renmonkyō "deceives the ignorant populace, sets morals in disarray, makes illicit gains, interferes with people's health, misuses people's daughters and makes them the object of its own carnal pleasure. Whether in matters of doctrine, ritual, or management, no part of it can be called Shinto."[45] The article ended with a demand directed toward the Home Ministry to save the Japanese population by disbanding the group.[46]

From 24 to 27 April 1894, the paper published a long essay outlining why it decided to target this group in particular. These can be summarized in four points: (1) the founder was an uneducated peasant woman who was not qualified to teach others; (2) she and her followers misled ignorant men and women; (3) Renmonkyō could not be called a religion because ceremonies were neither Shinto nor Buddhist; and (4) the use of "holy water" actually shortened life.[47]

REPRESENTATIONS OF SHIMAMURA MITSU

Focusing on stories of the founder allows the media to establish the tone and direction of debates about new religions. *Yorozu Chōhō* represented Shimamura Mitsu as a notorious figure who broke social conventions and contributed to general disorder. It claimed that she was promiscuous from her youth, that her parents disowned her, that she had numerous lovers and fell pregnant on occasion, and that she had at least one illegitimate child. As she made her way to Tokyo, she purportedly had liaisons with influential suitors who helped her acquire legal status for the group. In short, Mitsu was represented as an immoral woman who, together with her followers, engaged in shady business practices and sold fake "healing water" to gullible people. She was thus an evil "god" who not only did not adhere to a correct religious path, she was also the cause of social chaos. She stood accused of actively encouraging women to pursue an immoral spiritual path rather than encouraging them to live as role models who could raise their children within the traditional family structure to become good citizens and thus contribute to the nation's well-being. The thirteenth installment of the series related the story of a female believer who, despite the protestations of her husband, refused to give up her faith in Renmonkyō. Although she had three children, she neglected them completely, the report claimed. When her eldest son fell ill, she only gave him "holy water," thus causing his death. After attending Renmonkyō's church every day, the paper claimed, she fell pregnant although the identity of the father remained unknown.[48]

By taking a stance against Renmonkyō's alleged practices involving women, *Yorozu Chōhō* capitalized on the widely accepted discourse of gender relations. But these stories also provided significant financial opportunities for *Yorozu Chōhō* because of the salacious content that appealed to its readership. Thus Renmonkyō, as opposed to other smaller new religions, was a prominent and significant target. It also provided the paper with an opportunity to declare itself to be a defender of public interest. But closely linked with the issue of newspaper circulation was the ideological foundation of the criticisms of Renmonkyō. There were three main elements to this: the changing notions of gender relations and ideology; the issues of social class; and the developing discourse on Shinto in terms of "purity" and superstitions. At the deepest level, this final element—the notion that Renmonkyō's existence as a branch of Shinto degraded the nature of Shinto, and therefore the nation—was the consistent theme that underscored the entire campaign launched by the paper and taken up by other print media organs.

The theme of the potential damage new religions can cause society through disturbing a variety of people in society is powerful. *Yorozu Chōhō* argued in its first article that Renmonkyō threatened to damage society because it had attracted uneducated commoners and had infiltrated the middle and upper classes.[49] This inferred that Renmonkyō had the potential to infect society through gathering influential and important believers. Justifying its hard-line approach on Renmonkyō, the article held that while all new religions were "immoral," Renmonkyō stood apart from others because it had more potential to "poison" society due to its ability to work its way into every level of society. And to make this assertion more appealing for its readers, the paper claimed that the group lured its higher-class adherents through engaging in illicit sexual activities.[50]

The scandalous nature of these tales boosted circulation, resulting in a wave of associated publicity from other newspapers or media outlets. Furthermore, in this case, most of the newspapers also acted as both "servant" to national ideals associated with state-centered Shinto at that time, including reverence for the emperor and loyalty to the nation, and "watchdog" toward the bureaucracy and government authorities who were not fulfilling their duties in keeping the public safe from threats, real or perceived. *Yorozu Chōhō* tried to act not only as a definer of the issues but also as an empathetic guide for the public. Finally, the paper reproduced the dominant Confucian-based moralistic discourses of heterodoxy and orthodoxy that served to define religious boundaries in the early Meiji period.

THE AFTERMATH OF THE CAMPAIGN

Yorozu Chōhō's stories caused a sensation and triggered a remarkable response from the public, other print media organs, established religions, and government authorities. Renmonkyō issued its own response to the crisis it faced but this was ultimately ineffectual. Within days of the first article's publication, Renmonkyō's central shrine was attacked, as were regional facilities. It was denounced at public meetings and some demanded that it return financial donations.[51] *Yorozu Chōhō* reported all these events. Within days a number of other newspapers had taken up the story and continued to report on the unfolding situation; these included *Mainichi Shinbun*, *Yomiuri Shinbun*, *Jiyū Shinbun*, *Chūō Shinbun*, *Kokumin Shinbun*, *Niroku Shinpō*, and Kuroiwa's former paper, *Miyako Shinbun*.[52] Letters from members of the public were also published thanking the press for exposing Renmonkyō. Apart from newspapers, a number of books also appeared decrying new religions, particularly Renmonkyō. One such work, which was written from the perspective of an adherent to an established Buddhist group, was "Eleven Immoral Churches."[53] However, Renmonkyō was its principle focus. The content was almost entirely based on quotations of articles published in *Yorozu Chōhō*, and the claims were virtually identical.[54]

Yorozu Chōhō pursued Renmonkyō vigorously for many months. But not all newspapers accepted the paper's stance. *Kaishin Shinbun*, which was aligned with the Constitutional Progressive Party, initially defended Renmonkyō and raised questions about *Yorozu Chōhō*'s integrity. *Yorozu Chōhō*, on the other hand, inferred that corruption existed between Renmonkyō and the *Kaishin Shinbun*. Both papers criticized each other for their respective stances over a period of weeks. However, six weeks after *Yorozu Chōhō*'s initial article was published, Shimamura was stripped of her credentials as a religious instructor by government decree, and the *Kaishin Shinbun* found itself in a difficult position and retracted its criticisms of *Yorozu Chōhō*. *Yorozu Chōhō* again appeared to gain credibility as the *Kaishin Shinbun* lost public support.[55]

Established and officially recognized religious groups also responded to the issue swiftly. Buddhist groups, including the Jōdo and Tendai sects, joined in the criticism of Renmonkyō with gusto, "exposing" the dangers of all "immoral religions" in their own publications. *Jōdo Shinpō* published a month-long series from April 15 and ran a three-page editorial calling for Renmonkyō's dissolution. Given that Buddhism had only begun to recover from an intense period of persecution and was in the process of redefining itself, this clarification of the dangers and "heresy" represented by Renmonkyō was linked to Buddhism's sense of identity in the new social landscape. *Meikyō Shinshi*, a non sectarian Buddhist newspaper, reported approvingly of the media pursuit of the group and quoted extensively from the general newspapers.[56] Its editorial series added further pressure on the authorities by arguing that if a religion interfered with the nation's existence the government was bound to dissolve it under the authority of the Home Ministry.

Sectarian Shinto groups also responded to the situation. These actions could be seen as an attempt to present themselves as working for national aims and reinforcing their connection to the state. Members from the Shinto sect Misogikyō demanded that Taiseikyō take punitive action against Renmonkyō. It should be noted that Misogikyō had only just received status as a sectarian Shinto group from the government that year.[57] Misogikyō's demands could be interpreted as being connected with the group's desire to portray itself to the authorities and the public as upholding the "purity" of the Shinto tradition. *Yorozu Chōhō* duly reported the demands of the Misogikyō members, proclaiming that the reputation of this group was sullied because of Renmonkyō's inappropriate actions.

Renmonkyō was in a weak position compared to *Yorozu Chōhō*, which published accusation after accusation about the group. Through the persistent efforts of the paper, the group achieved an unprecedented level of notoriety. Under these circumstances, Renmonkyō's choice was to remain silent or defend itself against the charges. It chose to respond to its critics, a move which proved to be ultimately ineffective and damaging to its cause. It desperately needed to articulate and renegotiate its substantially weakened position, and subsequently issued rebuttals to each newspaper involved in the attacks. These were duly published together with other articles about the group and its activities. It placed advertisements in a number of newspapers including *Yorozu Chōhō* explaining to its members (and potential sympathizers among the public) that it was taking the action to fight against the fabricated charges of the newspaper. It also launched legal proceedings against *Yorozu Chōhō*. However, this strategy backfired after the group was criticized for choosing legal action rather than attempt to argue its case on doctrinal grounds, which was a position considered more appropriate for a religious group. Renmonkyō lost its public relations battle with the media, the numbers of believers lining up to receive "holy water" dwindled rapidly,[58] and it could not convince the majority of the public that it did not pose a serious threat to society.

During the sustained campaign of media and social criticism against Renmonkyō, Taiseikyō had not taken any action, preferring to delay any decision until it was forced to respond to outside pressures. *Yorozu Chōhō*'s campaign entered a new phase when it began to publish front-page reports that called on Taiseikyō to stop protecting Renmonkyō and take decisive action against the "heresies" committed by its affiliated group. The intense and critical media publicity against Renmonkyō coupled with the demands of established Buddhist and sectarian Shinto groups and the public outcry triggered a response from the government authorities. On 14 April 1894 the Metropolitan Police Department launched a surveillance campaign that focused on investigating local Renmonkyō churches through its bureaus. This official intervention caused Taiseikyō to finally capitulate and take action against the group. In the face of this, Taiseikyō forced Renmonkyō to accept a series of reforms. Renmonkyō was compelled to stop using paraphernalia connected with the Nichiren sect, to abolish the use of "holy water," and to cease performing rituals after three o'clock in the afternoon. These requirements essentially stripped Renmonkyō of its *raison d'être* as a religious group. After the sustained criticisms that peaked in mid-1894 and subsequent government actions, Renmonkyō's growth was curtailed severely. Although a final cholera epidemic broke out in 1895, the group could not capitalize on this through promoting "holy water" as a means of expansion. By the beginning of the twentieth century, Renmonkyō had all but disappeared.

MEDIA AND NATION

Yorozu Chōhō's campaign against Renmonkyō demonstrated that negative images of religions could generate substantial sales if they were packaged along the lines of moral outrage. Financial motives can certainly be considered and this argument could still be applied to some weekly magazines in relation to new religious groups in the contemporary period. But it was not simply profit that motivated the press attacks. Janine Sawada argues that Meiji "men of maturity" who envisioned systems of personal development more conducive to national unity were threatened by Renmonkyō because of its emphasis on a devotional leader.[59] Shimamura Mitsu became a figure of notoriety whose presence, at least in the media reports of her activities, served to confirm the potential dangers her group could cause to society.

Yorozu Chōhō's campaign against Renmonkyō was partly based on the developing ideas of state, nation, public morality, and safety. In its drive to increase circulation and position itself as a champion of the people, the paper articulated a vision of frightful social consequences that would occur if the alleged deviancy of Renmonkyō was left unchecked. Religious groups supported the newspaper's stance because of their own personal interest. Furthermore, its articles had generated strong reactions from the public. The authorities felt compelled to act under this type of pressure. Established religions tried to discredit Renmonkyō by claiming its illegitimacy. *Yorozu Chōhō* aimed at both increasing its circulation through titillating reports of Renmonkyō's alleged crimes and positioning itself as a defender of public morality. At the same time, its criticisms of the government could also be seen as a kind of insurance that could be used to garner public support in case the authorities introduced repressive legislation to curb its publication activities. And government authorities were certainly keen to be seen as acting to suppress groups that were widely perceived as presenting a threat to the social and moral fabric of the nation. Powerful actors, such as established religions, *Yorozu Chōhō* and its supporters, and government authorities each contributed to the developing ideas of nation and purity according to their vested interests. In the process of negotiating their own positions and asserting their views, the media and established religions made various truth claims that were juxtaposed to those of Renmonkyō. The opponents of new religions were not necessarily united in their motivations or methods of attack.

Yorozu Chōhō and other papers acted to reinforce national ideals associated with the emerging nation, including reverence for the emperor and loyalty to country. The process of creating a modern nation of loyal subjects entailed attempts to redefine the boundaries of acceptable behavior and thought through various social institutions. Religion was a key area that the state sought to assert its new ideals, and although the attempt to establish emperor-centered Shinto as the national faith failed, the state established an official system that recognized "religions." Renmonkyō had become affiliated with a recognized Shinto group but *Yorozu Chōhō* accused it of sullying the pure nature of Shinto—this could lead to, the paper claimed, the destruction of social morals and irreparable damage to the public and the nation. According to Tamaki Akira, the paper aimed to establish a dichotomy between people whose behavior should conform to the morals and standards of a modern, civilized, patriotic nation and those who represent the opposite qualities of licentiousness, immorality, and disloyalty.[60] The model of "how Japanese should be" incorporated elements of loyalty to emperor and nation, adherence to Confucian, patriarchal morality, and Western, scientific "rationality." Ethics taught in schools was conducted through using the vocabulary of Confucian morality, which emphasized the importance of fostering love for the nation and respect for the emperor. Terminology that derived from Confucian discourses on religion and morality, in which any practice not subservient to the state or "rational" Confucian interests was employed by bureaucrats and also the media. These terms reflected broader social and official attitudes and *Yorozu Chōhō* used it to great effect to describe Renmonkyō.

Takeda Dōshō argues that the incident involving Renmonkyō marks the first example of a "comprehensive, organic mobilization of the entire society which would become a hallmark of later persecutions of [other new religions like] Hito no Michi and Ōmoto under State Shinto."[61] He claims that Renmonkyō faced intense scrutiny and criticism because it stood apart from the national aims "within the context of what Murakami Shigeyoshi calls the religio-political institution of State Shinto."[62] Murakami holds that under the "emperor system," elites within the army, bureaucracy, and the police force, acting in the name of the emperor, imposed the central tenets of this institution, such as loyalty to the emperor and state, onto a subjugated population. Meanwhile, landowners and capitalists acted in collusion with the bureaucrats as participants in the state system.[63]

Murakami's theory of State Shinto, which directly links the early Meiji period with the fifteen-year war between 1931 and 1945, has been debated by scholars since his work came out in the 1970s.[64] Takeda, however, accepts Murakami's position and concludes that the mass media acted as one link in the official mechanism and served the role of supporting the authorities. He sets out a generalized pattern of oppression whereby (1) a new religion that is "at variance with the implicit assumptions of a State Shinto institution" triggers friction with surrounding society, and becomes the object of rumor; (2) the media seizes on the scandal value of the subject and stirs up public sentiment against the group, using "the dogma of the national polity" to censure it through public opinion; and (3) the public demands that the group be disbanded cause police and state authorities to intervene and oppress the group. In his conception "the media" as an entity was not only a link in the official mechanism they also spoke with one voice regarding groups that offended the orthodoxy, such as new religions.

Takeda's stance can be questioned, given there was some opposition to *Yorozu Chōhō*'s stance by *Kaishin Shinbun*, but it is true that the dominant tone of most media reports was highly critical of Renmonkyō. Another problem is that the vision of hierarchical domination and control exerted by a group of elites on the subjugated populace does not effectively explain the situation surrounding new religions at all times from the Meiji period to the late 1930s. Nor does it adequately explain certain developments after the Renmonkyō incident involving Deguchi Onisaburō, the multi-talented and self-promoting leader of Ōmoto, a new religion during the prewar period. Ōmoto and its media representations were to have a profound effect on postwar religions and the press.

2

Deguchi Onisaburō as a Prewar Model

IN EARLY 1949, freelance journalist Ōya Sōichi (1900–1970) contributed a series of articles to the *Tōkyō Nichi Nichi Shinbun* titled "An overview of newly arisen gods" ("Shinkō kamisama sōmakuri"). At this stage of his career, which spanned the prewar and postwar periods and eventually covered five decades, Ōya was concentrating on rebuilding his portfolio after a hiatus from journalism for the first years of the Allied Occupation. He began writing about new religions in 1931, focusing on large groups like Ōmoto and Tenrikyō. In his lead article published on 7 January 1949 in the *Tōkyō Nichi Nichi Shinbun*, he argued that these groups were the forebears of the postwar "newly arisen religions" (*shinkō shūkyō*) and that the founders and leaders of all other new religions had "passed through their gates." As with Satō Hachirō and others who framed stories of new religions for readers by recalling groups from former times, Ōya presented historical links between Ōmoto and Tenrikyō and the postwar new religions, proposing that the older groups were the models for new religions. As early as 1931 Ōya had discussed "prototypes" and "typical models" of "pseudo religions."[1] Ōya had first hand experience in dealing with new religions in the 1930s, including a number of interviews with leaders, including Ōmoto's flamboyant leader, Deguchi Onisaburō (born Ueda Kisaburō; 1871–1948). The exploits of Onisaburō, as he is often called, were widely reported in the media. Although he was quite distinctive in approach, the temptation to label him as a "model" was strong because he seemed to fulfill certain requirements. His group called for radical social change, he was personally very charismatic, and he came into conflict with the authorities.

This chapter examines the Ōmoto case with a particular focus on its relations with the media from the early 1920s until 1935, when the group was disbanded by the authorities. While the Renmonkyō incident provides insight into relationships between the newly established mass media, the state, and new religions, the legacy of Ōmoto is important.

Not only did the group have a profound impact on a number of new religions including Jiu, the media representations of Ōmoto during the prewar period influenced the reporting of new religions in the postwar period. Nevertheless, the notion of Ōmoto as a "model" is somewhat problematic because it allows for certain assumptions about one particular group within the specific social circumstances of the prewar period to be transferred to another group facing different conditions.

NEW RELIGIONS ON THE RISE

From the 1890s to the 1930s the numbers of Shinto-based new religions increased. Although the case of Renmonkyō caused a furor concerning issues of public morality and national identity linked to Shinto, the government did not make any significant moves to quell the rise of new religions during the late Meiji period. Rather, from that time the authorities increasingly neglected the area of religious administration.[2] Nevertheless, they attempted to reinforce the values of emperor-centered ideology through a variety of means. The state introduced lèse majesté laws in 1907 and the Peace Preservation Law of 1925, which became legislative tools for the control of new religions up to 1945.

The first two decades of the twentieth century saw a revival of interest in religious issues. The ideas of Nichiren, the thirteenth-century Buddhist priest, struck a chord with some people while others were drawn away from established Shinto, Christian, and Buddhist groups because of their perceived formalism and lack of affinity with the ordinary problems of daily life. New religions that espoused millennial messages combined with other ideas became more popular. However, such groups presented a threat to the state not only because their doctrines, which deviated from the mainstream, implied dissatisfaction with current social and political arrangements. The state was also concerned with their ability to accumulate large numbers of followers independent of government control. With the state increasingly attempting to inculcate centrally controlled views of loyalty to the nation through the education system, these groups were seen as a potentially destabilizing force.

After the failure of the initial attempts to impose Shinto as the national religion in the early Meiji years, the government tolerated existing religions to a certain extent and then incorporated established religions into the ruling structure.[3] In order to maintain the appearance of adhering to the separation of religion and state and religious freedom, Sect Shinto groups were barred from leading worship at public shrines after 1900. However, in 1908 the government nevertheless launched a campaign to encourage pilgrimages to shrines by schoolchildren in an attempt to inculcate the values of state-centered Shinto into the population. Other strategies later included encouraging compulsory shrine worship and the installment of Shinto altars in every home, but when this drew complaints from Buddhist and Christian groups the bureaucracy was forced to retreat. Sheldon Garon argues that "Home Ministry officials increasingly looked upon the established religions as natural allies in their managerial campaigns to improve social welfare, modernize daily habits, and ward off radical thought."[4] The established religions acted to maintain their own interests, including asserting the right to voice their opinions in religious and social policy. Part of their campaign, which was consistent throughout the period, was to urge tougher restrictions on the new religions, which were drawing believers from within the rapidly growing urban areas, thus competing with the established groups. Religious supervision within government departments was transferred from the Home Ministry to the Education Ministry. In 1919 the Education Ministry's Bureau of Religions issued a directive that called for prefectural authorities to strengthen surveillance over unrecognized religious groups. The term *ruiji shūkyō* ("pseudo religion") became part of bureaucratic terminology and was used to characterize groups that seemed to resemble established Buddhist and Shinto sects and denominations doctrinally, yet did not belong to them officially. It was also used in the media.

ŌMOTO'S ASCENT

From its humble beginnings in 1892, Ōmoto grew to become a large and influential new religion. It was founded by a peasant woman, Deguchi Nao, who lived in Ayabe, a rural area in Kyoto prefecture. Nao endured great suffering during her life and at age 55 had a possession experience which led her to believe she was part of a divine plan devised by a spirit known as Ushitora no Konjin. After she became convinced of her possession, she called for people to reform. The townspeople thought she had gone mad and she was imprisoned by the authorities on an arson charge. During her incarceration she started recording her divine revelations in a document known as *Ofudesaki*. After being released she began to make millennial predictions that foretold destruction of the present world followed by world renewal (*yonaoshi*). World renewal ideas were nothing new, although they varied from group to group and region to region. Yasumaru Yoshio presents cases of pre-Meiji social movements and new religions espousing world renewal ideas, whereas Miyata Noboru takes a different perspective by focusing on the "folklore of disaster." He discusses different variations of calamity and renewal that were discovered in a survey of mountain villages conducted in 1934.[5]

After Nao's dire predictions of destruction and resurrection, which were encapsulated in the phrase *tatekae, tatenaoshi* (demolition and reconstruction), failed, her followers largely abandoned her. This resulted in the elevation to the leadership position of her son-in-law, the remarkable Onisaburō.[6] Under his guidance, the number of adherents began to rise sharply from 1910, and in 1914 the group established its own magazine called *Shikishima Shinpō*.[7] This was a major step for a new religion and Ōmoto's use of the print media as a form of proselytization contributed greatly to its nationwide propagation activities. Asano Wasaburō, who was a well-known academic with a wide range of social contacts, joined Ōmoto in 1916 after hearing Nao's teachings. Asano had taught English at a naval academy, and his participation influenced a number of intellectuals and naval officers to join Ōmoto.[8] Claiming a high-profile figure such as Asano as one of its members was a coup for Ōmoto. Not surprisingly, Ōmoto tried to capitalize on his talents and his status. *Shikishima Shinpō* was changed to *Shin Reikai* and Asano became its editor. As Nancy Stalker argues, this publication provided the group with "not only a positive platform to publicize and defend its views and to connect the spiritualist community but also a national pulpit to critique other religions, an activity expressly prohibited among state-approved sects."[9] In 1917 Onisaburō presented an account of ancient gods in *Shin Reikai* that differed radically from the state-sponsored version, thus providing ammunition for the state authorities to clamp down on the group later.[10]

Asano's participation highlights an important theme that affected Ōmoto and other new religions. On the one hand, having intellectuals involved gave the group some kind of legitimacy in that they could not be accused of having a membership that consisted merely of peasants or people of lower classes. A group could utilize these figures to promote or defend their stance. On the other hand, they could be accused of duping the intelligentsia who were unaware of their wily ways, or of degrading national intelligence. Journalists such as Ōya Sōichi used this theme as a way of expressing concerns over the potentially dangerous social influence of new religions.

By the time of Nao's death in 1918, the organization had expanded its activities nationwide; official investigations into the group commenced around this time. Onisaburō soon revealed his remarkable talents as an organizer and leader, and his exploits attracted substantial attention from the public. Although some Meiji-period ideologues, including Inoue Enryō, worked hard to debunk various "irrational beliefs" and "superstitions" through scientific explanations, spiritualism in various forms enjoyed a boom during the Taishō years (1912–1926) in Japan. Ōmoto stood out among the new religions as the first successful promoter of mystic, spiritualist practices on a national scale. The spiritualist technique *chinkon kishin* (pacifying the soul and returning to the divine) helped propel the group from near obscurity in the 1910s to the third largest new religion in 1921.[11] At the same time, the practice also drew negative attention from the authorities.[12]

When Ōmoto purchased the large circulation daily newspaper from Osaka, the *Taishō Nichi Nichi Shinbun*, in August 1920, it became the first religious group to be closely involved in the operation of a mainstream publication. Asano became president of the newspaper and the articles blatantly promoted Ōmoto's philosophies while criticizing the political situation and the government. Major papers such as the *Asahi Shinbun* expressed reservations about Ōmoto's editorial control of the *Taishō Nichi Nichi Shinbun*, and some newspaper reports warned that Ōmoto would have a negative influence on the community because it had demonstrated some success in recruiting school and university students. Furthermore, some papers argued that the involvement of a number of high-ranking naval officers meant that Ōmoto's millennial ideas could infiltrate the military and thus threaten the state.[13] The ensuing controversy provided Ōmoto with more publicity. Nancy Stalker indicates that the police and Home Ministry often relied on media accounts for their own reports.[14]

Although Ōmoto had begun to attract adherents from a range of social groups, it was not so much its size initially that concerned the authorities but rather the nature of the teachings. The group intruded into political territory by calling for a "Taishō Restoration."[15] Apart from the publication and widespread distribution of Ōmoto's ideas through the *Taishō Nichi Nichi Shinbun*, the authorities were also concerned about the group's ability to accumulate large financial resources through contributions from followers. The police complained that the constitutional protection of religious freedom hampered their efforts to investigate further.[16] In August 1920 the Home Ministry issued a notification to tighten controls around the group. In February 1921 Onisaburō and two other leaders including Asano were arrested. They were convicted of lèse majesté and violations of the Newspaper Law on the grounds that the millennial prophecies published in the *Taishō Nichi Nichi Shinbun* presented a threat to social order.[17]

COMMENT FROM THE PRESS

In light of the substantial reporting concerning the build-up to the 1921 persecution incident, the initial reaction in the mainstream newspapers and magazines to the official actions was unremarkable.[18] The authorities placed restrictions on the reporting of the event, and the major newspapers did not report the arrests of the Ōmoto leaders until three months after the incident. When the restrictions were lifted, some newspapers carried reports alleging that Ōmoto was stockpiling weapons and conducting dangerous activities, in addition to sensational claims of mass murder and rape.

An editorial in the *Asahi Shinbun* on 13 May 1921 seems to exemplify the dual "servant" and "watchdog" traditions. It applauded the actions of officials during the trials but also criticized the authorities for ignoring the warning signs about Ōmoto, such as its "abnormal" growth. In a similar vein, the June issue of the *Chūō Kōron* contained an article that laid the blame on the Home Affairs Minister and the chief investigator for allowing the organization to commit lèse majesté no less than eight times over a period of two years. The 15 May editorial of the *Tōkyō Nichi Nichi Shinbun* (which later became the *Mainichi Shinbun*) argued that Ōmoto's growth could be attributed not to the power of its teachings or the delusions of its followers but its ability to fill in an empty spiritual space that lay in people's hearts. This was certainly no concession to the group, however, as the editorial went on to issue a warning that society needed to watch out for such groups with great care.[19]

The *Taishō Nichi Nichi Shinbun* folded after two years in operation. Onisaburō was sentenced to five years imprisonment but was released after spending four months in jail. He appealed against his sentence and all charges were dismissed on 17 May 1927 following a general amnesty after the death of the Taishō emperor. A number of the former leaders, including Asano, subsequently left Ōmoto after being released from prison in 1922. Undeterred, Onisaburō decided to attempt international expansion of the group. In 1923 he became affiliated with a philanthropic and religious association called Kōmanjikai Dōin or Red Swastika Society, a group that was based on the Chinese mainland and was then enjoying great popularity among the Chinese public because of its philanthropic activities. Kōmanjikai Dōin had become a very influential religious group in China and Manchuria and had the support of high-ranking officials and politicians. Young suggests that this may have been an attempt by Onisaburō to ameliorate the repercussions of his past crimes.[20] By establishing links with Chinese groups, he could be viewed as supporting the national policy of international expansion. Instead of seeking to affiliate with a sectarian Shinto group, as Renmonkyō and Tenrikyō had done in the past, Onisaburō could be seen to be acting in the interests of the state by connecting with Kōmanjikai Dōin. On the other hand, Kōmanjikai Dōin wanted to ensure its survival in a climate in which other similar groups in China had vanished.[21]

Ōmoto and Kōmanjikai Dōin shared a number of characteristics including voluntary membership, lay leadership, and texts and practices that distinguished them from established religions. The two groups were in a dangerous political and cultural climate because the Sino-Japanese relationship was becoming problematic. By making strong connections to a group from mainland China, Ōmoto could be seen by the Japanese authorities to be supporting the Japanese expansion into China. On the other hand, Ōmoto also adopted the technique of spirit writing using planchettes that Kōmanjikai Dōin employed.

Spirit writing is one technique of revelation among many that have been used in Chinese religious history, but it differs from spirit possession because of its literary aspirations. While groups employing these revelations focused on spiritual and physical healing, they were also concerned with reforming the world. From the perspective of the Japanese authorities they were highly problematic. According to Stephan Feuchtwang, in the early twentieth century when Taiwan was under Japanese occupation the Japanese regime banned spirit writing.[22] As this activity raised questions about the social and political circumstances through world reform, spirit writing was potentially subversive and destructive to the regime's controlling agenda.

Ōmoto's relationship with Kōmanjikai Dōin was formed ostensibly after a delegation from Kōmanjikai Dōin arrived in Japan in 1923 to provide humanitarian aid and financial assistance in the wake of the Great Kantō Earthquake. However, both parties had been in communication some time before this disaster. The earthquake may have provided an opportunity for them to show the Japanese government their mutual support for its expansionist policies. On 3 November the delegation visited Ōmoto's headquarters in Ayabe. Dōin established temple branches in Kobe, Ayabe, Kameoka, and Tokyo. Onisaburō also attempted to travel through Mongolia in 1924. This was an ill-fated trip during which he and members of his group, including the founder of the martial art Aikidō, Ueshiba Morihei, were kidnapped. Onisaburō's exploits caused his personal popularity in Japan to rise.[23]

CLASH BETWEEN WORLD RENEWAL BELIEFS AND THE AUTHORITIES

From the 1920s until Japan's surrender in 1945, an unprecedented number of new religions like Ōmoto espousing millennial renewal appeared and made a great impact despite the danger of suppression by government authorities. Tsushima Michihito holds that many new religions of the early Shōwa period developed concepts of world renewal that appeared to resemble classical myths that related to the emperor, the imperial line, and the nation. These concepts implied fundamental changes to the existing social arrangements because they tended to reflect values of direct imperial lineage whereby the people were viewed as playing a crucial role in the nation's development. These suggestions were radical at the time, given the attempts by state authorities to develop a unified state ideology. Most new religions of the prewar period were not directly critical of the emperor, and they were more inclined to place great hopes in him as the leader of world renewal and restoration.[24] Nevertheless, reinterpreting the role of the emperor was very dangerous, as groups like Ōmoto and Hito no Michi discovered.

It took some time for the state to develop the policies that were ultimately used to control religion under state-centered Shinto. In the 1920s the bureaucracy was not coordinated in the efforts to stamp out "pseudo religions."[25] Tenri Kenkyūkai was targeted by the authorities in 1927 on the premise of spreading a millennial message predicting the destruction of Japan. Its doctrines differed from groups like Ōmoto and Hito no Michi as the group claimed that the reigning emperor was an "empty person" (kūkyo no hito) without "imperial virtue" (tentoku) whereas its own leader was the "real emperor."[26] The authorities arrested many more people, including leaders and followers of the organization. Eventually, all defendants except for Tenri Kenkyūkai's leader were given suspended sentences, and in 1930 the Supreme Court acquitted the leader himself. The group was renamed Tenri Honmichi and the authorities again persecuted the leaders and followers, disbanding the group altogether in 1938.[27]

New religions remained a major concern for established Buddhist, Shinto, and Christian groups that were keen on asserting their authority within the state hierarchy and their identities as legitimate religions, as opposed to "evil cults" or "pseudo religions." Representatives supported the government in opposing communism, which was considered to be a threat to society and the national polity, and they passed a joint resolution at a conference on 15 March 1928 for further controls on leftist groups. But the government had difficulty imposing controls on religions because of the pressures brought to bear by established religions. Thus, it vacillated between relaxing restrictions on religions and attempting to place controls on their activities.

In 1924 a ban imposed in 1890 on religious education in schools was lifted with the proviso that religious sects could not claim primacy of their teachings over those of other religions. This appeared to be a concession to the established religions. However, in 1927 a religions bill that proposed to extend the limits of the state's powers over religions became the subject of fierce debate. The bill offered tax-exempt status and other legal protections to established groups (which meant that some Buddhist groups which had lost land in the early Meiji years could reclaim it at nominal prices), but many groups objected to heavy-handed state intervention into their affairs. But some aspects of the bill, particularly those which recommended restricting the growth of "evil cults" through such measures as demanding that religious leaders be required to have achieved educational qualifications of at least middle school level, met with widespread support from the established religions.

The bill failed to pass through the Lower House because it was deemed to be out of step with freedom of religion.[28] The differing demands of the religious groups and conflicting priorities of government departments contributed to this failure. Education Ministry officials, who had initiated legislation for religions in the 1920s, sought to apply administrative uniformity to religions. Although this attempt failed, clearly the authorities were moving toward greater controls over "evil cults," and the established religions enthusiastically endorsed this approach provided they were to be protected themselves.

In 1925 the Peace Preservation Law was introduced and was initially designed to punish groups that attempted to "bring about radical changes in the national polity" (*kokutai no henkaku*). A number of Communist groups were targeted under the law. It was amended in 1928 to allow authorities to invoke the death penalty, and was further amended in 1941 to include the punishment of any groups, and particularly religious groups that were found "desecrating shrines or the dignity of the Imperial household." Under the definitions of the law, the rule of the emperor was the underlying premise of the national polity. This law provided the legal framework for the severe measures that were to be taken by the authorities toward religious groups until 1945.

The extent to which doctrinal issues surrounding the emperor's position influenced the actions of the authorities toward these new religions is debatable. Ōmoto eventually became a staunch supporter of the emperor and the Japanese military, and Hito no Michi held daily worship services for the emperor and nation for thousands of people in the 1930s.[29] If it were simply a question of doctrinal concern, it would seem odd that the government allowed these new religions and many others to continue on into the mid-1930s and expand as much as they did. Although the state eventually suppressed these new religions with strong support from established religions, they were also targeted by intellectuals.

FROM IMMORAL SUPERSTITIONS TO SOCIAL ILLNESS

While many of the major themes in the reporting surrounding Renmonkyō in the mid-Meiji period concerned the "immoral" nature of the founder and her teachings, which were derided as superstitious, by the 1920s a different "scientific" theme, which began to develop from the emerging field of psychology, concerned new religions and their proponents as manifestations of social disease. These criticisms provided a more "scientific" basis for the continuing accusations of immorality and superstition. This represented an intellectual challenge against new religions, particularly ones that enjoyed huge popularity or were reported widely in the press. The potential psychological danger "cults" can inflict on the purportedly gullible and the spiritually weak continues to be a major theme in modern societies.

Two of the main proponents of this theme were Nakamura Kokyō (1881–1952) and Morita Shōma (1874–1938). Both men believed that the activities of new religions and psychological illness were closely linked.

They considered new religions to be psychopathological phenomena that incorporated spirit possession. Morita was famous for developing a therapy for treating obsessive-compulsive and nervous disorders. Nakamura, a psychologist, founded the Japanese Association of Psychiatry (Nihon Seishin Igakkai) in 1917, which was a semi-academic association composed mostly of nonprofessionals.[30] He began publishing *Hentai Shinri* (Journal of Abnormal Psychology), which contained articles on supernatural phenomena such as telekinesis, mind reading, spiritualism, prophetic dreams, ghosts, and life after death. Nakamura was intent on exposing and eliminating "superstitious and evil cults."[31] Morita, who wrote an article entitled "Meishin to mōsō" (Superstition and delusion) in 1917, concentrated his argument on Tenrikyō and Konkōkyō. His opinions were, not surprisingly, similar to Nakamura's.

In 1920 Nakamura published a widely read book entitled *Ōmotokyō no kaibō* (Analyzing Ōmoto). He then produced a series of other works throughout the 1920s and 1930s including *Meishin to jakyō* (Superstition and evil cults, 1922) and *Meishin ni ochiiru made* (Falling prey to superstition, 1936). These works and others included Ōmoto and other new religions such as Hito no Michi and Seichō no Ie. Nakamura viewed Tenrikyō and Konkōkyō as classic examples of "suspect religions" (*giji shūkyō*), even though they had incorporated into the state's system by affiliating with Shinto sects.[32] But he was particularly opposed to Ōmoto's growth after Nao's death. Nakamura did not simply conduct a paper war against new religions. Appointed as an instructor at the Tokyo Police Academy, he not only trained the next generation of law enforcement officers about "evil cults," in the lead-up to the first suppression he repeatedly urged the authorities to act and urged the Home Minister to take action against Ōmoto.[33]

Nakamura's criticisms of new religions focused on the leaders and followers of the movements. He described the founders of Konkōkyō and Tenrikyō as being deluded and mentally ill, and labeled Deguchi Nao a psychotic whose family had mental problems. Her successor, Onisaburō, was a swindler and a master manipulator who deceived people with false predictions and spiritual sophistry.[34] As for the followers, he argued that although most had some form of psychological illness, the reason why intellectuals and other higher class members, including soldiers, businessmen, teachers, prosecutors, and lawyers were joining new religions was because they did not have a solid grounding in psychology. These types of people were fooled, he claimed, because they lacked proper education and were therefore unaware of the true nature of new religions.

Nakamura and his colleagues were intent on promoting their scientific, rationalistic approaches as appropriate avenues to solve individual and social problems. New religions that purported to treat people through alternative means were therefore an appropriate target because they were perceived as not only unscientific but also quite opposed to the interests of the nation. While the authorities did not use Nakamura's ideas specifically to justify their actions in the first Ōmoto incident, the theories did provide a type of conceptual framework for later activities against the group. Therefore, the newly developing concepts involving scientific rationalism combined with notions of the state and Shinto under the emperor.[35]

Another group of intellectuals, Shin Bukkyōto (New Buddhists), were also active in their opposition to new religions. This group of scholars from Waseda University urged the public and the government to examine the dangers posed by Ōmoto and other new religions. Although Shin Bukkyōto had been generally opposed to government interference in religious affairs since its inception in 1899, it deemed "superstitious" religions to be an appropriate target. Members apparently held different views on whether the government should opt for outright oppression of new religions. However, after the second Ōmoto incident in 1935, the leader of Shin Bukkyōto urged the authorities to continue to clamp down on such groups and "stage one massive roundup, concentrating fire on those groups possessed of quackery, whether they be established religious bodies or the newly arisen pseudo religions."[36]

In contrast to Nakamura and Shin Bukkyōto, a small group of intellectuals took a different view. Nakayama Keiichi and others began researching groups like Kurozumikyō, Tenrikyō, and Konkōkyō, and they produced a book called *Kyōha Shintō no kenkyū* (Research on Sect Shinto), which emphasized the "religious creativity" (*shūkyōteki sōzōsei*) of such groups.[37] But these scholars, who seemed to see some positive value in the groups, were clearly in the minority.

By the early 1930s the number of new religions seeking government authorization through the Education Ministry's Religious Affairs Department had jumped from 98 in 1921 to 414 in 1930. The numbers increased dramatically by 1935 when a total of 1,029 groups applied for official recognition. In response to the growing number of new religions, the language of scientific modernism combined with the

Confucian, moralistic, patriarchal judgments carried over from the past. The increase in new religions captured journalists' attention. The magazine *Bungei Shunjū* published an article in July 1931 describing how "strange, evil cults" (*jakyō kaikyō*) were causing problems for the Home Ministry and the Education Ministry. But journalists also began to incorporate the more modern arguments, which can be seen in the writings of Ōya Sōichi. He picked up on many of the ideas offered by Nakamura and other intellectuals and used them to significant effect for the rest of his career.

ŌYA SŌICHI AND "MODELS" OF NEW RELIGIONS

Ōya Sōichi was a highly prolific writer, and he wrote on a wide variety of subjects in newspapers, magazines, and books. At the time of his death in 1970, he was widely praised by his media colleagues as a true iconoclast and hailed for the "heckling spirit" (*yajiuma seishin*) he had cultivated throughout his career. Ōya's "heckling spirit" is perhaps no more apparent than in his sometimes relentless pursuit of new religions in both the prewar and postwar periods. During the prewar period, he published work critical of groups including Ōmoto, Tenrikyō, and Hito no Michi, while in the postwar period he aimed his pen at Tenshō Kōtai Jingū Kyō, Sōka Gakkai, Reiyūkai, and many other new religions. Ōya wrote about what he saw as the common traits of these groups and their leaders. His writing expounded the idea that new religions had certain models from the past they looked toward, whose ideas they borrowed while adding their own slight variations to suit their audiences.

Ōya maintained an active interest in religion throughout his career as a journalist. While he did attend church in his youth, this was apparently to take advantage of the English conversation lessons offered.[38] By the time he began his writing career after dropping out of Tokyo University in 1925, he was well versed in Marxist ideas, as were many journalists of the period. He was closely involved in socialist movements during the 1920s and early 1930s. Gradually his view toward all religions, established or new, became critical, and he admits to thinking at that time that belief in any religion was irrational and unscientific.[39]

In 1931 Ōya began to write of an "age of religious inflation" (*shūkyō infure jidai*).[40] He argued that although some groups had developed their doctrines and policies over a number of years, a significant proportion of them were only at an embryonic stage in their lives. Nevertheless, they still sought official authorization. In calling them "newly arisen religions" (*shinkō shūkyō*) he implied that the apparent faddish nature of new religions was potentially dangerous for society.[41] Ōya applied a variety of terms to new religions depending on the occasion. He observed that before the 1930s the followers of "newly arisen religions," which, he argued, were formerly labeled "evil cults," were mainly farmers and people of lower classes. In an article written in 1936, in which he listed the reasons for the "flood of pseudo religions," he argued that established religions actually have "tendencies of a pseudo-religious-type," and questions whether such groups can apply the term "evil cults" to "pseudo religions."[42] Nevertheless, in listing the reasons for the explosion of "pseudo religions," he ultimately dismissed them as "evil cults" (*inshi jakyō*), borrowing the Meiji-era term.

But while he was an aggressive opponent of new religions, Ōya did not hold back in his criticism of established religions either. He argued that established religions themselves were "pseudo religions" when they were formed. "Of course," he wrote, "it is clear that pseudo religions are complete fakes, but it goes without saying that all established religions are not exactly paragons of virtue. Originally religions were not differentiated with artificial categories such as 'authorized' or 'unauthorized.' But if we look at religions from another angle, they are all irrational and unscientific."[43] Such opinions most likely made for uncomfortable reading for established religions at a time when the definitions of heterodoxy and orthodoxy were under significant negotiation. Nevertheless, the reported growth of new religions allowed established groups to focus on a common target that could be used to divert attention from any lingering "superstitions" they themselves might be accused of holding.

By the mid-1930s Ōya had developed a degree of familiarity with new religions. It was around this time that his ideas about "models" of new religions solidified. Although he saw the solutions to individual and social problems that religions offered to be antiquated and counterproductive, he argued that leaders of new religions had suspect motives, promoted potentially dangerous practices, and ultimately drained society's resources by drawing away people's energies. Numerous groups, he argued, were breeding like diseased cells, which were breaking up and causing havoc across the country. He claimed that while similar "questionable groups" in previous times attracted mainly uneducated peasants and people of lower classes, by 1935 the pernicious effects of such groups presented a significant danger to society because of the participation of the middle class, including soldiers, educators, government officials, company workers, and "quasi-intellectuals." He also questioned the validity of groups like Tenrikyō and Konkōkyō because although these officially recognized religious bodies could no longer be called "pseudo religions" as such, they continued to display a "pseudo religious flavor" (*ruiji shūkyōteki*). Borrowing from the ideas of the psychologist Nakamura and his scientific colleagues, he concluded that the public in general, and particularly intellectuals, lost the power to criticize and that this was a major factor in the rise of the "pseudo religions." These circumstances provided the "ideal hotbed" for the "pseudo religions" to flourish.[44]

Ōya also wrote about the changes he perceived in the methods of "pseudo religions" in the mid-1930s. Before this period, he claimed, most new religions attracted ignorant people through primitive superstitions or visited the houses of sick people to sell various healing potions. However, the new religions that had appeared recently, particularly Ōmoto and Hito no Michi, had begun to use the print media with great effectiveness. Some of them had "captured" the public's attention in this way because people had great reverence for the written word. It is ironic that Ōya raises this point about "pseudo religions" employing the print media to spread their ideas without reflecting on his own work. His arguments about irrationality, superstition, and changing social structures show his proactive engagement in defining for his readers the limits of acceptable social behavior, which he supported with modern social theories and prescriptions for social disease.

Ōya backed up his ideas about new religions through extensive fieldwork. Rather than being deskbound and relying on secondhand reports, he actively sought out leaders and members of new religions and then wrote about his experiences. One of his first meetings was with Deguchi Onisaburō, who rarely missed an opportunity to engage in self-promotion. Onisaburō was, of course, a perfect subject for Ōya's attention. Multitalented and bold, he was a charismatic leader who took great risks and had widespread influence.

This meeting, held in the autumn of 1931, apparently had a profound impact on Ōya's view of new religions.[45] He met with Onisaburō again a few years later at the request of the *Mainichi Shinbun* and the Shinchōsha publishing company. He later wrote of his experiences in 1950 in the *Sandē Mainichi* magazine, stating that although Onisaburō was not unlikable, he was a "master in the business of religious management" (*shūkyō keieisha*) who got his start in the "religions biz" (*shūkyō eigyō*) by swindling people.[46] This description of Onisaburō, which shows him as slightly roguish yet potentially dangerous, is revealing. For Ōya, Onisaburō was a problematic figure who deserved attention if only to point out the damage he and those like him could cause to society.

DEMISE OF AN "EVIL CULT"

By the early 1930s Ōmoto had become a significant social and political force, and rumors appeared in the press concerning its activities. While there were a number of right-wing radical groups that appeared advocating an emperor-centered view of national identity, Onisaburō promoted a version of right-wing patriotism that called for an era of divine governance. His views on *kokutai* (national polity) differed from the official view, and while he felt that Japan had a special mission to guide the development of Manchuria and Mongolia he was concerned that this be carried out through Chinese cooperation rather than Japanese force. Onisaburō had a guiding hand in establishing and directing the Shōwa Shinseikai, a nationalistic movement that included well-known public figures and politicians and had links to both right-wing groups and the military.[47] The press had printed rumors since the formation of the Shinseikai in July 1934 about Onisaburō's significant influence in Asia and his connections with the Kōmanjikai Dōin, which was accused in some papers of being a radical and militaristic group.

The Special Higher Police were elite law enforcement officers whose activities were reported in the monthly bulletin *Tokkō Geppō*, which began publication in March 1930. Although *Tokkō Geppō* initially reported on investigations concerning Communists and student and labor movements, by March 1936 "the situation regarding religious movements" was receiving significant attention in the bulletin, reflecting the outcome of the second suppression of Ōmoto on 8 December 1935. The Special Higher Police, together with the Justice Ministry and the Prosecutor's Office, worked to develop a case against Ōmoto a year earlier. On 8 December 1935 the authorities suddenly raided the group's headquarters, arresting the leaders and destroying buildings within the grounds. The group was charged under the provisions of the Peace Preservation Law for lèse majesté and the authorities asserted that Ōmoto was attempting to change the national polity. Additional charges were laid under the laws relating to the establishment of religious buildings without a proper permit. Over one thousand suspects were arrested. On the day of the arrests, the *Tōkyō Nichi*

Nichi Shinbun reported that the chief of security of the Home Ministry stated that the authorities had acted because of the suspect nature of Ōmoto's doctrines. In this report he denied the rumor that the arrests were made because of Ōmoto's alleged influence on Japanese society through the Shōwa Shinseikai.

The actions of the authorities in clamping down on new religions were generally met with press approval. Morioka Kiyomi claims that the prewar press would print the fabricated charges of the police against new religions, such as Hito no Michi and Ōmoto. The prime motivation for this, he argues, was the potential profits the press could earn from the ensuing scandals.[48] Profit may have been one motivation, but this did not mean that the press reached unanimous agreement over the actions of the authorities. As was the case of Renmonkyō, some of the press concerning the suppression of Ōmoto appeared to reflect the dual traditions of "servant" and "watchdog." Similarly, Ōya Sōichi's articles were not just attacks on Ōmoto and religion; they were also thinly veiled critiques of state policy and the actions of the authorities. In January 1936 Ōya argued in *Nippon Hyōron* that while many newspapers had published articles on the Ōmoto incident, the actual details of the crimes reportedly committed by the group were abstract and unclear. Furthermore, he held, the claims that the group committed lèse majesté seemed extreme and that the application of the Peace Preservation Law was unnecessary. He wrote that "one gets the feeling that the arrests were carefully planned and politically motivated. It seems clear that the aim of the authorities was to use this opportunity to suppress completely this evil cult." He went on to describe a trip he took to Manchuria, where he claimed Japanese new religions like Ōmoto and Tenrikyō were attracting large numbers of followers. He commented that a Chinese follower he interviewed considered Ōmoto to be the best of the Japanese religions and that it appeared to be a real driving force for the world promotion of the Japanese people. Ōya questioned the value of the government-directed suppression when Ōmoto had been trying to unite the people, albeit in an unconventional manner. He argued that the nation could have used Ōmoto as a political tool in order to achieve its expansionist aims. Furthermore, if the authorities were serious about uncovering "evil cults," there were plenty of others still around. He advised the police to dispense with them quickly without imposing an extra burden on the long-suffering public.

Although Ōya was not standing up for new religions, it could be argued that he tried to focus his attention on "evil cults" in order to negotiate and protect his own position. In 1933 he was arrested for being a Communist party sympathizer and imprisoned for ten days, an incident that was reported in newspapers at the time.[49] Many of Ōya's press colleagues were arrested in different incidents; some, in fact, died as prisoners of conscience. Yet Ōya survived. On the one hand, the reported exchanges between Ōya and his interrogators appear to show Ōya's strong anti-authoritarian stance, a factor that led to him becoming known in the postwar period as a journalistic "heckler" who showed no favors to any particular group in society. Yet Hasegawa Kunio, the editor of a magazine that was in competition with a magazine Ōya established and edited during the 1930s, commented that Ōya's real genius lay in the fact that he managed to save himself during a time of rampant fascism.[50] Therefore, an alternative view might be that Ōya had the capacity to adjust to the circumstances for self-protection. After that time, his writings were strongly in favor of state policies such as the military advance into China. New religions served as an effective target for him to demonstrate his capacity as a "watchdog" on government actions which, in the case of the persecution of Ōmoto, fell short of the current national aims of mobilization and expansion. His support of these national aims shows a willingness to act as "servant" to the state at a time when other colleagues had fallen foul of the authorities for their political views.

Ōya was not alone in his criticism of the authorities in terms of their handling of the Ōmoto incident. *Yomiuri Shinbun* ran an article which agreed in principle with the actions of the authorities during the Ōmoto suppression and hailed them as successful, but also complained that the government had not acted quickly enough to deal with the situation. *Kokumin Shinbun* took a similar position to Ōya in arguing that it was not just "newly arisen religions" but also established groups that were causing problems for society. On the other hand, *Chūgai Shōgyō Shinpō* argued that the problem lay in the current education system. It claimed that the large number of intellectuals who were involved in such groups indicated that society did not provide appropriate positions for the intellectual classes.[51]

Meanwhile, Nakamura zealously continued his crusading pursuit of new religions, and in particular Ōmoto. At the time of the second Ōmoto incident in 1935, he proclaimed there was nothing more fearful in the world than a group like Ōmoto. He also gloated about how his predictions had come true, and joined in the chorus of opposition against "false religions," calling on the police to start with the officially recognized Tenrikyō and work their way downward.[52]

When Ōmoto began to make significant progress in the first decades of the twentieth century, ideas of scientific rationalism and psychology became part of the developing themes in the press about new religions. Religious authorities and representatives of established groups continued to criticize new religions. Arguments over genuine religion and superstitions were important for establishing authority and protecting their own positions. Such claims continued through to the postwar period. By the time the government comprehensively suppressed Ōmoto in 1935, financial factors may certainly have been at play but most journalists avoided speaking out against the authorities, or at least, the ideals of the nation state under the emperor. The general consensus was that Ōmoto threatened society on a number of levels; the suppression was the culmination of a number of factors that had been building over the years. Onisaburō was paraded in the court of public opinion as a prize catch; the manifestation of deviance. Following the Ōmoto incident, the authorities disbanded Hito no Michi in 1937 and Tenri Honmichi was dissolved under the same provisions of the Peace Preservation Law in 1938. While it had become extremely difficult for new religions to promote their activities in public without risking the danger of arrest, criticism of the military regime by journalists was also a perilous path to follow.

Despite successive prosecutions of new religions, the authorities considered the Peace Preservation Law of 1925 to be inadequate. In 1941 the law was revised with clarifications that mentioned "pseudo religions" in particular. The revision contained an important change in the wording, from targeting groups that were attempting to "change the national polity" to groups that "denied the national polity" (*kokutai no hitei*).[53] The provisions held that if a religious group worshipped different gods or *kami* other than those worshipped at Shinto shrines or contained in ancient myths, it would be denying the national polity and would be liable for prosecution. The state's powers of control were extended in 1939 with the extremely intrusive Religious Organizations Law. This law effectively subordinated all religions under the cult of the emperor. Officials could legally destroy groups whose teachings wavered from those of state-directed Shinto. Many established religions survived during the war by accepting the absolutism of this policy and escaped persecution. Not all new religions were targeted, but those that did not cooperate with the demands of the state or whose teachings were deemed intolerable by the authorities were likely candidates. In addition to Ōmoto leaders, those of Sōka Kyōiku Gakkai and Hito no Michi were also persecuted and imprisoned.

ONISABURŌ AS "MODEL"

State authorities did not necessarily have control over new religions, nor did they seek to control them in any comprehensive and unified manner until the persecution of Ōmoto in 1935. They were not always clear about their own aims with regards to religious policy, nor did they present a coordinated and consistent approach with regard to religions. Established religions, while agreeing with measures to curb the growth of new religions, did not necessarily accept the government's position in all aspects of policy. And the press did not always agree with the authorities' handling of new religions. A kind of evolving consensus developed over new religions, one that was negotiated among such disparate groups as government authorities, the press, established religions, and academics.

Renmonkyō in the Meiji period was described in language that implied it was a threat to the social fabric because of its illicit and immoral behavior. Furthermore, its teachings were against the interests of the nation because they defiled Shinto under the emperor. Terms like "pseudo religions" and "evil cults" were partly formed from a combination of Confucian-based morality and Western scientific rationality. This developed further with media reporting of subsequent new religions, such as Ōmoto and Hito no Michi. Proponents and practitioners of psychology, grounded in the ideas of scientific rationality, viewed new religions as dangerous because they led normally intelligent people away from dealing with life's problems through psychological methods. As psychology from the early Taishō period was developing as a method for treating all kinds of disorders, attacking groups that promoted healing practices and espoused personal and societal change through spiritual means was one way to justify their claims. On the other hand, groups such as the New Buddhists and other sectarian organizations were also keen to distinguish and define new religions as antisocial in order to strengthen their own social standing.

As discussed above, the idea that certain new religions or their leaders can be "models" is questionable. The distinctions between groups and individuals in terms of activities and motivations are often quite extreme. Nevertheless, in order to make sense for the reading public, the press often draws on popular notions and terms that will be easily understood. In 1930s Japan, representations of Onisaburō and his activities blended with developing ideas about the role of new religions in early Shōwa society. He drew attention to himself through his extensive efforts at self-promotion and expansion, which were intended to present his activities in a positive light. However, the mass media focused on him as a notorious figure who broke social conventions and promoted irrational teachings. The media used pre-developed notions of new religions by appropriating the language of the past while encouraging new terms that fit in with modern society (such as acknowledging "fads"). Opinions of psychologists fueled Onisaburō's notoriety as did complaints from other religions. Journalists still saw their role as educating the public and trying to keep the authorities accountable, at the same time as negotiating the treacherous line between supporting the nation and being accused of treason or crimes again the emperor. Ultimately, Onisaburō remained a mysterious figure to the public whose fate was decided by the state. Yet celebrities must deal with the media attention they receive and sometimes crave. Onisaburō certainly sought publicity and recognition for his actions. His intention as the leader of Ōmoto was to promote his beliefs and activities. Although the media brought him to the public's attention, his notoriety ultimately contributed to his downfall. Any discussion of Onisaburō's "legacy" or his role as a "model" of new religions needs to take this into account.

3
The Birth of
Two Celebrity Gods

WHILE large new religions like Ōmoto and Hito no Michi made an impact on prewar Japanese society, there were many other smaller groups that were far removed from the public spotlight. Although they became nationally notorious in the immediate postwar years, the leaders of Jiu and Tenshō Kōtai Jingū Kyō, Nagaoka Nagako and Kitamura Sayo, were virtually unknown to the public during the prewar years. Both women were highly charismatic leaders who inspired intense devotion among their followers. The conditions of pre-1945 society had a significant effect on their identities in terms of their eventual relationships with the public, the authorities, and the media during the Occupation and immediate postwar periods.

PART I: BEFORE JIKŌSON

Nagaoka Nagako (sometimes referred to as Yoshiko) was born in 1904 to a relatively prosperous farming family in Okayama prefecture. She finished one year of junior high school and then became a student nurse at an ophthalmology clinic. In 1924, she moved to Kobe and worked during the day as a nurse, and studied at a night school. However, she had a weak constitution and contracted tuberculosis. She was forced to return to Okayama in 1927. During the period of recuperation she stayed in a local Zen temple for a time. This experience marked the beginning of her religious career. In 1925 she married a seaman and moved with him to Yokohama. Her husband was often away from home and she soon became bored with married life. Although the next few years passed without remarkable incident, in 1928 she began to suffer intense fevers. After the fevers, she would fall into a trancelike state. These incidents occurred once every three months on average.[1] The high fevers and spiritual possessions continued, and a doctor diagnosed her as having a kind of infantile paralysis. It appears that she neither received nor sought treatment for this condition.

According to her account that was related to a researcher from SCAP's Religions Division in 1946, she received a revelation on 20 September 1934 in which she was guided "under the leadership of a white-bearded old man, through the celestial spheres... [and saw] the supreme goddess for the first time." During this journey, which apparently took four-and-a-half hours, this deity told her to "teach the eternal unchanging truth, save the people and work for the nation in a time of dire need."[2] In another separate interview with a Religions Division staff member, she stated that she had seen "not only the Supreme Deity but the souls of deceased persons both high and low, beginning from Buddha, Avalokitesvara [sic], Jesus Christ, Emperors Jinmu and Meiji down to common people."[3] This spiritual awakening indicated a self-realization of a special mission to save the nation from calamity. She saw herself as a messenger of a deity that passed on to her various predictions of calamities and told her of people's past lives. This experience had a profound effect on those who eventually followed her but also became the subject of mocking in the press later.

Nagaoka's beginnings as a shamanic medium have some resonance with the female founders and leaders of new religions described by Carmen Blacker, which include Tenrikyō's Nakayama Miki, Ōmoto's Deguchi Nao, and Tenshō Kōtai Jingū Kyō's Kitamura Sayo. She held that *kyōso*, who were mostly women, were

> sickly, neurotic, hysterical, odd, until a moment comes when, exacerbated by suffering, these symptoms rise to a climactic interior experience of a mystical kind. A deity, by means of a dream or a possession, seizes them and claims them for his service. Thenceforward they are changed characters. Their former oddity and sickliness give way to a remarkable strength and magnetism of personality, which is conferred on them, together with various supernormal powers, by the deity who has possessed them and who henceforth governs their lightest move.[4]

Ellen Schattschneider describes spirit mediums located in Aomori prefecture in northern Tohoku, Japan, as women who are "usually called into sacred service later in life through revelatory visions or profound illness."[5] This description also shows similarities to Nagaoka's experience. Accounts of visionary journeys have long been part of Japanese religious consciousness, and these include Buddhist tales and other stories. Yet Nagaoka's experience is also reminiscent of the remarkable story of a journey by Ōmoto's Onisaburō, whose descent into a hell then back to a heaven also included an encounter with a white-haired old man.[6]

The ideas of Ōmoto under Onisaburō eventually had a significant impact on Nagaoka, as they did with a number of new religions, such as Sekai Kyūsei Kyō, Seichō no Ie, and Mahikari, whose founders and key members were directly associated with him or were his disciples at some stage. Nagaoka may have been strongly influenced by Ōmoto's world renewal ideas, and Jiu also took up spirit writing, which Ōmoto had promoted through its connection to the Chinese new religion Kōmanjikai, mentioned in the previous chapter.

Nagaoka's close followers told vivid stories of the visions she experienced and their effects on those around her. Katsuki Tokujirō (1905–2008), who became Jikōson's successor after her death, offered detailed descriptions of her sharp insight into people's lives, including the famous followers, Futabayama and Go Seigen, who became part of the group for a time.[7] Another strong supporter, Yamada Senta (1923–2010), first met Nagaoka in 1956, which was long after the period of intense notoriety at the hands of the press she experienced in the immediate postwar period. He stated that her perceptive powers were so extraordinary that famous people from the worlds of politics, letters, and entertainment sought her advice throughout her life.[8] A number of figures called upon her during the 1950s, including the founder and first president of the Heibonsha publishing company, Shimonaka Yasaburō, and Tokugawa Musei, a former silent film voice-over performer (*benshi*) and radio star. The experiences of these close followers suggest the extent of her charisma within the group itself and their immediate circle. Her position within the group remained unchallenged until her death. Nevertheless, her talents, or the claims to those talents, were mercilessly ridiculed by the press as representing irrational and possibly dangerous beliefs.

From around 1935, she attracted a small circle of people by her spiritual pronouncements and activities. As her spiritual career developed, she began to detest married life, and she pressed her husband for a divorce. But married life had taken a toll on him as well. After returning from long stints at sea, he would return to find the house occupied by Nagaoka's followers. He finally left the house in 1935.[9]

During the initial stages of her spiritual quest, Nagaoka was preoccupied with esoteric Shingon mysticism. She divided her time between Kamata ward in Tokyo and Yokohama where she conducted informal sessions for people seeking to cure their illnesses. She apparently achieved some success and grateful customers named her "the mother of Kamata." In time, she attracted followers not only from

Tokyo, Yokohama, and Kanazawa, but also from Hokkaido and parts of Aomori prefecture.

Although Nagaoka is usually referred to as the founder of Jiu, its roots lie in an organization founded in 1941 by Minemura Kyōhei, a Shinto practitioner and businessman who was actively involved in mining development and farming. It was made of two separate groups: the first, Kōmanjikai Dōin, had had close connections to Ōmoto since 1923, as mentioned in chapter 2; the second, Kōdō Daikyō, was a Shinto-based study circle unaffiliated to an officially recognized sect. Kōmanjikai Dōin and Ōmoto formed alliances in China and Japan, and two men associated with Ōmoto, Ōshima Yutaka and Ōta Hidehito, joined Kōmanjikai Dōin in 1929.[10]

A CHILD GENIUS IN THE GAME OF GO

Although Ōshima and Ōta were key people in the foundation of what eventually became Jiu, the figure who became widely recognized for his association with the movement was the Chinese-born Go Seigen (Ch. Wu Qingyuan). Go is considered to be one of the greats of the game of go, or Japanese chess. He was a child genius and was courted by Japanese professionals who visited China. Through the lobbying of politicians and philanthropists, he went to Japan in 1928. Upon his arrival, the young Go was immediately awarded a high ranking in the professional league. By the time he was eighteen, he was part of a small group of elite players. In 1933 he was instrumental in producing a new ground breaking opening strategy that was very influential in the world of go, thus cementing his position as a player.

Although Japanese newspapers began to support the game in the first decades of the Meiji period, it was the failed assassination attempt on prince regent Hirohito on 27 December 1923 that had a significant effect on the game's eventual success. The head of the Tokyo police, Shōriki Matsutarō, was forced to resign over the affair. He then took up a new career as president of the *Yomiuri Shinbun*, which was going through difficult times. Shōriki proved to be a brilliant publisher and entrepreneur who used sensational news coverage and various gimmicks to boost sales. He had a major impact on baseball in Japan and founded the Yomiuri Giants, but under his leadership the newspaper also influenced the fortunes of go and sumo. Go Seigen gained substantial publicity through Shōriki's support. His genius was widely lauded in the print media and although Go was not a national hero of the stature of the sumo great Futabayama, who eventually joined him in Jiu, he was nevertheless an important figure whose presence in Jiu boosted the group's news value. New religions that have followers who are widely recognized as having made significant achievements in their fields can sometimes use them to acknowledge the group's position in society and even legitimate their activities. Go's own memoirs[11] and the depiction of his life in the film *Go Seigen*,[12] in which he served as an advisor, show that he was deeply concerned with spiritual matters at the time.

On a visit to China in 1935, Go joined Kōmanjikai Dōin. He was drawn to its spiritual teachings and placed great faith in the oracles that formed the basis of its practices. In 1938 Ōta and Ōshima approached Go to enlist his support in establishing a new chapter of Kōmanjikai Dōin in Japan. Together they tried to register the group as a religious organization, but the government apparently refused permission on the grounds that a Chinese religion could not be introduced to Japan.[13] Not to be defeated, they decided to form a Japanese support base for the group. It carried out clandestine activities in order to avoid the authorities' attention. The worsening military situation between the two countries meant that developing meaningful and effective activities was impossible, and the group made little progress.

Kōdō Daikyō, the second group that Jiu developed from, was established by Minemura Kyōhei and his brother-in-law Mitsuo, who was a medium of some repute. Minemura felt he had been granted a divine mission, and he saw his mining activities as contributing to the economic and spiritual wealth of the nation.[14] As Minemura's various business ventures floundered, he became more involved in religious pursuits. Kōdō Daikyō apparently emphasized unity with the emperor and service toward him, the followers worshipped Amaterasu Ōmikami, the sun goddess, and their business concerns were mingled with religious activities.[15] Minemura advocated the idea of "the oneness of faith and business" (*kyōgyō icchi*), and the members chanted this phrase. He reasoned that the number of believers would increase, and finances would improve through the joint promotion of religion and business.[16] Although Minemura tried to apply his business acumen to his group, he was not a spiritually charismatic figure. Instead, his brother-in-law took the lead in conducting rites. The main spiritual inspiration for Kōdō Daikyō came through Mitsuo in the form of oracles (*shinji*), which were used to guide the mining development activities. Despite his efforts, Mitsuo could not stimulate the flagging Nagano project and it ultimately failed.

Ōta and other supporters of Kōmanjikai Dōin lived near some members of Kōdō Daikyō. Due to similarities in the spiritual aspects of each group, relationships began to form between their members, and Ōta and Go became closely involved with Kōdō Daikyō. However, Ōta and the other Kōmanjikai Dōin supporters were in a precarious position. The Special Higher Police continued to investigate religious groups, and those that advocated their own interpretations of the emperor and imperial system were likely targets. After some negotiation among themselves, they decided to enshrine their object of worship at Kōdō Daikyō's base. This arrangement suited Minemura because Ōta, who had various contacts in the business world, agreed to try and secure funding for Minemura's mining enterprises. The young Go benefited from the merging of the two groups as he met his future wife, Nakahara Kazuko, through Minemura's introduction. Ōta concentrated more on business dealings than religious activities, and he sought financing from banks and from the munitions ministry for Minemura's projects. Kōmanjikai Dōin supporters' group dissolved in 1940 and a number of the members joined Kōdō Daikyō.[17]

THE BIRTH OF JIU

In 1941, the group changed the name Kōdō Daikyō to Jiu.[18] Go, Ōta, and Ōshima were all closely involved in the organization.[19] Although the group began to advocate world renewal ideas around this time, they could not easily spread these teachings due to pressure from the authorities. Nevertheless, the group made various attempts to reestablish effective communication with the headquarters of Kōmanjikai Dōin in China. Ōta and Go travelled to China in March 1942 and visited the headquarters in Beijing. Minemura wanted to renew the ties with Kōmanjikai Dōin's leaders. However, due to the continuing conflicts in China, Kōmanjikai Dōin decided not to send a delegation from China to Japan. It would have been virtually impossible for a Chinese-based religion to gain any official approval from the Japanese government to establish a branch in Japan at that time. Ōta and Go returned to Japan three months later, having failed in their mission to establish effective ties. It was sometime after this that Nagaoka became involved in Jiu.

She first went to Minemura's house in Tokyo from her home in Yokohama at the request of one of her followers, a businessman from Aomori prefecture who was involved in the mining business. He commissioned her to conduct rites to improve the fortunes of his flagging copper mine. Each summer, from 1936 until sometime in 1942, she travelled to the site to administer rites and offer him guidance on his business based on the oracles she received. However, despite her efforts toward resuscitating the business, the mine did not yield significant results. She went to Minemura for financial assistance and their relationship began to deepen.[20] They were on good terms with each other and Nagaoka made a favorable impression on those who gathered at the house. She began to make regular visits and performed divinations, which impressed Jiu members. Her popularity as a medium grew rapidly. In fact, Minemura and his brother-in-law Mitsuo entrusted her with taking over the task of spiritual guide and interpreter of revelations during times when both were away on business or other matters. Their absences became more frequent, and as a result, their influence on the followers diminished while Nagaoka's increased. According to a Religions Division report based on an interview with Go, after he met her he decided to "devote himself to her teachings and gave up playing go in compliance with her request." He eventually resumed playing, with her permission, in July 1946.[21]

A POLICE RAID

Nagaoka's spiritual convictions solidified when she was introduced to some of the ideas associated with Ōmoto through her contact with other members of Jiu. Her ideas on world renewal were similar to those promoted by Ōmoto before the second persecution in 1935.[22] Nagaoka firmly believed in the religious authority of the emperor, and she participated in rituals involving emperor worship. She shared with other members of Jiu the conviction that Japan had a special mission to save the world through the emperor. This particular brand of *yonaoshi*, which placed Japan at the center of the universe, certainly appears to be nationalistic, and Jiu was eventually accused in the postwar period of promoting ideas that were against democracy.

A pamphlet of Nagaoka's teachings called *Makoto no hito* (True people) was published in the autumn of 1943. It was a significant publication that indicated Nagaoka's strengthening role within the group, particularly in terms of spiritual ideas and philosophy. The pamphlet proclaimed that after the present dire circumstances had passed, a period of world renewal would begin. While ideas of chaos followed by world renewal had played a role in a number of religious movements from the early modern period, during the early Shōwa period it was a particularly risky form of social protest, as Ōmoto and Tenri Honmichi discovered. *Makoto no hito* argued that the only way for the Japanese to achieve this would be for them to do away with individualism, liberalism, and materialism and become "true people."

In fact, the police had been closely watching Jiu for some time. Although they were aware that a form of world renewal comprised part of Jiu's beliefs, the main reason for the investigation was to probe aspects of Minemura's business activities, particularly those relating to mining. While the police decided that Jiu posed no major threat to public safety, they conducted a raid on the premises where Nagaoka and some of her followers were living in Yokohama on 8 February 1945. They uncovered a copy of *Makoto no hito*, which contained references calling for "cooperation in the realization of imperial ideals" and "the end of the holy war." Tsushima holds that even though there were references relating to world renewal and "the holy war," the pamphlet did not display any blatant disrespect toward the emperor.[23] Nagaoka was immediately arrested and imprisoned for some weeks. A report of the Education Ministry's Religious Affairs Section published in 1950 claims that the reason why Nagaoka was arrested was because she formed a group called the "Society for World Renewal" (Yonaoshi Kai) with a number of her followers.[24] Although this does indicate how potentially dangerous world renewal was viewed at the time, in fact the source of this particular claim and the reasons for her arrest are unclear. Nevertheless, the raid marked the first official attempt to control Jiu and the beginning of her difficult relationship with the Japanese authorities, which was to continue into the postwar period.

Go Seigen tried to appeal directly to the Home Minister for her release, and although it is unclear whether his efforts had any effect, she was released on 3 March 1945 and was sent to a hospital immediately because she had been coughing up blood during her detention.[25] She returned to the house in Yokohama after a brief period of recuperation. From that time on, according to her loyal supporter Katsuki Tokujirō, Jiu was under constant police surveillance.[26]

Over the next few months Nagaoka strengthened her position within the core Jiu community as a result of Minemura's deteriorating physical condition and increasingly erratic behavior. His brother-in-law had taken control of the mining business but it soon folded. The defining moment of the leadership change from Minemura to Nagaoka came when the air raids of the Allied forces hit Tokyo on 25 May 1945. A group of ten members of Jiu, including Go, his wife, her sister, and

Nagaoka were forced to flee Yokohama because of the intensive bombing. They managed to reach Minemura's house in Tokyo but it had sustained major damage. Nagaoka and Minemura then decided it would be best to split up. He and several of his close supporters left Tokyo while Katsuki, Go Seigen and his party, and others stayed with Nagaoka. With the loss of the house and his departure, Minemura effectively relinquished leadership of Jiu.

LIVING BY ORACLES

Nagaoka's group moved to another temporary residence in Tokyo on 31 May. That day, she delivered an oracle that was to have a significant effect on the group's future: it declared a new era for Jiu centering on Nagaoka. It signaled major changes for the group, and marked the beginning of an intense period of tension within Jiu and between the group and the outside world.

According to Yamada Senta, the method of recording the oracles was influenced by Ōmoto's adoption of spirit writing rituals.[27] During this process Nagaoka first offered prayers in front of the shrine to various deities (*kami*). Go's wife Kazuko and her younger sister Kanako acted as mediums and transmitted the messages or guidance from the deities. Kazuko then fell into a trance-like state after emitting high-pitched sounds and began to receive messages from the deities. Kanako held out a piece of paper while Kazuko used a pen to record the messages or instructions from the deities. On other occasions Kanako would record the messages, or Kazuko would write them down without Kanako's help.[28] Although Nagaoka did not verbalize or record the messages, she always took spiritual leadership because she called forth the deities.[29] According to Katsuki, Jiu members referred to each other as "comrades" (*dōshi*). They did not consider themselves to be "believers" (*shinja*) because they felt they were all equal under the eyes of the gods.[30] This, however, was not how the authorities or the press later viewed the situation. There appeared to be no question that Nagaoka was the leader. The group conducted its activities based on her convictions and revelations, and they looked to her for guidance.

An oracle recorded on 31 May 1945 called for the members to take Nagaoka's message of world renewal to the outside world. Apart from Minemura's business activities, the group had remained extremely insular and the members eschewed contact with those outside their circle; they did not make significant public efforts to propagate their beliefs widely. It is likely that the change in the group's activities mirrored the changing conditions of society. By the middle of 1945, many people were starving and the country was in crisis. The record of the oracle delivered at this time essentially marked the "reestablishment" of Jiu and a defining of its mission. However, the actual official ceremony formally establishing the renewed Jiu took place some six months later on 15 November 1945.[31]

Virtually all courses of action and activities Jiu attempted from 31 May 1945 onward were based on the oracles. They concentrated on restructuring the current social systems and world renewal and did not recommend overthrowing the emperor but rather reaffirmed the importance of imperial rule. The sun goddess played the main role in the achievement and administration of world renewal whereas various buddhas and bodhisattvas had the task of saving people and cleansing spirits. For example, the founder of Shingon Buddhism, Kōbō Daishi, and the bodhisattva of compassion, Kannon, were extremely important in the second task. The group also chanted *tenji shōmyō*, which was a prayer specific to Jiu.[32] When Nagaoka took over the leadership, oracles became the dominant part of Jiu's spiritual activities and direction. They were believed to have infallible authority and each member of the group, including Nagaoka herself, was compelled to follow their instructions. Despite her being leader of the group, she was bound to follow the instructions contained within the oracles as the others were. Apparently Nagaoka herself would express surprise and shock at the types of activities Jiu was required to perform by the deities.[33]

The members felt a sense of great apprehension because the oracles required each member to participate in activities that broke the boundaries of social convention and common sense. They were constantly torn between the fear of repercussions that might occur because of the demands placed upon them, and also great hope for the achievement of world renewal and eternal peace.[34] On the one hand, there was a sense that the messages were coming directly from deities who were directing the "comrades" to carry out a holy mission for which only they were qualified to carry out. This inspired them and solidified their sense of belonging and self-worth. It also provided encouragement that the goal of world renewal was drawing closer. On the other hand, they could not predict what sort of commands the deities would give them, and there was always the possibility that the oracles would call on the believers to perform actions that would cause friction between Jiu and the world outside. Nagaoka was highly sensitive and would experience extreme physical distress if she felt the presence of malignant spirits around her. Her reaction would then trigger off a sense of desperation and fear among other members of Jiu. They interpreted Nagaoka's suffering as a warning from a powerful god that they should personally reform and strengthen their resolve to carry out their assigned tasks for world renewal.[35] The core group's communal lifestyle served to intensify the feelings they shared. Many of them had been living together in one place for a long time, and together they had endured evacuation and relocation after the fire bombings in Yokohama and Tokyo. When the headquarters was reestablished in Tokyo, there were between ten to thirty people living in the same house. As the community was strengthening internally, it isolated itself from the world outside. The group saw its headquarters as a model of the original imperial palace, a pure holy world that had to be completely separated from the corrupt society outside. According to Go, the lifestyle was one of monastic stoicism, and no contact with the outside world was permitted for the believers.[36] Any contact that had to be made was done with great care, and Nagaoka in particular would not permit casual visits or grant an audience (*hai'etsu*, which usually means "an imperial audience") with outsiders such as landlords.[37] This isolationism contributed to inevitable conflicts with landlords and neighbors.

From 31 May 1945 the oracles were delivered with increasing frequency, sometimes at the rate of four or five per day. These were all recorded in notebooks and continued to be written down until November 1946 when Jiu moved to Kanazawa. The subjects covered were wide-ranging and the central themes were the design of world renewal under the *kami*, blueprints on post-world-renewal society, and its administration under the *kami*. A number of oracles concerned detailed directions for the day-to-day activities and lives of Jiu's "comrades" and administration of the group, including leadership roles and plans for building a financial base for future activities. In effect, their lives were controlled by the dictates of the oracles.[38]

THE APPEARANCE OF JIKŌSON

The oracle delivered on 31 May 1945 set the framework for the reestablishment of Jiu including detailed instructions on the daily activities of the group. Following this came an oracle that outlined aspects of the practice (1 June), one that announced eight leaders within the group (6 June), and another that proclaimed that the group must unify around

Nagaoka (17 June). The word "Jikō" (璽光) first appeared through an oracle delivered on 22 June 1945. This was an important message because it meant that Nagaoka was not a leader in the mundane, human sense: she identified with a deity sent to save the world.[39] Her followers referred to her as Jikōson from then on.

A key issue concerning Jikōson is one that affects many charismatic leaders of religious movements. Did she dominate her followers to the extent that they simply obeyed her dictates, or was she a spiritual leader whose guidance they sought freely? Did they view her as a living god (*ikigami*), which is how the postwar press portrayed her? The memoirs of the people closest to her reveal conflicting opinions. Go Seigen and his wife were both key members but they had left the group by the end of 1948 in a rather acrimonious split. Go made some remarks that were repeated in the press about Jiu and Jikōson that were taken by its members as derogatory.[40] Go claims that she simply declared herself to be a deity and assumed the name Jikōson, implying that she had become the leader who assumed absolute spiritual authority.[41] A report made by two representatives of SCAP's Religions Division who visited Jiu headquarters in September 1946 seems to indicate her dominance over people at that time: "[Jikōson's] adherents obey her completely and are eager to perform what she tells them, however absurdly her words may sound; they salute her with the most respect imaginable."[42] While Katsuki claims that she did not dictate orders but merely acted as a conduit for the various deities, it is clear he believed she had powers beyond ordinary people.[43] Yamada Senta's view is that Jikōson was definitely an *ikigami*, the manifestation of the universal light that could shine on all humanity. Sometime after their first meeting, Jikōson said to him, "You might think you are looking at the real Jikōson. In fact, this body is just one form of Jikōson. The real Jikōson is always around and never goes away."[44] Rather than any kind of human leader, for him Jikōson was simply imparting universal truths, and was therefore a living god.

Once the basic structure and operations had been put into place, Jiu began to direct its world renewal activities toward the outside world. The first plan was to send Go and Katsuki to Manchuria to tell Emperor Puyi about Jiu and seek his cooperation. At the time, a number of Kōmanjikai members in China were close to the emperor. Although the plans came close to fruition—Go had apparently even arranged a military aircraft through his contacts—the trip did not eventuate. Instead, just before their departure, Jikōson and Katsuki were suddenly arrested by the police in Tamagawa in early July 1945.

The police had maintained a close watch on the group since Jikōson's initial arrest. The group spent most of its time in rented lodgings chanting and praying for the arrival of Amaterasu Ōmikami to save the world from impending calamity. Their landlord, who clearly had some issues with the group, told the police that the group held questionable beliefs centering on the sun goddess. The leaders of Jiu were arrested on suspicions of lèse majesté. Although Jikōson was released after ten days, Katsuki was detained for a period of five weeks.[45] Records do not show why Katsuki was held for that period of time, but one possibility is that the police believed that he, rather than Jikōson, actually controlled the group. Eighteen months later, in the Kanazawa incident of 1947 Katsuki was named in a press interview of one of the arresting police officers as the probable mastermind of the group.[46]

Jiu moved into another house owned by a sympathetic supporter. He may have donated his house to the group for a time. Jiu usually survived on donations from followers or relatively wealthy benefactors. By this stage, the group was convinced that it was time for them to spread the messages of world renewal that were contained in the oracles to the outside world. Although they had spent most of their time cloistered in their lodgings, the messages of the oracles demanded that they take radical action. Jiu entered a period during which it attempted quite audacious actions that ultimately led to its decline. The new landlord was charged with the first mission. It was his unenviable task to inform the emperor directly that Jikōson had arrived and that she and her followers were ready to carry out the essential task of world reform. He did not even attempt to do this and the next oracles received harshly criticized those who failed in their duties.

In the last days of the war, Jiu continued to hold high hopes for the emperor to lead in the holy mission of world renewal. The official state ideal of "the whole world under one roof" (*hakkō ichiu*) centering on the emperor had been part of their plan for the future. This concept was viewed by the Allied Occupation as being connected to state-centered Shinto, militarism, and ultranationalism, and its use was prohibited under the so-called Shinto Directive.[47] Yamada Senta argued that *hakkō ichiu*, in Jikōson's interpretation of the term, had nothing to do with state-enforced Shinto ideals and right-wing nationalism but was instead an all-encompassing view of the world that recognizes and respects all people and creeds: "The world under one roof doesn't mean everyone follows Shinto under the state. It means tolerance for all people and beliefs."[48] Nevertheless, while this is how he expressed his understanding of Jikōson's beliefs more than sixty years after the fact, she appears to have supported Japan's expansion during wartime. While her views may have been deemed to be at variance with the official line, they were colored with strong nationalistic ideals of the day.

Jikōson was convinced that she was sent to act as assistant to the emperor in order to fulfill the wishes of the sun goddess to bring about a "restoration of imperial power" (*kōi ishin*). An oracle, delivered and recorded on 12 July 1945, held that "Jikō" was the representative of Amaterasu Ōmikami sent to help the emperor. To Jikōson the emperor was not only a living god, but also the rightful ruler of Japan and the entire world.[49] Consequently, the group's activities became focused on the imperial family. Jiu saw Japan's worsening domestic situation toward the end of the war as a sign of divine punishment. The members believed that the gods had abandoned the nation and that the destruction surrounding them indicated that the time for world renewal had arrived. They equated the bombings of Tokyo and Yokohama with an intensification of "holy war." By the time of the surrender and the arrival of the Occupation troops, Jiu clung onto these beliefs, and it felt ready to launch into its second phase of activities toward world reform. The group became more daring and reckless in its attempts to influence society in order to realize its self-appointed mission.

By the end of the war, Jiu had a solid, if small, core of members who were determined to pursue their own path of world renewal. Their close connections with Ōmoto and Kōmanjikai Dōin certainly informed their spiritual practices. The unwanted attention from the authorities contributed to the group's sense of mission in that they saw their task as dangerous but vital. The demands of the oracles that Jikōson passed on from the "gods" were increasingly extreme, requiring absolute adherence to the divine dictates. Thus, the blueprint for Jiu's postwar actions was set in the prewar period through a combination of social and internal pressures that grew more intense for them as the new period of religious freedom was imposed on the country at the beginning of the Occupation. Although Jikōson's closest supporters considered her to be an unparalleled mystic, if not a living god, the police and other authorities viewed her as potentially troublesome.

PART II: BUILDING A "KINGDOM OF GOD"

The woman most often compared to Jikōson in the Occupation-period press, Kitamura Sayo, the founder of Tenshō Kōtai Jingū Kyō, came from an entirely different background to Jikōson. Born on 1 January 1900 into a farming family in a small village in Yamaguchi prefecture, she was the fourth daughter of nine children. Her formal education ended after she completed primary school. Her spiritual journey in the prewar and postwar periods is contained in the group's doctrinal text *Seisho* (生書, "Book of Life").[50] This work appears to be the only source of information on her activities in the prewar period. Although it is hagiographic, postwar sources, including SCAP and Japanese government reports and print media publications, indicate that *Seisho*'s descriptions of some of her character traits and attitudes are accurate. The passages from *Seisho* dealing with Kitamura's life before she experienced the religious awakening that profoundly influenced her activities until her death indicate her determination, resilience, and unwillingness to compromise. As with other hagiographies, *Seisho* is designed to highlight the achievements and qualities of the founder in order to reveal her characteristics as an exemplary person. These are traits that characterized her postwar activities and were recognized by journalists and the authorities alike.

In *Seisho*, a childhood friend recalls that Sayo as a young girl was quite manly, funny, was good at climbing trees, and argued frequently.[51] In 1920 she married the thirty-seven-year-old Kitamura Seinoshin, a resident of Tabuse in Yamaguchi prefecture (a "weak and colourless man," in Carmen Blacker's assessment).[52] He had spent time working in Hawai'i and returned to Japan to live with his mother. This woman was a strict taskmaster and serial mother-in-law, having driven away her son's former wives after using them to work the family fields for a season and then forcing them to divorce by the time of the next harvest. Kitamura was bride number seven, but she was stronger than her predecessors and withstood her husband's mother's constant haranguing without complaint. She bore Seinoshin a son, Yoshihito (1922–2007). Her mother-in-law eventually recognized her redeeming qualities, and just before she died in 1940 she entrusted her with the farm finances. Kitamura later expressed gratitude for having had the opportunity to go through these trials with this woman because of the great virtues she learned.[53] While dealing with her new family, Kitamura earned the respect of others in the village. People noted that she had extraordinary physical strength and endurance. She broke a number of social conventions such as wearing *mompe* (trouser-like garments) before the trend took on among women during the war. She also rode a bicycle around town at a time when it was unusual even for men to do so. During her involvement with local women's associations, she developed firm views about fighting social injustice.[54]

THE FIRST "DIVINE TEST"

Kitamura's life changed dramatically on 22 July 1942 after some buildings on the property were destroyed by a fire that had been deliberately lit. This was the first "divine test" that initiated her spiritual awakening. She was overcome with guilt and consulted a local faith healer who told her to pray at a local Shinto shrine in order to find the culprit. Despite spending days in intense prayer and taking cold-water baths as penance, the culprit's identity remained a mystery. Based on the healer's advice she continued to pray and gradually came to experience a sense of great joy. Although she still wanted to find the culprit, an assistant police officer remarked offhandedly that she should just let things go and forgive the arsonist. His words made a deep impression on her, and she realized that if it had not been for the arsonist and the fire she would not have been able to achieve such a state of spiritual fulfillment. She continued on with her practices along the path to self-realization until one day, in March 1944, the healer told her that she would become a living god.[55]

On 4 May 1944, she felt the presence of a being in her stomach that she eventually identified as the "absolute god of the universe" (*uchū zettai naru kami*). Although the being first declared itself to be a snake by the name of Tōbyō, it eventually revealed itself to be Tenshō Kōtai Jingū 天照皇大神宮, a combination of the female Amaterasu Ōmikami and the male god Kōtai Jin. At first Kitamura thought she had been possessed by an evil spirit, and she intensified her practices in order to expunge it. The being told her that these practices were completely useless, and it advised her to cleanse her soul, to "go to god" (*shinkō*), and "achieve a divine union between the person [that is, Kitamura herself] and god" (*gasshō*).[56] It further commanded that she recite the phrase *na-myō-hō-renge-kyō* one hundred times per day. The phrase *na-myō-hō-renge-kyō* 名妙法連結教 is quite different to *namu-myōhō-renge-kyō* 南無妙法蓮華経, the *daimoku*, of the Nichiren tradition.[57] Thus began an internal conversation with a deity that was to drive her activities until the end of her life.

The being within her continued to demand things, such as forcing her to chastise passersby in the street for their "sins." It began to take scores of her resistance and compliance. Once when she tried to ignore the commands, it threatened to punish her and offered her a choice of punishment, either a cerebral hemorrhage or internal hemorrhage. Nevertheless, the being was not entirely malevolent. It gave her accurate weather forecasts, guided her toward the efficient completion of household chores, and even gave her cooking lessons. It also revealed her previous lives, discussed the state of the war, and made some predictions, such as Japan's surrender. Although she had an extremely difficult time dealing with the being, Kitamura finally resigned herself to accepting its dictates. When she did this, she found that she could perform feats of great physical strength. For example, when she responded willingly to its demand that she do some gardening around the farm, she was able to pull out particularly tough weeds with one hefty tug.

"GOD'S MAIDSERVANT"

As she began to realize that she needed to submit to these kinds of orders, she began to pour forth sermons and songs that seemed to flow endlessly. In fact, despite the belief that she was the mouthpiece of the deity, Kitamura became well-known for wordplay. For example, concerning the expression mentioned previously, "going to god" (*shinkō* 神行) is a homonym for "belief" (*shinkō* 信仰), and "a divine union between the person and god" (*gasshō* 合正) is a homonym for "joining one's hands in prayer" (*gasshō* 合掌).

It is unclear whether this use of words was *kotodama*, which is a belief in the magical power of words and sounds. *Kotodama* is believed to have a foundation in folk belief in Japan. Some interpretations hold that *kotodama* is an extension of animism, whereby beliefs in the spirits can be extended to inanimate objects. Esoteric Buddhism in Japan used chants and mantras, and various key figures, such as Kukai and Saichō, claimed that these words had the power to protect the nation. New religions also incorporated *kotodama*, and Nancy Stalker points out that it was an important facet of Ōmoto's teachings under Onisaburō. She also notes that early scholarly criticisms of new religions that used *kotodama* ignored the long history of appropriation by established groups.[58] Some of Kitamura's critics in the postwar period seized on phrases to claim that she was appropriating commonly understood religious concepts without producing anything original herself. Although Kitamura later claimed that her revelations were purely from the absolute god of the universe and that her teachings came directly from this being, a SCAP report lists identifiable elements from at least four other religious traditions in her teachings.

The name Tenshō Kōtai Jingū Kyō, which could be read as "the teaching of the shrine of Amaterasu," clearly contains strong Shinto elements.[59] The term *rokkon shōjō* (六根清浄) in Buddhism would normally mean purification of the six sense organs, but Kitamura used the homonym *rokkon shōjō* (六魂清浄), meaning the purification of the six worldly desires. There are a number of Christian elements such as the concept of angels, the notion of a divine land (like heaven), and the concept of a god in heaven. She also used terms from other new religions, such as Tenrikyō.[60] Although journalists and critics did accuse her of lacking originality, they could hardly accuse her of not having a sense of humor. One example of this is her self-description as "god's maidservant" (*onna yakuza* 女役座), a homonym for "female *yakuza* [gangster]." Her use of humor and phrases that evoked not only familiar religious ideas but also famous figures and current events continued on until her death.

CRITICIZING AUTHORITY IN PUBLIC

While Kitamura gradually became used to the being's remarkable predictive powers, she was stunned when it began to criticize not only high-ranking army officers but also the emperor. She knew that there could be grave consequences if such criticisms were aired in public. One day the being in her body suddenly made a shocking announcement, describing the emperor as hardly a living god, but someone who was packed in a tightly nailed box and given the role of an idiot.[61] When she questioned these extreme statements, the being replied that it was simply telling the truth that would soon be realized by all. Some days later it told her that speaking out against the emperor was not disrespectful or insulting because he had abandoned the nation but did not realize he was being led in the wrong direction. Nevertheless, it warned her that she would probably be arrested if she spoke about the emperor that way in public, and if she was arrested various misfortunes would befall her.

Despite these warnings, by the beginning of 1945 Kitamura began to voice criticisms of the emperor and the imperial institution. John Dower notes that before the end of the war, police in some areas reported an increase in direct criticism of the emperor. Some police reports included cases of children singing songs about the imperial palace burning down together with other examples of offences that were punishable under the laws of lèse majesté.[62] When the Occupation began, the charge of lèse majesté became invalid after the war. Thus, it is worth considering the claims contained in *Seisho* relating to the public criticisms of the emperor expressed before the surrender.

She was highly critical of existing social structures, including the imperial institution, during the Occupation and later postwar periods,[63] and her uncompromising position and sharp critiques of society appealed to many people who felt abandoned or betrayed by the government and even the emperor. *Seisho* is the only source of these prewar critiques, and their publication could be seen as a tactic by the group designed to attract people who were disillusioned with the wartime regime's promotion of the emperor. This would lend substance to the idea of Kitamura as a fearless leader, thus giving her some credibility during the postwar period when the imperial system did receive some public criticism. While on the available evidence it is difficult to either confirm or deny whether she actually did make these statements, it is sufficient to observe that these claims in the hagiographic account promote the founder in a positive light with respect to her postwar image of an uncompromising yet perceptive leader.

Kitamura's moment of spiritual realization came when the being told her that she would have to sacrifice her own life and those of her family members in order to ensure the salvation of the country. When she replied that she would submit to its demands completely if it meant saving the country, the being told her that she had grasped the meaning of "going to god." It then raised her two feet in the air, and she had finally realized her mission.[64] From that time she preached everyday and walked into the town spreading the message of world reform.

THE MAGGOT WORLD

After the being entered her body, Kitamura's personality changed quite remarkably from humble, polite, and modest to aggressive, forthright, and to many people, quite rude. If she started to talk to former acquaintances or relatives who did not meet with the being's approval, it ordered her to cease at once. Eventually she criticized virtually everyone she met on the street. She decreed that society had become the "maggot world" (*uji no sekai*) and she stopped using honorific terms of address, choosing terms like "maggot beggars" (*uji no kojiki*), "beggar officials" (*hotoi no kojiki*), or "traitor beggars" (*kokuzoku no kojiki*) depending on their status and the occasion. The being demanded she use rough, unconventional language. Kitamura once explained to Carmen Blacker that the reason why she wore men's clothes was because it would look incongruous for such language to come from someone in female attire.[65]

After seeing this change, most people avoided her for fear of censure or public humiliation. They thought that she was mad because it seemed she had turned completely irrational and had also sent her only son to war. After Kitamura's spiritual breakthrough, all the problems she had experienced—her irascible mother-in-law, a weak and unreliable husband, and a son who had gone to war in a foreign country—simply became fuel for her fiery tongue. She criticized the war, the army, the government, the emperor, people who she thought were spiritually impure, and other religions.[66] On New Year's Day 1945 she sang a song that outlined the basic doctrine used for the creation of a "kingdom of god." The lyrics contained a message of the human world coming to an end "in a sea of furious flames." This clear exposition of Kitamura's own version of *yonaoshi*, in which she predicted destruction then world renewal with the promise of salvation for those who listened to her message, served as a kind of template for her postwar activities.

In the final months of the war, Kitamura made more contact with the local community. She was invited by the head of the Tabuse Women's Association to address a meeting at the local primary school.[67] The principal and a teacher at the school were also scheduled to lecture at the gathering. She launched a stinging attack on the teacher, whom she accused of stealing from the army and making profits on the black market. Despite feeling greatly embarrassed by her outburst, the host invited her to join the other speakers for refreshments. She refused, saying that unlike the "lecture beggars" she would not accept gifts. Despite this behavior, she was invited to another meeting at the local school where she stated after the enemy's bombs fell, all people could do was polish themselves and repent. Kitamura suggested that a meeting be held at her house. This marked a turning point in her religious career.

Later that night, the being told her, "Shout, O-Sayo! Shout at the top of your voice until your throat bleeds. The more you shout, the more people will understand your teaching, especially those who are sincere and conscious. You should travel at your own expense, carrying a celestial sack on your shoulder.... You have been appointed to perform a Salvation Dance [*muga no mai*] when the present world is on the verge of collapse."[68] The *muga no mai* (often translated as the "dance of ecstasy") became one of the core aspects of the practice of the group and one of the main sources of ridicule in the postwar media. While it appears to be a free-form movement that involves the whole body, the practice is aimed at bringing the practitioner "closer to god."

On 22 July 1945 Kitamura preached her first sermon at her house. Approximately fifty people gathered in the morning, but the numbers swelled as the day wore on. Although most were concerned about the state of the war, after hearing Kitamura sermonize on the war, daily life, and numerous other issues, her listeners apparently experienced a great sense of relief. Her sermons were a combination of songs and monologues interspersed with occasional dancing. The content of the sermons was sometimes quite specific, and it usually concerned people she was censuring or praising. Word about the sermons began to spread among people in Tabuse and other communities and localities.

Kitamura's pronouncements about Japan losing the war disturbed some people to the extent that they alerted the police from the nearby town of Hirao. When she appeared on August 14, the police chief demanded that she stop making such speeches. She agreed to stop and no further action was taken. This was the first time Kitamura's activities attracted the attention of the authorities. Two days later the news of Japan's unconditional surrender to the allied forces by the emperor was broadcast to the nation.

People continued to appear at her house in increasing numbers, especially after the surrender was announced. Eventually supporters referred to Kitamura as Ōgamisama ("Great God"), indicating an acknowledgment of her status as a living god. As with Jiu, the people who joined Kitamura were known as "comrades" (*dōshi*) because she insisted that they were not "followers" (*shinja*) because they were working together "to establish god's kingdom." Some participants were "educated people with much knowledge of modern science." [69] Although enthusiastic "comrades" began to take her message to the town themselves where they exhorted passersby to go and listen to her speak, it was Kitamura's powerful and uncompromising presence that made the deepest impressions. Among the various stories of her early activities, one of the most compelling is her confrontation with Kishi Nobusuke (1896–1987), the future prime minister of Japan whose hometown happened to be Tabuse.

A PROPHECY COMES TRUE

Kishi served in various governmental capacities in Manchuria from 1936 to 1939 and was a skilled bureaucrat. He rose up the ranks quickly to become a member of the wartime cabinet of Tōjō Hideki from 1941 to 1944, although his success was cut short by Japan's defeat in 1945. SCAP labeled him a "Class A" war criminal and he was imprisoned until 1948. His part in Kitamura's story began just before he was sent to Tokyo's Sugamo prison. By war's end, he had returned to Tabuse to await judgment by the victors. On 13 August 1945 Kitamura Sayo paid him a visit. In her recollection of the events, she found him suffering from severe leg pain and told him she would take the pain back to her home as a gift to him. She returned to his house on 17 August and scolded him and his wife. Although friends and relatives had gathered around to commiserate over his impending arrest, Kitamura told him that he would leave for a period of three years, reflect on his behavior, and then become the prime minister. This prophecy eventually came true. The politician and the god developed an unusual relationship of politics and religion that would continue for some years.[70]

According to another account, not everyone gathered at Kishi's house appreciated her presence. Some demanded that she leave but she refused and began to pray. Kishi even joined in the prayers, "pausing occasionally to swallow down a cup of sake." After a few minutes, Kishi's secretary demanded to know why the gathering was letting "an old fool of a woman" take over the solemn occasion. Kitamura lashed back at him, shouting, "You will drop dead within a year." This prophecy also came true.[71] On 12 September, Kishi received the arrest order from the Occupation authorities, and he went to prison five days later.

Years later, Kishi and his wife did not forget Kitamura. After Kishi was elected prime minister, Kitamura visited Tokyo in March 1957 to congratulate him on his appointment. Kishi visited the group's headquarters in Tabuse on 4 May 1957, and although he never became a "comrade" himself, he was sympathetic toward the group. According to some "comrades," while Kishi was a high profile supporter who expressed gratitude toward Kitamura, he did so with an eye to attracting votes. It is likely that through the connection to Kishi, a young Nakasone Yasuhiro, who was to become prime minister during the 1980s, also visited the headquarters on 26 March 1958 with a journalist named Satō Seichū.[72] Kitamura did attempt to use her connections with the politician to promote herself and her powers during sermons. On one occasion, in front of a group of scholars, she related her experiences with Kishi and made special mention of her accurate predictions. Although Kishi had returned back to "the world of worms where he belongs," she felt that he and his wife remained grateful for what she had done for them.[73]

By the end of the war, Kitamura Sayo had laid the foundations of a new movement in her local area. She developed a distinctive style of preaching that combined contemporaneous songs and spoken sermons about social conditions and the state of the country. The number of supporters was still very small at war's end but grew steadily in the first year after the surrender. By 1947 the momentum had picked up: Kitamura and some companions began travelling to different parts of the country to spread the teachings. It was around then that the stories about Kitamura began to appear in documents other than *Seisho* and other publications produced by Tenshō Kōtai Jingū Kyō, such as newspapers.

DIFFERENT HISTORIES, DIFFERENT GODS

Jikōson and Kitamura Sayo came from different backgrounds and their spiritual experiences were unique. Both were highly charismatic women who elicited enthusiastic support from sometimes surprising quarters, and they also promoted their own versions of world renewal. They emerged around the same time, and the oracles and prophecies they promoted were against the backdrop of war and escalating social crisis. Furthermore, they both used images of the sun goddess and referred to the emperor—one of them venerated him while the other blamed him for the war. But there were significant differences in their relative stances toward the outside world. Jikōson's followers protected and isolated her from society up until the end of the war. This cultivated an appealing air of mystery for some followers at the same time as feeding suspicions about the group. Over time the members developed notions of purity and impurity that distinguished them from those who were not part of their inner circle. Jikōson's position as the sole source of revelations was never questioned, and as such she developed a powerful position in the group. Jiu's insularity and the intense conditions that threw the group together combined with oracles that demanded extreme actions from them. These had a cumulative effect on their awareness, or lack thereof, of the social and political environment. They appeared, at times, to be untouched by the affairs of the outside world, instead choosing to live in accordance with the oracles. Jikōson and Jiu cultivated an image of secrecy, but this may have been the result not only of Jikōson's own unique experiences, but also due to years of avoiding the authorities.

Kitamura Sayo was quite different to Jikōson in attitude, temperament, and outlook. Once she became attuned to her singular spiritual mission, she not only dedicated her life to its fulfillment, she went to exceptional lengths to spread the word of her mission. Even in the latter years of her life she embarked on incredibly taxing world tours while still continuing to preach daily. Rather than cultivating an image of secrecy, her attitude was to promote her vision as widely and to as many different people as possible. And while she was certainly concerned with how her image was portrayed in the media, and how the Occupation authorities in particular viewed her, fundamentally her mission was one of active and constant promotion in "the maggot world" of the message she had realized.

Despite these differences, Jikōson and Kitamura Sayo were represented in most print media reports as being remarkably similar. They were generally portrayed as mad women who had the potential to cause havoc to society with their irrational behavior and actions. Images of *kyōso* of other new religions who preceded them played a major role in the media representations, but another significant factor was the drastic changes to Japanese society once the Occupation began.

While the backgrounds and temperaments of these women played an important part in their worldview and the paths their lives eventually took, the tumultuous events of Japan's loss in 1945 and the subsequent Allied Occupation also had an enormous effect on their careers. The following chapter deals with the structural changes relating to religious administrative policy that impacted not only on their lives but continues to affect understandings of religion in Japanese society today.

4

Bureaucracy, Religion, and
the Press under the Occupation

AT NOON on 15 August 1945, the Japanese emperor, who had never before spoken directly to his subjects, made a radio broadcast to the nation bringing the news of Japan's defeat. When the Allied Occupation (henceforth referred to as SCAP) took over control after Japan's surrender,[1] the new regime's agenda was clear: demilitarization and democratization, which were enforced through a combination of hard-line controls and idealism. SCAP had originally intended to govern Japan directly through a military government, as occurred with Germany in the immediate postwar period. However, this plan changed quite suddenly just before the Occupation and SCAP decided to use the Japanese bureaucracy to carry out its directives. Although Japan's military establishment was eliminated, the civilian bureaucracy remained virtually unchanged and the emperor was retained.

In order to grasp the issues during this period that affected Jiu and Tenshō Kōtai Jingū Kyō, it is necessary to examine the changes that affected various authorities. The first section of this chapter considers various challenges SCAP and the Japanese bureaucracy faced in dealing with the new rules of postwar Japan. The differences in attitudes between the two sides had a significant effect on the trajectory of all religions in postwar Japan, and new religions in particular. The second section deals briefly with the impact of SCAP's policies on the press with a focus on the reporting of religion in the immediate postwar period.

RELIGION UNDER THE OCCUPATION

The question of dealing with state-centered Shinto and religions in Japan was among the priorities of the occupying forces. At the popular level, there were wartime propaganda films like Hollywood director Frank Capra's theatrically released troop indoctrination documentary-style work *Know Your Enemy—Japan* (dir. 1945). This work employed a sense of drama, graphic imagery, and sweeping generalizations about Shinto and emperor worship to instill fear and hatred against Japan

90

Lieutenant Robert L. Eichelberger, commanding general of the
Eighth US Army, standing in front of the Kamakura Buddha.

in US troops and viewers at home. It conveys the image of emperor-
worshipping drones that slavishly followed the beliefs of "the way of
the divine gods, or Shinto" in their quest to conquer the world under
the "mad, fanatical doctrine" of *hakkō ichiu*. The film begins with the
words, "We shall never completely understand the Japanese mind. But
then, they don't understand ours either," before presenting Shinto as a
set of simple folk beliefs and emperor worship as the dark side of religious control. Although the SCAP officials who were charged with the
task of dealing with postwar religious policy were equipped with more
nuanced information regarding the religious situation in Japan than
Capra's wartime propaganda film, these opening lines did reflect to a
certain extent the gap in the understandings of religious freedom and
democracy in the initial postwar years. This section considers the positions of the major players in the Religions Division, who were essentially temporary "overseers" until the end of the Occupation. It also
examines perspectives of their Japanese bureaucratic counterparts and
others on the receiving end of the newly imposed policies. It discusses
the conflicts they faced, the sometimes uncomfortable resolutions they
reached, and the impact of the decisions they chose.

SCAP's agenda of complete religious freedom was a radical departure from the pre-surrender situation whereby government bureaucrats effectively controlled religious affairs. SCAP officials, the Japanese government bureaucracy, and established religious groups faced a number of problems as a result of the introduction of the new regime. SCAP utilized religious organizations, the Religious Affairs Section, and other Japanese government agencies in the implementation of the religious objectives of the Occupation.

On 28 November 1945 SCAP's Religions Division was set up within the Civil Information and Education section (hereafter CI&E) as a counterpart to the Education Ministry's Religious Affairs Section (Shūmuka).[2] Although there were numerous changes relating to religion that were introduced, three in particular stand out: first, the abolishment of state-controlled Shinto and what was termed the "*kokutai* cult," a system of officially imposed teachings, rites, and practices that centered on the notion that the emperor and the state formed one entity and that the emperor was divine;[3] second, establishing freedom of religion; and third, the remarkable surge of new religions as a result of these policies. All these factors are of great significance to the postwar stories of Jiu and Tenshō Kōtai Jingū Kyō.

John Dower argues that the victors had little choice but to govern "indirectly" through existing organs of government because they "had no linguistic and cultural entrée to the losers' society."[4] In SCAP's Religions Division, however, this group included United States citizens, such as William P. Woodard (1896–1973), a former missionary who had previously lived in Japan for many years, William Kenneth Bunce (1907–2008), an academic who had taught in Japan before the war but had no previous experience with religious policy, and Walter Nichols, a staff researcher who was not a religion specialist but had grown up in Japan. As Walter Nichols was the son of the one-time Episcopal Bishop of Kyoto, he was not unaware of religious issues in Japan and no doubt his fluency in Japanese and understanding of the culture helped him develop connections with the leaders and founders of new religions, including Kitamura Sayo.[5] The division staff also relied heavily on Japanese nationals to advise and interpret in certain situations, and individual staff members belonged to different religious traditions.

KEY PLAYERS IN SCAP'S RELIGIONS DIVISION

Any examination of religion during the Allied Occupation necessarily requires close attention to William P. Woodard's *The Allied Occupation of Japan 1945–1952 and Japanese Religions,* a detailed record of religious policy and implementation.[6] William Bunce, the former chief of the Religions Division, wrote the preface to this book, stating that no one was better qualified than the author to write on the religious policies of the Occupation and their impact on Japan.[7] According to one reviewer, Woodard's detachment and critical wording ensure that it is "an authoritative source of information of the first rank."[8] Woodard not only interviewed significant participants, he painstakingly worked through original documents. He claimed that his own role was "more like that of an observer than an active participant."[9] Others have acknowledged Woodard's book as the *sine qua non* for research on the Occupation and Japanese religions, while not being the final word on the subject.[10]

Woodard was an "old Japan hand" who first moved to the country from the United States as a missionary of Congregational Christian Churches in 1922. He lived in various parts of the country before leaving in September 1941 amid the worsening political conditions preceding the United States' entry into the war. From 1942 to 1947 he served in the US Navy and returned to Japan in October 1945. In 1946 he was appointed as Chief of the Religious Research Branch, Special Projects Officer, and Advisor in Religions and Cultural Resources within the Religions Division, which was part of CI&E. Woodard worked closely with Japanese religious leaders on issues relating to Yasukuni Shrine and other shrines, and was involved with the development of the Religious Corporations Law of 1951. In the post-Occupation period, he left Japan in 1952 and returned again, serving as the director of the International Institute for the Study of Religions and editor of its English language journal, *Contemporary Religions in Japan,* the precursor to the *Japanese Journal of Religious Studies.* Before returning to the United States in 1966, he was still actively involved in meeting Japanese religious leaders.[11]

William Bunce played a central role concerning religions in Japan during the Occupation. Bunce lived in Japan for three years during the 1930s before returning to the United States to complete a doctorate in history. He joined the Naval Reserve in 1943 and later helped plan for the Occupation. He was initially assigned to SCAP to take charge of the reorganization of university education in Japan. Upon his arrival in Tokyo, however, he was given the task of handling Shinto and religious policy. SCAP had no plan for establishing the principle of freedom of religion, and none of the staff of SCAP's Religions Division, including Bunce, had experience in the area. The result was that SCAP policy was misinterpreted by its own officials at SCAP headquarters in Tokyo, and also in regional and prefectural areas.[12]

One of the most important Japanese advisors to SCAP's Religions Division was Kishimoto Hideo (1903–1964), a professor from the Department of Religious Studies of the University of Tokyo. Kishimoto was the son-in-law of the famous religious scholar Anesaki Masaharu, and he had studied at Harvard. He became closely associated with SCAP and the Japanese authorities as a liaison officer in a non-paid, informal capacity. Bunce relied heavily on his expertise and received a crash course in Japanese religious traditions, dedicating himself to this study and making a special effort to understand Shinto.

SCAP'S AGENDA

The major policy documents of the Occupation in matters concerning religion were the Civil Liberties Directive of 4 October 1945 and the Shinto Directive of 15 December 1945. The former clearly articulated freedom of religion (and also affected freedom of speech and the press, as will be discussed below), whereas the latter established the principle of the separation of religion and state. The Shinto Directive prohibited State Shinto while providing Shrine Shinto the same protection extended to all religions. It permitted voluntary private support of all Shinto shrines previously supported in whole or in part by public funds. While the legislative effect of the Shinto Directive only lasted until the end of the Occupation in 1952, the principle of the separation of religion and state became entrenched in subsequent Japanese legislation, particularly the Constitution of Japan in 1947 and the Religious Corporations Law of 1951.

SCAP's main targets were the prewar Japanese home ministry and the Education Ministry, and The Greater Japan Wartime Patriotic Association of Religions (Dai Nippon Senji Shūkyō Hōkokukai), a prewar semi-governmental body chaired by the Education minister, was among the first organizations to change under the new regime. This body actively promoted the war effort through spiritual mobilization of the people, and its functions included the observance of rites for the war dead.[13] After the surrender, all government officials resigned from their prewar positions and the association was renamed the Religions Association of Japan (Nihon Shūkyōkai) on 14 September 1945. It was then renamed the Japan Religions League (Nihon Shūkyō Renmei) in 1946 and consisted of official representatives from Buddhist, Shinto, and Christian groups. Further changes included the dismantling of the powerful wartime Shrine Board, removal of the Peace Preservation Law, and the abolition of the Special Higher Police, which had played a significant role in crushing a number of new religions, as discussed previously. Furthermore, SCAP abolished the official recognition system that was administered through the wartime Religious Organizations Law by the Education Ministry.[14] Given the rather radical changes that took place in a short space of time, it is not surprising that errors occurred and misunderstandings grew. The conflicts between the Religions Division and the Education Ministry's Religious Affairs Section show not only culturally different perspectives but also the strains each side faced under unusual pressures.

PRESENTING THE "JAPANESE SIDE"

Woodard's book is a crucial document among relatively few firsthand accounts of religious administration and policy during the Occupation. Therefore, his claims and representations of the Religions Division's activities and stance regarding its Japanese bureaucratic counterpart, the Education Ministry's Religious Affairs Section, require consideration. Fukuda Shigeru, chief of the Religious Affairs Section from May 1946 to June 1948, provides an occasionally bitter account of the situation these opposing bureaucracies faced. Before the Occupation began, there were concerns within the Allied forces regarding how the Japanese people might react to the defeat.[15] Capra's *Know Your Enemy* had depicted ordinary citizens as besotted minions enslaved by an ideology that taught them to never surrender and to die for the emperor. It is not surprising that there was some anxiety among the Occupation participants. But for a lifelong bureaucrat like Fukuda, seeing armed guards stationed outside the small Religious Affairs Section office came as a shock. He was also surprised to learn the tantalizing (but unfounded) rumors of a stash of jewels and cash allegedly kept in the office. These details, noted in a roundtable discussion held in 1984, provide a sense of the tumultuous times that followed regarding religious administration and the differences between perceptions and realities on both sides.[16] Although the mundane activities carried out in the Religious Affairs Section office were a far cry from the anticipated mayhem at the beginning of the Occupation, Bunce and others within CI&E were nevertheless uneasy about the existence of a Japanese government office that was concerned solely with religious matters, fearing that it was symbolic of past control of religious bodies by the government.

Religious administration in the immediate postwar period involved some conflict between the Japanese bureaucrats and the Occupation officials. At the end of the first year of the Occupation, Bunce concluded in a weekly report in November 1946 that "the Religious Affairs Section had no understanding of what the principles of religious freedom and separation should mean and no desire to find out."[17] Given his stance, it is no surprise that he clashed with Fukuda, who began his job as section chief in the same month as Woodard arrived in Tokyo to work for CI&E. By this stage, Kishimoto's visits to the Religions Division had become less frequent. Woodard states that Kishimoto's efforts contributed to the "smooth relations" that existed between CI&E and the Education Ministry.[18] Fukuda's recollections, however, present the relations as being somewhat troubled. He was working in the archives division of the Education Ministry when the Occupation began. Given that throughout his period of tenure his own position as head of the section was under threat, it is not surprising that Fukuda's memories of Bunce are less than fond. The American's initially warm demeanor betrayed his stubborn nature, and many people on the "Japanese side," including Fukuda's colleagues and subordinates within the government bureaucracy, felt Bunce was rather cruel and coldhearted.[19]

Once the Occupation began, the Religious Affairs Section was stripped of the supervisory responsibilities held by its wartime predecessors in connection with religious organizations and religious functions. It mainly dealt with the allocation to religious organizations of rationed goods such as paper, clothing, utensils, and materials for rehabilitation of war-damaged facilities. It also handled the disposal of state-owned precincts of temples and shrines. The headquarters of denominations and sects of Buddhism, Shinto, Christianity, and other religions, together with religious leagues and associations, such as the Japan Religions League, the Buddhist Federation, the Shrine Association, the Sectarian Shinto federations, and the Christian Federation, were involved in the implementation of the objectives. The Central Liaison Office, the Japanese government authority that served as a link between SCAP authorities and Japanese government departments, contacted relevant areas within the bureaucracy concerning religious matters.[20]

Woodard's account and the records of the Religions Division present the Religious Affairs Section as having a rather non-compliant attitude when it came to SCAP policies. This is challenged by Fukuda, who argues that "the Japanese side" did not consciously resist the Religions Division's demands with respect to the policies. He also claims that Woodard took a more proactive role concerning the formulation of religious policy than his book would indicate. Woodard was certainly more participant than observer in the negotiations surrounding the introduction of the Religious Corporations Law of 1951, and he was instrumental in producing a draft of the law. Fukuda similarly takes issue with Woodard's admission that the law was ultimately the product of negotiations between the Japanese government, Japanese religious leaders, and the Religions Division.[21] Fukuda's recollections serve as an important reminder of the need to consider the position of Japanese bureaucrats, not merely the records of the occupiers. Nevertheless, Woodard indicated that his book was "not a definitive discussion of any of the problems raised."[22]

Fukuda holds that the Education Ministry had held discussions immediately after the surrender relating to a number of issues including the handling of religious groups after the Religious Organizations Law had been removed. "The Japanese side," he argues, was faced with a set of extreme circumstances in the immediate postwar chaos that did not allow them to act sooner to implement SCAP's policies of freedom of religion and removal of government control.[23] SCAP's Religions Division also faced its own difficulties. Even though it did have talented people with significant Japan experience, Bunce was not an "empire builder" and the Religions Division ran with a small number of staff. Yet Bunce seemed convinced that the working methods of the bureaucracy under the wartime government would persist into the Occupation, firmly believing that once the Occupation was over the prewar status quo would return. On the other hand, Fukuda and his staff had been trained under the prewar system yet they were required to follow rules imposed by the conquerors. Ultimately, the section survived throughout the Occupation. Nearly twenty years after the Occupation ended, Bunce expressed surprise that most of the reforms introduced by SCAP in the area of religion still remained in place.[24]

THE "KARMIC DISEASE OF THE RELIGIOUS WORLD"

The Constitution of Japan promulgated in 1947 radically differs from the Meiji Constitution of 1889 with respect to religion. Whereas Article 28 of the Meiji Constitution contained a highly qualified freedom of religion that allowed government authorities to control the emperor's subjects when they posed problems for "peace and order" or acted contrary to their "duties," Article 20 of the new constitution guarantees freedom of religion "to all." Furthermore, state sponsorship of religious organizations is explicitly prohibited in Article 89. Certainly this represents a significant rupture from the past, and while the unconditional nature of these guarantees provides some of the clearest guidelines of any country concerning freedom of religion, there have also been numerous problems concerning the nature of the "freedoms." In the initial years of the Occupation, part of the mission of SCAP officials was "to develop a desire for freedom of religion."[25] This was no easy task. The changes that eventually took place concerning religions involved compromises that left representatives of SCAP and the Japanese authorities not entirely satisfied. In the area of religious affairs, a number of problems developed because of discrepancies between the idealized visions of SCAP and the realities of religious administration.

The Religions Division faced some resistance to its policies and actions from representatives from a number of established religions. Woodard claims Japanese religious leaders found it strange that SCAP called for separation of religion from the state yet at the same time encouraged respect and freedom for all religions. There was apparently a strong suspicion among religious groups that SCAP was intent on secularizing Japan.[26] From their perspective, Woodard argues, official recognition of religion itself represented respect for religion. Although religious groups expected a relaxation of the draconian prewar system, a number of them appeared to desire a continued government involvement in religious affairs.[27] According to the *Sengo shūkyō kaisō roku* (1963), a volume of recollections concerning events in the religious world during the Occupation, the stance of established religions toward government authorities represented their "worship of authority" (*kenryoku sūhai*). On the one hand this work is an important primary source that contains valuable information, including Kishimoto's own recollections of the period. On the other hand, the publisher was connected to PL (Perfect Liberty) Kyōdan, one of the new religions to appear in the postwar period (September 1946) from the ashes of the prewar Hito no Michi, which was suppressed by the government in 1936 and disbanded a year later. Given the organization's history of resistance and then repression by the state, it is not surprising that the publication is quite critical of the relationship between state authorities and religions. In the book, this "worship of authority" is described as "a karmic disease of the religious world" (*shūkyōkai no gōbyō*).[28] This term reflects the idea that religious groups who were used to years of state control simply felt attached to the status quo and deferred to the orders of bureaucrats above them. Connected to this is the issue of legitimization through government recognition. Since the Meiji period, some religious groups sought incorporation under the state's religious policies in order to demonstrate that they were genuine religions, as opposed to "pseudo" or "heretical" religions, as a number of new religions came to be viewed. This affected not only established religions but also new religions, such as Tenrikyō, who actively sought government recognition as a means of survival.

Representatives of established religions were not sure how SCAP would treat their groups in the days immediately following the surrender. Some made overtures toward the staff of SCAP's Religions Division in the hope of receiving favorable treatment. They offered unsolicited suggestions about how religious policy should be administered. Not surprisingly, suggestions for "improvements" to policy were not generally enthusiastically received from the division's advisors. It was not just representatives of established religions who tried to either exert some influence on the division's staff or develop relationships with them that might help their cause. SCAP records reveal that a number of people from new religions tried to elicit information, or even tacit support, from division advisors. Certainly this was the case with Kitamura Sayo. She frequently visited the division, sought the opinions of advisors on a range of issues affecting her group, and also often sent news of her latest activities to various staff members, including Bunce.

While Woodard holds that SCAP's Religions Division did not "allow itself to be identified with any religion or any religious organization or movement," there were some incidents whereby Occupation officials did attempt to co-opt Japanese religious organizations into SCAP's official programs.[29] The division mainly dealt with policy matters, and its officers did not consider themselves to be religious reformers. Nor did they generally offer suggestions on how religious organizations could be made more effective.

CONFLICTS AND COMPROMISES

The circumstances surrounding the introduction of the Religious Corporations Ordinance (Shūkyō Hōjin Rei) on 28 December 1945 provides a good example of the conflict that occurred during the early part of the Occupation. The new ordinance sought to liberalize and simplify procedures for incorporation, remove the necessity for "recognition" as a prerequisite to incorporation, and deprive government agencies of any control over the internal affairs and religious activities of religious organizations. Fundamentally, CI&E believed that it was not necessary to introduce a new law to replace the Religious Organizations Law for the incorporation of religious organizations, and the Religions Division proposed that all incorporated religious organizations be reincorporated through other legal means.[30]

This proposal met with strident opposition from officials of the Education Ministry's Religious Affairs Section.[31] While the representatives may have believed that the interests of recognized religious organizations could be best served by special legislation, the proposal threatened the existence of the Religious Affairs Section. This sent the bureaucrats into a flurry of activity to produce proposals of laws that SCAP would find acceptable. The Education Ministry released a report in three sections on 15 October 1945 to CI&E proposing the following: an imperial ordinance abrogating the Religious Organizations Law would be ready for promulgation within a week; religious organizations (including denominations, sects, religious associations, temples, and churches) could be established without government authorization; and all legal restrictions on freedom of religion would be abolished. A copy of the imperial-sanctioned ordinance arrived a few days later, together with the news that ministry officials had discussed the situation with religious leaders, who had approved its contents.[32]

The new ordinance removed sections of the Religious Organizations Law deemed objectionable by SCAP but retained others relating to the incorporation of religious bodies. Although a SCAP advisor believed the ministry officials had acted in good faith by attempting to carry out the spirit of SCAP's reforms, the proposed document fell short of what SCAP wanted. Bunce judged that the officials were "caught in the meshes of an irrational and irresponsible system of government." In explaining the new ordinance to religious leaders, according to Woodard, the Education Ministry appeared to regard its passing as almost a formality. However, after checking the ordinance, the Religions Division eliminated references it judged to be inconsistent with the principles of religious freedom and the separation of church and state.

A meeting was held between CI&E staff, Education Ministry officials, and representatives of established Buddhist, Shinto, and Christian groups. The chief of CI&E, Colonel Ken Dyke, asked whether the religious leaders felt that a new law was necessary. SCAP advisor Kishimoto attended the discussions on the proposals for the Religious Corporations Ordinance as moderator and interpreter. Woodard argues that he was "exceedingly disappointed, not to say disgusted by the pusillanimous attitude of the religious leaders who did not express any opinion other than that which they had been instructed to offer by the Education Ministry." CI&E fully intended to separate all government involvement and decision-making with regard to religious incorporation. However Woodard holds that the religious leaders present at the meeting were "imbued with the idea of accepting whatever was handed down by those who governed and of not speaking out against those in power." During the meeting the Education Ministry officials made a number of suggestions for a new draft but, as Bunce put it, they exhibited an "inordinate fondness for certain terms and expressions" that characterized prewar thinking and ideology.[33] Dyke insisted that religious leaders be consulted before any draft of the ordinance could be approved, and seventy copies were sent to all the sects and denominations of Buddhism, Shinto, and Christianity.[34] Fifty-seven replies were received, and nine of them (mainly Christians) wanted more safeguards against "unhealthy and injurious sects." On other occasions, individual Buddhists and Christians informally sought government action to ban sects considered unhealthy or injurious.[35]

An acceptable draft for the ordinance was finally approved by all parties and introduced. While one source claims that agreement on the final draft was reached through a process of "negotiations" between government officials and religious leaders,[36] Woodard states that the word "negotiate" was hardly an accurate description of how the consultations actually proceeded. His comments reveal that although CI&E did listen to the opinions of the other parties, it always remained in control of the ultimate direction of the draft. He holds that "CI&E frequently consulted with government officials and religious leaders before deciding what course would be followed, but in no sense did it ever regard these consultations as negotiations." These comments are interesting to consider in the light of SCAP's official document on the outcomes of the Occupation in the field of religion up until 1948, which was published as *Religions in Japan*. It held that the religious groups "were practically unanimous in feeling that the ordinances were necessary and in indicating complete satisfaction."[37] SCAP was clearly determined to promote the idea that its policies were a resounding success by claiming the general acceptance of the policies by religious groups.

Before it was promulgated, forty-three sects and denominations incorporated under the Religious Organizations Law. Less than two years after the new ordinance was promulgated, their numbers had increased to approximately five times that figure.[38] The ordinance differed from the previous law in that it was a notification system that removed the necessity for government recognition as a prerequisite to incorporation. No government agency had any control over the activities or the organization of incorporated religious groups. It was concerned primarily with property, and when a group met the required conditions it could become a religious corporation. For the first time, complete religious freedom was granted, and any religious group was allowed to organize and qualify for tax exemptions as a religious body.

The shortcomings of the ordinance were significant. First, officials of CI&E removed words that were deemed not to reflect the principles of freedom of religion and the separation of church and state. This effectively sanitized the draft produced by the Education Ministry. Thus the ordinance was "a hybrid document that belonged neither to the old era nor the new era."[39] Second, despite CI&E's best intentions, the process encouraging the principles of democracy was quite difficult to carry out. Also, staff of SCAP's Religions Division appeared to assume that the representatives of Buddhist lay believers were democratically elected. In fact, they were generally close friends of chief priests or even self-appointed local bosses. Third, although complete eradication of all traces of prewar government control relating to the organization and polity of established religions was SCAP's ideal, the existence of a government office that dealt with religious matters was not.

In SCAP's eyes, representatives of the established religions, in their desire to approve what the Education Ministry had drafted, clearly exhibited obsequiousness toward government authority that had characterized the previous era. This was hardly an ideal environment to "encourage the desire for freedom of religion." Thus the plans of CI&E officials were not met with complete acceptance or understanding. Finally, the ordinance provided no criteria for determining the qualifications for incorporation or guidance for officials in administration of the ordinance. Although it specified that "anyone who desired to create a denomination, sect, order, shrine, temple or church" was required to provide certain specifications regarding control of its property, any individual or group that applied could incorporate regardless of whether it was a religious organization or not.

The result was a chaotic system that was left vulnerable to unscrupulous individuals or groups who might take advantage of the situation. Ultimately, the SCAP authorities (and the Japanese government) interpreted the principle of freedom of religion too literally, resulting in a chaotic and poorly controlled system.[40] Applications for incorporation were accepted indiscriminately. Many new groups arose, claiming to be legitimate religions in order to receive tax exemptions and other privileges. These groups contributed significantly to the negative image of new religions during the period, and there followed "five years of freedom, license, and confusion."[41] The two main effects of freedom of religion that came from the introduction of the ordinance were the secessions that plagued established organizations and the growth of the new religions. Some of the new religions were genuinely "new" in the sense that they began after the postwar period. But the majority of them were postwar versions of groups that had either been persecuted during the prewar years or had some trouble with the wartime authorities, such as Jiu, or had simply escaped their attention, such as Tenshō Kōtai Jingū Kyō. The rise of new religions combined with the difficulties of the legal situation was taken up in the media.

A DRASTIC PROPOSAL

In 1947 problems between the Religions Division and the Religious Affairs Section came to a head. Bunce, who remained firm in opposing a Japanese government section specifically for religious affairs, finally drew up a memorandum suggesting the elimination of the section.[42] A SCAP report indicates that Kishimoto appears to have supported him, and that some representatives of established religions did not support the Religious Affairs Section.[43] Although Kishimoto, who was still acting in an advisory capacity to the Religions Division, had initially felt that the Religious Affairs Section should be allowed to continue, Woodard suggests he changed his mind as the problems came to the surface. At a Religions Division conference on 13 November 1947, Kishimoto expressed some reservations about the Religious Affairs Section, stating to division representatives that he had been

> considering recently the desirability of retaining or abolishing the Religious Affairs Section (RAS) of the Mombusho. It is Prof. Kishimoto's opinion that the RAS is attempting to gain as much control as possible. He has insisted all along that there is a place for the RAS, but he feels less sure of it now than formerly. He believes it is desirable to retain a small unit to gather and maintain statistics and to serve as a research agency to supply information for interested ministries of the government. It would deprive the RAS of all administrative functions.

During a conference on 11 December 1947 with a number of Religions Division officials, two representatives of the Religions League of Japan advocated abolishing the Religious Affairs Section. They argued that the existence of the Religious Affairs Section weakened the position of the Religions League of Japan itself and its members, and expressed their belief that the section was determined to "make it difficult for religious bodies to remain entirely free of government restraint."[44]

Nevertheless, Kishimoto continued to criticize established religions and their attitudes toward authority. He wrote in an article published in the *Tōkai Mainichi* in January 1948. He expressed his concerns that the leaders of established religions continued to cling to the belief that government concerns should be placed above those of the people. He also stated that these religions felt honored to be participants in governmental projects and were eager to carry out the intentions of government.[45]

Fukuda holds that there was a perception from some leaders of established religions and bureaucrats that Kishimoto actually pressed Bunce to call for the abolition of the section. However, Fukuda came out in support of the SCAP advisor "for the sake of Kishimoto's honor." Fukuda claims that Kishimoto apologized to him many years later for not doing enough to strengthen the position of the section at the time, and claims that although Kishimoto wanted to help the Religious Affairs Section, he was placed under pressure by Bunce. Fukuda states that Kishimoto recommended that the statistical gathering powers of the Religious Affairs Section be maintained but that its administrative function be abolished.[46] Woodard also offers support to Bunce's former advisor, stating that "culturally, Kishimoto was a man facing two ways, and for this reason those who were committed to only one way, whether Buddhist or Shinto, sometimes found him difficult to understand."[47]

When the Education Ministry was reorganized in 1948, it was informed by the Religions Division of CI&E's intention to abolish the Religious Affairs Section. Fukuda recalls Bunce informing him of this development in May 1948, and he subsequently made strenuous efforts to generate public opinion within religious circles in favor of maintaining the section's existence. He managed to enlist support from various religious representatives, and claims that religious groups criticized SCAP's rashness.[48] Fukuda's efforts bore fruit; SCAP placed great value in "public opinion" and the Religions Division could not ignore the voices of major religious groups supporting the section.

A survey in the religious newspaper *Chūgai Nippō* showed that among representatives of religious organizations, chief priests of large temples and churches, officials in charge of religious affairs of each prefectural government office, and men of learning and experience, only 19.8 percent were in favor of abolition while 79.7 percent wished to keep the section. According to the survey, the major reason given by respondents in favor of the continuation of the Religious Affairs Section was that they considered it necessary for a government organ to administer the Religious Corporations Ordinance. Some called for religious administration to be upgraded from a "section" to a "bureau," as had occurred in the past. In fact, 26 percent of the survey respondents felt that such an elevation would be indicative of the state's respect for religion. However, it is possible to interpret this overwhelming support as being evidence of the "worship of authority."

Religions had sought government recognition since the Meiji period to legitimize themselves in the eyes of bureaucrats and general society. Although some during the Occupation period were wary of a return to the harsh government controls and directives of the 1930s and 1940s, most appeared to expect that a government office specifically dedicated to religious administration was a necessary and desirable thing.

This attitude was apparent when two representatives of the Catholic Church visited SCAP's Religions Division on 4 June 1948. They argued that the Religious Affairs Section should continue to exist for three main reasons. First, they claimed that if there were no government agency dealing with religious affairs, the public would believe religion was not considered important by the government. They claimed that abolishing the section would ultimately weaken the effects of SCAP's policies of religious freedom because the people would probably assume that religious groups that did not have government recognition were "bogus" religions. Second, they held that the Religious Affairs Section served as an important source of information concerning the activities of new religions. Third, they maintained that a single government agency handling religious affairs was of benefit to religious institutions because of the information and support it provided to them.[49] There was clearly a difference between these views and those of members of SCAP's Religions Division.

Despite Bunce's own concerns, he reluctantly accepted the position that religious circles wanted to keep the Religious Affairs Section alive. He presented the following statement at a press conference in Tokyo on 12 October 1948:

> When such an organ as the Religious Affairs Section exists, religious organizations will forever be depending upon it and cannot become autonomous. Because, under the new Constitution, no section of the government is allowed legally to interfere with religions, the ideal for religious organizations would be to establish a strong autonomous organ apart from the government and to employ specialist lawyers to negotiate efficiently with the government. On the other hand, however, as the religious world in present-day Japan has no such central organ and no quick establishment thereof is desired, it is unavoidably recognized that it is necessary for an organ to exist which deals with matters of liaison between religious organizations or between the government and religious organizations.[50]

Bunce was clearly disappointed with the result and he considered it to be one of the failures of SCAP's religious policies. On the other hand, Fukuda claims that if the Religious Affairs Section had been abolished, the section's talented and dedicated staff of specialists would have disappeared and the establishment of the Religious Corporations Law of 1951 may not have gone smoothly. Fukuda notes drily that contrary to Bunce's own assessment, his perceived failure to abolish the section was ironically a success for him.[51]

"ARE THERE SUCH THINGS AS *KAMI* OR BUDDHAS"?

The phrase that best encapsulates the uncertainty and confusion concerning religions at the time was "are there such things as *kami* or buddhas?" In noting the popularity of the phrase, Takagi Hiroo, one of the first Japanese religious studies scholars to examine new religions in the postwar period, holds that it was more indicative of a rejection of the power and authority of Shinto and established religions rather than a denial of the various deities of the "newly arisen religions."[52] The February 1947 edition of the religious weekly *Nippon Shūhō* stated, "if the expressions of the various religions in this country immediately following the surrender are classified according to color, Shinto may be said to have turned black with perplexity, Buddhism grey with impotence and Christianity rosy with hope amid the sorrows of defeat."[53] Established religions suffered enormous physical damage during the war: 23 percent of Christian churches, 15 percent of Sect Shinto churches, and 6 percent of Buddhist temples were destroyed. Yet only 1 percent of Shinto shrines were damaged. This situation was in marked contrast to a number of new religions that appeared, or reappeared, in the immediate postwar period and flourished.

Fukuda Shigeru claims that despite the Religions Division's aims of treating all religions fairly and equally, Christianity received favorable treatment over Buddhist and Shinto groups. He asserts (without offering evidence) that some members of the Religions Division who visited shrines and temples acted in a threatening and intimidating manner.[54] Occupation policy certainly did not call for any special treatment of Christianity, and there is no strong evidence to indicate that the Religions Division itself made special concessions to the faith. Nevertheless, Woodard admits that material and moral support was given to Christian groups by General MacArthur, GHQ, CI&E, and the occupying forces.[55] MacArthur's public pronouncements regarding the inferiority of the "indigenous faiths" compared to Christianity caused great consternation to the Religions Division. He ceased releasing official statements regarding Christianity after 1 January 1948.

Due to the changed conditions, Buddhist and Sect Shinto groups faced a number of difficulties, including loss of lands and secessions. At the same time there was a brief "boom" period for Christianity. The introduction of religious freedom and the Religious Corporations Ordinance contributed to various secessions within Sect Shinto. Groups affiliated with these sects before the surrender became independent. Most Shinto shrines lost financial resources because under the stipulations of the Shinto Directive shrines lost government protection and were treated the same as any other religious organization. With the abolition of the wartime Shrine Board in February 1946, Shinto groups were faced with major challenges to their existence. But Buddhist groups did not fare well either. Buddhism had existed for a long time under the protection of the state, and before the surrender the government had forbidden temples to establish new sects, to be independent, and to transfer from one sect to another. Some sects, such as the Sammon and Jimon sects of the Tendai school, had differences that had existed for many years. Despite the fact that they were forcibly merged during the war, they had continued to fight among themselves. However, after the government's controls were removed in the postwar period, old rivalries reemerged and groups bickered among each other. These sects reverted to being separate entities under the Religious Corporations Ordinance.[56]

Many cases of secessions were brought before the courts, and a number of ugly disputes attracted public attention. Some financially rich temples also seceded from their sects and became independent. The internecine battles that occurred in the immediate postwar period between various groups, such as disputes within the Nichiren and Sōtō sects, received substantial coverage in the press. But with the new constitution, the prewar system of family support for temples was officially broken down. Although the effect of this was not immediate, it undeniably had significant ramifications for the Buddhist world.[57]

According to *Sengo shūkyō kaisō roku*, many perceived that the established Buddhist sects could not meet the religious and spiritual needs of the people, evidence of corruption within administrations and internal power struggles existed, and temples were damaged due to wartime hostilities and faced with financial difficulties due to farmland reform introduced in 1946. Many shrines and temples possessed extensive landholdings before the surrender, and some temples survived on the income generated from the land. The impact on established groups in a material sense and in terms of public perceptions was substantial.[58]

In the early years of the Occupation, public opinion polls were conducted on a range of subjects by a variety of organizations, including media companies. The Jiji News Agency conducted a series of national polls regarding religious beliefs. In 1946, the number of people who professed faith in religion was 56 percent. In 1947, 71 percent replied in the affirmative whereas 29 percent replied in the negative. The poll conducted in 1948 showed that 59.7 percent believed in religion whereas 34.7 percent did not.[59] In 1949 the poll revealed that 56.4 percent stated that they believed in religion in contrast to 43 percent of the respondents who claimed to have no religious beliefs. The next year the numbers shifted, with 71.2 percent professing belief and 28.8 percent denying any belief. The figures show the instability of the immediate postwar period for religions. The shifts in positive responses could indicate the disillusionment people felt toward established religions and the open criticisms of established religions in the media. The significant fluctuations in the numbers of those professing belief in religion may have also reflected the growth of the new religions and the impact they made during the initial postwar years.

"A HOT HOUSE OF NEW RELIGIONS"

In addition to the secessions that occurred among Buddhist and Shinto groups after the introduction of freedom of religion, the other major characteristic of the initial postwar period was the rise of new religions. Japan became "a hot house of new religions," to use Woodard's phrase, and this was a completely unintended result of religious freedom. He indicates that new religions were a constant problem for the Religions Division, which often had visitors expressing concerns about "the way in which the Japanese people were being exploited and frequently asked that the new movements be suppressed."[60] Despite figures showing the increase in religious groups recognized by the Religious Affairs Section, it is difficult to estimate the actual numbers of new religions that appeared.[61] Not all the groups were incorporated under the Religious Corporations Ordinance, and some were postwar versions of prewar new religions. Sōka Kyōiku Gakkai was renamed Sōka Gakkai, and Hito no Michi split into PL Kyōdan and other groups.

What were the reasons for the growth of new religions during the so-called "rush hour of the gods"? One well-known critique is H. Neill McFarland's, which sees the new religions as reactions to social crises.[62]

His analysis reflects Takagi Hiroo's opinion concerning two main reasons for this development. First, Japan's defeat had a major impact on the public consciousness, and previously held beliefs about the emperor and nation were completely overturned. State-sponsored emperor ideology collapsed and was followed by the victory of Allied forces, unconditional surrender, rampant inflation, starvation, and a general collapse of values that characterized the previous era. In the search for new ways of dealing with the various problems associated with the defeat, a number of people turned to new religions. Second, given the serious problems faced by established religions (apart from Christianity), such as secessions and loss of land, many people felt that Buddhist and Shinto groups were inextricably associated with the wartime regime and could provide no answers for them in the mayhem of the years immediately following the Occupation. But it is also important to consider the impact of the freedom of religion.

A large number of new religions sought legitimization through both the Japanese and Occupation authorities. Registering under the Religious Corporations Ordinance of 1945 (and later with the Religious Corporations Law of 1951) provided groups with benefits afforded to religions under the freedom of religion, including tax breaks and government "recognition." Government recognition of religions before 1945 meant that they were officially sanctioned under the state system. Under the new rules the Japanese authorities could not discriminate against any religions. But for religious groups who had the "karmic disease of the religious world," recognition by the authorities was still an important acknowledgment of their legitimacy.

There is no doubt that a number of the new groups that appeared were corrupt and attempted to abuse the favorable postwar laws and conditions. The most notorious cases were Denshinkyō and Kōdō Chikyō. Denshinkyō aimed to "popularize electrical science and express gratitude for electricity," and had three deities including Thomas Edison.[63] It flourished for a brief time as a body incorporated under the Religious Corporations Ordinance. However, its status was revoked after revelations that the founder, who was based in Osaka, was actually an electrical goods dealer. According to a report from SCAP's Religions Division, this particular group was mocked in the press and not treated as a serious threat to public safety and morals.[64]

In the case of Kōdō Chikyō, the "founder," Kifune Seizen (also Naotarō), managed to set up an elaborate business scheme over a number of years and thus abused his group's tax-exempt status under the Ordinance. The legislation at that time allowed for any business enterprise to register as a religious corporation. The operations of Kōdō Chikyō followed this pattern: the premises of registered businesses were labeled "religious buildings," the owners "chief priests," and the customers "believers." Kifune appeared in the official documents registering his religion under impressive-sounding titles including supervisor (*shukansha*), superintendent (*sōkan*), and chief abbot (*kanchō*). Kōdō Chikyō consisted of a headquarters and some ten subsidiary organizations (or church branches). Each had Kifune's name listed as the senior figure. Although the headquarters' documents listed doctrines explaining that the religion had Confucian roots and followed the principle "life is religion" (*seikatsu soku shūkyō*), subsidiary organizations cited Shinto and Buddhist deities as well. Within a two-year period from 1947 to 1948, Kifune oversaw a thriving business of registered religious facilities that included coffee shops, brothels, barbershops, radio stores, fishing businesses, and ironworks. By early 1949 it became clear that religious doctrines had nothing to do with his true purpose. The Japanese authorities had accumulated a substantial amount of information about the group and its operations were finally terminated. Watanabe Baiyū, academic and advisor to the Education Ministry's Religious Affairs Section, reported these details to SCAP's Religions Division, noting that if the system were left uncontrolled it could cause ruin to the national taxation system because there were other equally unscrupulous individuals who would try to copy Kifune.[65]

With the new religious policy in place, the emergence of the new religions with no government controls had been greeted with concern by the established religions. Some individual Buddhists and Christians informally sought government action to ban sects considered by them to be dangerous. Furthermore, suggestions were made by established groups that the new religions be dissolved under the authority of the Organization Control Order of April 1949, which was designed to ban subversive organizations. However, this order carried a specific prohibition against interference in any way with religious freedom, and SCAP advisors advised against the possible misuse of this order.[66]

An important factor in considering new religions during the "rush hour of the gods" is the press. The Religions Division had to contend with religious administration, the growth of new religions, and also the inquiries of journalists seeking stories on the groups that were appearing. In order to consider media representation of new religions during the period, the effect of SCAP policies and the relationship between SCAP's Religions Division and the media require consideration.

SCAP'S IMPACT ON THE PRESS

SCAP's reforms introduced fundamental changes to Japan's media industries that had, up until the Occupation began, been under state control. In the wartime years, the media acted more as "servants" to the state, rather than "watchdogs." Journalists who may have opposed state policies on ideological grounds were imprisoned or used in the service of the state for the war effort. Ōya Sōichi, for example, began working as an army journalist in 1937. For the next six years he spent time on the Chinese mainland, Taiwan, and Java, among other areas, writing reports that shone a favorable light on Japan's military activities. For a time during the war, Ōya also held responsibility as a film director with a wartime detachment that was active in Manchuria. In the first edition of the magazine *Tairiku* (The Continent) in June 1938 he wrote about the situation in China: "The advance into the continent has been a long-held dream of the Japanese race.... The flag of the Rising Sun has crossed the Great Wall and traversed the Yellow River. In other words we are conquering China."[67] Matsuura Sōzō, one of Ōya's colleagues, holds that Ōya's postwar critics cite passages like these as evidence of his wartime complicity. He believes that Ōya became a film director simply to escape arrest and imprisonment, and that his work as a war journalist reflected more his instinct for survival rather than genuine support for the motives of military advancement. In this sense, Matsuura argues, rather than being an actual supporter of the war, Ōya participated in order to protect himself.[68] However Ōya may be judged on his wartime record, he undoubtedly had a talent for protecting himself from the social and political vicissitudes of the times. After the war was over, he did not publish any work for a few years.

SCAP recognized the importance of the press in presenting the ideals of democratization in a society that had been under strict control. Indeed, the press had been targeted during wartime as one of the most important weapons the military government had in controlling the people and spreading propaganda. A few days before the surrender, the major papers continued to function as mouthpieces of the government, and ran articles touting wild claims and fantasy about the impending invasion of Japan by foreign troops.

When it became clear that newspapers and radio broadcasts were reporting false rumors about the Occupation, SCAP issued one of the first non-military formal directives on 10 September 1945. This directive, SCAPIN 16, ordered "freedom of discussion of matters affecting the future of Japan." It indicated that SCAP wanted an absolute minimum of restrictions on publishing and broadcasting as long as reporting adhered "to the truth" and did not disturb "public tranquility," and threatened to suspend any publication or radio station that acted against this. In addition to listing the restrictions, the directive also warned the Japanese press not to publish or broadcast "rumors" or "destructive criticism of the Allied Powers."

The *Asahi Shinbun* tested the mettle of the new regime by attacking the American use of atomic bombs and criticizing the Occupation. On 18 September it was suspended for two days. The English-language newspaper *Nippon Times* was suspended the following day for twenty-four hours for the same reason. After this, however, the tone of reporting suddenly became almost obsequious, with the *Nippon Times* leading the charge. A few days after its suspension, the chastened newspaper "expressed thankfulness that the Americans, endowed with all possible human virtues, had come to liberate the Japanese people from thraldom to their erstwhile military masters."[69]

Another phenomenon began to develop. Journalists who had supported the Japanese military in their adventures in the Pacific theatre came out strongly as advocates of postwar democracy, criticizing wartime bureaucrats and military figures for their role in the war. As John Dower explains, the Allied version of the war that SCAP was attempting to present was one that "the media had to endorse by acts of commission as well as omission."[70] After the Civil Liberties Directive was issued, editors and publishers were called into the CI&E office and encouraged to openly criticize the government, engage in debate about the emperor system, and even advocate Marxism. While this seemed to be an official invitation by the conquerors for the media to stop acting as "servants" to their former masters, clear limits were set on the kinds of permissible materials. Criticism of the Occupation forces, defense of war propaganda, and militaristic and nationalistic propaganda were proscribed. Ironically, at the same time as encouraging freedom of expression, SCAP imposed wide-ranging censorship, which began on September 1945 and continued until September 1949.[71] As the occupying power, SCAP did not permit any criticism of its own operations or officials. The literary critic Etō Jun later made a controversial criticism of this censorship by claiming that SCAP launched a campaign against Japanese culture and ideas through the censorship process. He argued that because of this the Japanese people ultimately lost their national and cultural identity.[72]

Robert Spaulding, who worked as a censor for SCAP before he became a historian of Japan, appeared to show little patience for such arguments. He challenges critics who argue that the Allied Occupation was dictatorial and that, among other things, it restricted freedom of the press:

> All military occupations are dictatorial. All military occupations restrict press freedom. What is exceptional, almost unique, is that the Occupation of Japan used dictatorial means to create democratic liberties—and even gave the Japanese press an opportunity to avoid censorship by exercising voluntary restraint.[73]

Although CI&E had primary responsibility for the press, the Civil Censorship Division (CCD) of the Civil Intelligence section, which was part of the vast G-2 intelligence network of SCAP, dealt with censorship. Within two months of arriving in Japan, the SCAP press staff had established policies for a free press independent of government control. But this did not necessarily mean that the press meekly followed SCAP's orders to the letter. Part of the problem was that although SCAP had removed government control of the press, its officials had no intention of controlling the press themselves or imposing restraints (apart from censorship) upon it. However, a spontaneous movement aimed at eliminating the old leadership of newspapers developed.

The *Asahi Shinbun*, for example, began to reorganize itself. On 21 October policy-making officers down to bureau chiefs resigned their positions en masse. On 26 November the management of the *Mainichi Shinbun* bowed to the staff's demands. While the president of the *Yomiuri Shinbun*, Shōriki Matsutarō, initially resisted the demand to resign, he was forced to do so because he was apprehended as a war criminal in early December. The newspaper's top staff resigned from their positions on 11 December 1945.

Although Japanese journalists initially appeared to expect SCAP to give them guidance on how to report on various issues, Occupation officials offered nothing. CI&E officials realized the nature of the problem, and a meeting was held on 24 October with editors and publishers of leading newspapers, together with broadcasting executives. After this meeting, there were notable changes in the way the press approached issues. They began to discuss war crimes and political issues, and wrote more about world events.[74] SCAP held a series of conferences with newspaper editors, columnists, and reporters to discuss issues facing the country, such as separating Shinto from state control and the Tokyo war crimes trials. SCAP continued to hold conferences until the press in general appeared to show some "improvement," and over time it found that the aims of the Occupation required less explanation to the media. On 8 December 1945, a new left-wing Tokyo daily newspaper, *Minpō*, published an editorial declaring the emperor bore responsibility for the war. This marked a new phase in the plan to introduce freedom of speech.

In SCAP's official history on the media, the *Asahi Shinbun*, the *Mainichi Shinbun*, and the *Yomiuri-Hōchi Shinbun* (the "Big Three") are listed as the dominant forces in the Japanese press, and "editors throughout the country consciously imitated the Big Three and strove to produce faithful local images" because there was a pervasive idea that important and significant news emanated from Tokyo.[75] The larger papers used various means such as a so-called "exchange agreement" on news and features to cultivate smaller regional papers as their unofficial affiliates. They would supply the smaller papers with feature material and pictures free of charge, and in return "the smaller papers presumably were expected to pattern themselves editorially along the lines of their benefactors."[76] This assessment is accurate with respect to the stories of new religions that appeared in the postwar period. When the larger papers paid attention to new religions, the articles were often reprinted word-for-word with the same photographs.

In accordance with the SCAP policy of not giving preferential treatment to particular journalists or papers, CI&E and the Religions Division released news to all newspapers simultaneously, regardless of their size or location. There were also no favors given over supplies of the much-valued newsprint. During the war, newspapers had been reduced to single sheets printed on both sides. Although the newsprint industry made a gradual recovery after the Occupation began, supply was quite critical for a number of years. It only began to improve by August 1948, when all newspapers were given a special ration to produce a weekly four-page issue. In spite of numerous difficulties with the paper-rationing system, there was a rapid growth in the postwar press. Total circulation for Japan's fifty-three daily newspapers at the end of the war was around 9,500,000. By July 1948 the circulation had climbed to around 19,000,000, and there were 158 newspapers. The *Mainichi Shinbun*'s circulation rose from 2,412,000 at the start of the Occupation to over 3,369,000 in January 1948—the *Asahi Shinbun* reported a similar rise. The *Yomiuri-Hōchi*'s circulation rose from 1,456,000 to 1,654,000 by 1948.

RELIGIONS AND THE PRESS

The immense changes that had occurred concerning religion from the start of the Occupation were also covered in the press. Newspapers generally criticized Buddhist and Shinto groups for colluding with military authorities during the prewar years and failing to provide any moral opposition to the policies that led Japan to war.[77] But the media attacks became more focused on the numerous social problems that the country faced after the defeat. Various Buddhist and Shinto groups were reported in the press as having failed to provide any answers or relief to the suffering masses in the postwar period.

From the Religions Division's viewpoint, press relations were occasionally difficult. Press interviews were apparently quite problematic because of great variations in the backgrounds, abilities, and motivations of the interviewers. As a result, division staff members were always concerned with what would finally appear in print. According to Woodard, interviews "were often difficult to handle because the correspondents expected exact information and quotable quotes, neither of which the Division was prepared to give. It was not its mission to keep the world informed on the state of Japan's religion, and it should not have been expected to do so." Some journalists complained that the censorship under SCAP was, at times, harsher than the limitations placed on them during wartime. Decisions to censor articles or passages relating to religious matters were sometimes made over the telephone with only a brief extract on which to base the decision. On one occasion, the keen eyes of a somewhat overzealous CCD censor deleted a reference to Amaterasu Ōmikami because the Shinto writer had referred to her in terms of praise. "This apparently was regarded as a form of ultranationalism, and the shrine sponsoring the publication not unnaturally resented this interpretation."[78]

One subject that concerned the Religions Division was a tendency within the press to equate new religions with "superstition" and irrational thought. Given the prewar terms such as "pseudo religions" and "evil cults" that had been part of bureaucratic and media discourse, and that new religions had been attacked by psychologists for a number of years, the division went to some lengths to promote the idea of freedom of religion. Bunce held a press conference in October 1946 and discussed issues related to superstitions and freedom of religion. During the conference he argued that it was difficult to differentiate between superstition and "genuine religion" because of the subjective nature of what constituted "religion." He held that "what some may call religion, others would call superstition. Furthermore, some people consider all religions to be superstitious, and some of the greatest heresies within Japan have had official sanction."[79] This could be seen as his attempt to subvert prewar discourses of superstition and alert journalists and the public to his own concerns regarding the possibility of postwar government interference and control over religions.

Despite this, the press for the most part continued to criticize new religions, although some adjustments and concessions to postwar conditions were made. While new religions had long been criticized for promoting superstitions and irrational thought, in the prewar era, particularly by the mid-1930s, groups like Ōmoto and Hito no Michi were accused of acting against the emperor and state. In the postwar era of freedom and democracy, some press reports represented new religions as being problematic because not only did they manifest superstitions and irrational thought, they could not be easily controlled by the authorities. Similarly, some representatives of established religions were keen to see limits set on the activities of those groups that they saw as promoting superstitions. The journals and newspapers of established religious groups mounted concerted campaigns criticizing new religions by arguing that they were illegitimate and a danger to society. A number of books appeared on the subject written by priests from various Buddhist sects. The Religions Division received letters of complaint about new religions from Zen priests, and on one occasion on 12 September 1946, Reverend Kozaki Michio, a representative of the United Church of Christ, visited the Religions Division to lodge a complaint about "quacks playing on the superstitions of the people." He told the staff that "Japan needs some regulations to protect the right sort of religion and guard the people from … impostors. The laws controlling religions under the previous regime were too severe, but Japan is hardly advanced enough to be able to get along without some sort of control of religious bodies."[80] Although such opinions were patiently listened to and recorded, SCAP was clearly not interested in introducing any form of controls on religion. According to SCAP's official record on religion, Christian leaders petitioned the government to control superstitions that (most, if not all) new religions allegedly used. The calls obviously had some effect because the Education Ministry's Religious Affairs Section began an investigation into prevailing superstitions, which SCAP's report on the history of the Occupation suggests was not completed due to lack of funds.[81] Another SCAP report, *Religions in Japan*, raised the issue of "true religion" and "superstition" in the following manner:

> Understanding the true meaning of religious freedom comes slowly to the Japanese people, long accustomed to governmental paternalism and

police scrutiny and curtailment of religious activities. Unwholesome "religious" sects will undoubtedly appear as a result of the new freedom. There are those who look upon this phenomenon with alarm and sigh for the return to administrative officials of arbitrary power to determine what should be permitted as "true religion" and what should be forbidden as "superstition." There is ample provision in the criminal law, however, to protect the public welfare. Time will be required, of course, before complete adjustment to the new situation is attained.[82]

Despite the somewhat condescending tone that appeared to demand that Japanese suddenly accept the "true meaning of religious freedom" against the prewar "governmental paternalism," clearly the Religions Division was determined to eradicate any possibility that Japanese government officials could determine "true" and "false" religions. However, it also appeared to acknowledge that under a free press, the prewar images of new religions as unhealthy, dangerous, and promoters of a variety of superstitions and unwholesome practices would continue to exist.

By late 1948, stories of new religions were becoming more frequent in the press and SCAP's Religions Division checked these reports carefully. The Religions Division was often seen as a potential source of information and tidbits about the activities of new religions. Bunce was constantly asked for his opinion about new religions by reporters, and on 6 October 1948 he spoke to a non-Japanese reporter who had heard about new religions in Japan and wanted to learn more:[83]

> The opinion was given that it is easy to exaggerate the significance of the so-called new religions. Many of them are groups which formerly enlisted as a part of larger recognized groups. Others arise as a result of a feeling of insecurity on the part of the Japanese people. The total number of followers of these groups is very small, even compared with one large sect of Buddhism. Rather than to say that these groups are degrading Japanese culture, it would probably be more accurate to state that they represent the real level of Japanese culture and are a product of it rather than its creators. More disturbing than the rise of new religions themselves is the fact that the great mass of the Japanese population is highly susceptible to the influence of quacks of all kinds. The only apparent remedy is the slow one of education. The people can be saved from the effects of unwholesome religions only by educating them to the point where they are immune to the grosser forms of occult appeal.

Despite Bunce's views, this kind of response hardly made for good copy. Salacious tales concerning various groups of money laundering, drug use, sexual deviance, blind faith, and perverted beliefs were much more interesting material for the press. For example, the *Hōchi Shinbun* published an article on 16 November 1948 that claimed that

> heretical religions covet more profits than black marketers, squeezing human blood under the pretext of curing diseases by prayers and incantations. We cannot stand aloof saying that this all comes from social defects. Of course the solution of social problems is the fundamental cure. But, at the same time, we should cultivate the people's power of judgment and encourage scientific spirit in order to exterminate these objectionable sham religions.

The question of people's intelligence also featured in an editorial titled "Skepticism and Science" which appeared in the English-language paper *The Mainichi* on 24 August 1950. The writer claims that the problems caused by "pseudo religions" and "postwar bogus religions" would be solved "naturally" if common people attained a higher intellectual level because "fake religions would die a natural death." The writer argues that people should decide "with the national intellectuality which comes from democracy whether this god or that god of bogus religions is genuine and true or spurious and false." Thus, according to the writer, one of the natural effects of democracy is intellectual development that would lead people to realize irrationality of "pseudo religions."

POSTWAR CHALLENGES

It is not surprising that SCAP faced opposition regarding the changes in religious administration. Not only did the Religions Division find that Education Ministry bureaucrats showed some resistance to the new policies, its officers were also perplexed when they realized that representatives of established religious groups that had long been used to government control and recognition indicated their desire for government involvement in religious affairs. The struggle over the Japanese Religious Affairs Section revealed significant gaps between the understandings over the interpretation and administration of religion under the new "democratic" regime. For established religious groups that were used to government control and clung to a "worship of authority," the change was also difficult. In the prewar era, such groups could criticize the new religions that were popular by demanding official recognition and calling for harsher government controls. However, the new rules for religious freedom made way for a number of new religions to surface and evangelize, ostensibly free from government interference.

Despite complaints about the activities of certain groups, the argument for government controls on religion was firmly rejected by SCAP.

In the midst of these significant changes, stories concerning the growth of new religions in postwar society once again attracted the attention of the press, which had been released from the previous controls of the wartime regime. Although they were allowed freedom of expression, it was ironically curtailed by SCAP censorship. Criticism of the former military regime was permitted yet criticism of SCAP was off-limits. The press was encouraged to reassert a "watchdog" role but within certain limits. Journalists and intellectuals who had supported the wartime military turned against their former masters and began praising the merits of democracy. This sudden change had a major impact on religious movements. Social institutions or movements deemed "undemocratic" became a target for press criticism. In the case of the postwar new religions, exemplified in the cases of Jiu and Tenshō Kōtai Jingū Kyō, prewar critiques that raised concerns of superstitions and irrational thought were reformulated to fit in with the new era of democracy.

5

Jikōson and Jiu
Battling with Celebrity

JIKŌSON, who had struggled together with her followers during the prewar years to fulfill her millennial visions that conflicted with official state policy, established herself as the undisputed leader of Jiu by the beginning of the Occupation. Within a few years, she would become notorious for a brief period due to intense national media coverage. The group's appeals for the emperor to change direction and realize the importance of Jikōson's message were not unlike the attempts by other individuals in the immediate postwar period to reach out to the imperial family. Yet its methods stood out for their sheer audacity. Jiu's spectacular plans of world renewal, which included trying to gain support from the Supreme Commander of the Allied Powers, General MacArthur, stood in stark contrast to the intense isolation and exclusive internal workings of the group. Part of Jiu's appeal for the media was this isolation because the secretive nature of the group aroused curiosity and suspicion. But the most appealing aspect of Jiu for the media was the presence of a genuine superstar, Futabayama, who lent the group cultural capital that deteriorated almost immediately after his involvement was revealed.

Crucial to the Occupation's aim of democratization was eliminating any aspect of spiritual control of the people under the umbrella of state-centered Shinto and emperor worship. When the emperor issued an imperial rescript as part of a New Year's statement on 1 January 1946 in what became popularly known among non-Japanese as his "declaration of humanity," it was seen by Westerners as an effective repudiation of prewar emperor worship and ultranationalism. Dower argues, however, that in the original Japanese the declaration was far less the sweeping renunciation of divinity than they had wishfully imagined. In reality, however, for ordinary Japanese, questions of the imperial system and the national polity mainly ranged from "mild attachment, resignation, even indifference."[1] Although those who spoke out against the emperor during wartime risked being charged with lèse majesté, by the end of the war and in the months that followed, the emperor became the butt of jokes and a source of rumors and conjecture.[2]

One revealing indication of the emperor's changing position was the appearance of a dozen or so people who claimed to be the legitimate heir to the imperial throne or the direct descendant or incarnation of the sun goddess. Although the reporting of these various claimants was entertaining for the reading public, Occupation officials did not ignore them but rather treated them, at least initially, as serious cases within the study of a shattered society under the drastic circumstances of recovery. One prominent example was Kumazawa Hiromichi, a fifty-six-year-old shopkeeper from Nagano, whose claim to legitimacy based on historical grounds came to SCAP's attention in September 1945. The case first appeared in the US military newspaper *Stars and Stripes* on 18 January 1946 and then received international attention in the 21 January issue of *Life* magazine. Over the next few years, Kumazawa became somewhat of a celebrity, gathered a small group of supporters, and continued to appear periodically in newspapers throughout the Occupation. Kumazawa made a number of public statements, including the following that was published in *Life*: "The reigning imperial household has aggressed on me and my rights and on the rest of the world.... I consider Hirohito a war criminal. MacArthur is heaven's messenger to Japan." In addition to publically challenging the emperor, this statement could also be read as a cynical ploy to curry favor with the Occupation through praising the supreme commander.

"THE SACRED CHILDREN OF THE *KAMI*"

Although Kumazawa's case is noteworthy, Jikōson's is no less remarkable. She claimed a very different connection to the imperial line. Japan's defeat in the war, the entry of Occupation troops into the country, and the subsequent changes in society appeared to have little effect on Jiu initially. In their minds, Jiu was "the true imperial palace in which the sacred children of the *kami* reside."[3] After presiding over the group in the difficult wartime years, Jikōson's charismatic and spiritual authority remained unquestioned. The early stages of new religious movements are often characterized by rapid changes founded on the experiences, understandings, and visions of their leaders. As Ian Reader has pointed out with Aum Shinrikyō, these changes can also be the reason new members are attracted to the group because of the excitement and sense of dynamism generated.[4] But for Jiu, at least in the initial few months of the immediate postwar period, the concentration was not gathering new members but contacting the imperial family to encourage them to recognize the role that was planned for them in Jikōson's visions of world renewal.

Under Jikōson's mediumship, oracles were divined on a daily basis and these contained increasingly urgent demands that the members enact world renewal. Before Japan's surrender, Jikōson and her followers remained firm in their conviction that Japan was sacred and indestructible, and that world renewal centering on the emperor was not only possible but essential for the survival of the world. She predicted that a series of great calamities would occur during the process of world renewal, which would be followed by the restoration of the imperial family whereby the emperor would take his rightful place as ruler and world leader. Jiu believed that the emperor or members of the imperial household would eventually realize that the time for world renewal was imminent, and that Jiu would be recognized for its role in establishing a "restoration of imperial power." Furthermore, they felt that once the emperor became involved in Jiu's world renewal activities, his subjects would naturally gather and support this new order. Nevertheless, on 5 September 1945, an oracle indicated that while contact with the imperial family was important, Jiu should carry out philanthropic activities in order to help members of the general public stave off the ravages of hunger and illness during the coming winter months. This was an early indication of the group's intention to step out into society and propagate its message.

Jiu's attitudes toward the circumstances of Occupied Japan affected internal group dynamics and its relationships with outside society. Jiu effectively ignored the Occupation for the first few months and continued to cling to a sense of alienation and persecution that arose partly from previous conflicts with the Japanese authorities. They took the drastic post-surrender circumstances to be further evidence that the nation was receiving divine punishment from various *kami* for its failure to recognize the "true" path.[5] This caused the bonds between the live-in members to strengthen considerably.

Go Seigen, who halted his brilliant go career temporarily to follow Jikōson, recalls a strict lifestyle with no privacy for individuals and states that during this period he only associated with other Jiu members.[6] By living a cloistered existence, the group had little concept of what was happening in society outside their "palace." The members lived in a constant state of tension because their lives were essentially controlled by the oracles and they were always uncertain of the demands of the *kami*. Furthermore, Jikōson's physical condition fluctuated quite drastically depending on the importance of the oracle's messages. Their insularity thus intensified their desire to accomplish world renewal, but their actions triggered a series of remarkable events that led to the group's ultimate downfall.

"RELOCATING THE PALACE"

Jiu's activities immediately after the surrender concentrated on laying the foundations for world renewal under the emperor. Despite the grand and ambitious nature of the plans, the group acted with caution initially. After Jikōson's arrest earlier in the year and the arrival of the Occupation forces, they were unsure about how the new regime would react. Meanwhile, a steady stream of oracles provided statements and directives concerning their day-to-day existence and blueprints for a new political structure under the emperor.

Jiu moved its "headquarters" over a dozen times from August 1945 up until July 1948, finally settling in a house offered by a supporter in Yokohama. The members saw the instructions to "relocate the palace" (*sengū*) that appeared in the oracles as messages from various *kami*, yet such messages came when the group was about to be evicted or when the police stepped up surveillance. Jikōson refused to recognize or accept anything other than donations or offerings, including accommodation, despite a number of opportunities that arose for the group to settle permanently.[7] Jiu members believed that Jikōson provided a connection to the worlds of humans and *kami*, and that offerings to her (and the group) were the means for people to secure divine protection. On the other hand, Jiu was later widely portrayed in the national press as a group that preyed on ignorant people in a cynical fashion and procured goods through coercion. Much of the criticism Jiu eventually faced in the print media focused on rumors that the group thrived through ill-gotten gains.

Jiu's plans for world renewal began to take shape through a series of oracles delivered from August 1945 to February 1946, when they lived in Koganei, Tokyo. Oracles outlined proposals to strengthen Jiu's organizational and financial status, and reconfirmed Jikōson's status as the undisputed leader. After a formal ceremony marking the group's establishment on 15 November 1945, the oracles revealed an ambitious plan to establish eight chapters of the group around the country, with eight leaders, thirty ordinary members, and three hundred supporters.[8] While some oracles predicted that the emperor or members of the imperial family would contact Jiu concerning their role in world renewal, others indicated that Jiu had to take complete responsibility for the task at hand rather than relying on the imperial family. By December 1945 Jiu had received no clear messages from the imperial family that it was aware of its activities and the members began to feel that some kind of obstacle was preventing effective communication.

One oracle declared that those who did not fulfill their mission would be punished by the *kami*, which could be seen as a direct criticism of the imperial family for failing in their mission. An oracle delivered on 8 December declared that Jiu's headquarters was not only the true imperial palace but also "the general headquarters of salvation." Jiu was required to establish guidelines for the structure and operation of world renewal rather than wait for acknowledgment from the imperial family.[9] But despite the criticisms of the imperial family in the oracles, Jiu still hoped for its support.

Jiu's isolationism was shattered on 1 January 1946 when the emperor made his "declaration of humanity." Although this news came as a great shock to the members, they remained convinced that serious obstacles kept him from assuming his proper role. However, they believed the cause was not lost, and they began planning to make direct contact with the emperor or members of the imperial family. During the first few months after the arrival of the Occupation forces, oracles advised the group to wait until they were contacted by the imperial family with instructions for their mission. With no clear message from them, Jiu was essentially faced with a crisis of faith. If the prophecies failed, and if they were unable to make meaningful communication with the emperor, both the spiritual authority of the oracles and Jikōson could be questioned.

By the beginning of the New Year, the tone of the oracles changed. Rather than waiting for members of the imperial family to acknowledge their mission of world renewal, the oracles told Jiu to take a more active role in world renewal. They commanded the members to step outside the "palace" and openly propagate Jikōson's ideas to the public. As part of this campaign, Jikōson began sending messages to famous and influential people from various fields, ordering them to pay a visit to the "palace." She would continue to do this long after her most celebrated moment under the media spotlight, the "Kanazawa incident," was over.

A CABINET FOR WORLD RENEWAL

Social movements seeking to make an impact in society generally try to generate support for their causes through various means. It is not unusual for new religions to attempt to attract well-known people or celebrities of some social standing to their cause or help promote their aims. Regardless of the motivations of groups appealing to famous figures or the motivations of the individuals in question, their participation draws attention to the group because of their status. Nevertheless, public perception is not easily controlled, and these attempts may have a negative impact. In the early 1990s Aum Shinrikyō's leader Asahara Shōkō held discussions with various Japanese academics and celebrities, which were eventually published, and he also met the Dalai Lama. Aum had faced criticism from elements of the press and in the late 1980s was struggling to be recognized as a legal religious corporation. Thus, Aum was motivated to present itself in a positive light to the public in order to create a more positive perception of its activities and goals. In other words, the group made a conscious effort to improve its public image after being accused by some elements of the media of kidnapping and other criminal activities. It managed to present an image of itself as an open organization on a genuine religious quest. The campaign appeared to work for a time and the group received some positive appraisals from various commentators.[10] Thus, Aum tried to overcome external pressure by asserting or clarifying its position in the hope of gaining sympathy.

Aum Shinrikyō and Jiu were both torn between two competing aspects, one insular and the other promotional. Groups that are attempting to establish a public identity tend to waver between these aspects, reverting from one to the other depending on the circumstances. The insular aspect is that of a close-knit hierarchy that is centered on a charismatic leader whose messages promise changes to the social order or structure that only insiders can access. Outsiders are shunned because their presence and lack of understanding or sympathy with these aims represent a threat to the hierarchy. But the group may realize the limitations of this approach because of the need to protect itself from outside suspicion or to realize the visions of the founder. This leads to the development of the promotional aspect. Aum tried to improve its public image through promoting connections with well-known figures. Jiu's tactic was to attempt to use celebrities and well-known figures of political authority to draw attention to its cause. The consequences of this choice contributed to the group's spectacular public downfall.

Go Seigen was a significant figure within Jiu's hierarchy. Although he was a well-known figure given his profile as a go-playing star, he had been somewhat out of the public eye since he stopped playing matches. As Jiu began to emerge into the public sphere, Go became a vital key in its promotion. When the oracles Jiu received warned of obstacles blocking the emperor from fulfilling his role of taking the lead in world renewal, Jiu's promotional desire took over from its insular tendency. While it had maintained a low public profile until that point, an important oracle delivered on 23 January 1946 contained a proposal announcing the establishment of a "Jiu cabinet." According to a SCAP document, oracles that appeared soon after listed a total of thirty potential candidates, including the emperor, General Douglas MacArthur, and Yoshida Shigeru, who was to become prime minister in May 1946. The "cabinet" included senior Jiu figures such as Katsuki Tokujirō and Go Seigen,[11] with Jikōson acting in an advisory capacity. These oracles required Jiu to inform the various individuals of their duty to participate in this cabinet of celebrities. Usually Jikōson wrote letters that were sent to people. In the case of MacArthur, however, Jiu took a different approach that was to have significant ramifications for the group.

In some ways, it is not surprising that MacArthur was chosen as a member of the cabinet. On the one hand, it could be said that Jiu was oblivious to and ignorant of the realities of Occupied Japan in its attempt to co-opt MacArthur into a plan of reuniting the world under the emperor. But Jiu was not alone in viewing MacArthur as having a special spiritual function in the postwar years. A number of groups and individuals in the Occupation period with religious or spiritual aspirations looked to MacArthur as a figurehead to participate in their own movements; others attempted to use his name to lend some credence to their own quests to save the world.[12] Furthermore, Jiu had lived for years in hiding, attempting to avoid potential persecution from the authorities.

Although the group had initially ignored the Occupation, the members now recognized that SCAP represented the dominant secular power in Japan and that MacArthur was the leader of the new regime. Jiu eventually interpreted the activities of the Occupation forces as representing the will of the *kami*, and in the members' eyes, the Japanese people had been unwilling to carry out world reform, hence the defeat. As MacArthur was leading the Occupation forces in dismantling the previous wartime structure and revolutionizing society, Jiu justified their view of his role in world renewal as being the will of the *kami*.[13] It should be remembered, however, that this ambitious plan did not become public knowledge: the group still needed to establish other forms of outside support.

GOING PUBLIC

One of Jiu's first attempts at public proselytization occurred on 18 February 1946, which was followed by a number of other efforts to gather outside support.[14] The group displayed an image depicting the traditional thirty-three forms of the bodhisattva Kannon that represented the salvation of the people. (This number reflected the number of people involved closely with Jiu, including Jikōson, Go's wife Kazuko and her sister Kanako, who were the mediums, and thirty others.) Participants were encouraged to offer prayers and pay homage to Jikōson. After offering prayers, the participants ate rice gruel which had been donated to the group. On one occasion, at least one hundred people attended the event. While some of the participants may have been genuinely touched by Jikōson's message, others may have been attracted by the prospect of receiving free food.

There were massive food shortages by the end of the war, and many foodstuffs and crops were only available on the black market. Malnutrition was a major problem, and there were delays in the delivery of the meager food rations. Although both the Occupation and government authorities were engaged in the collection and distribution of basic foodstuffs, the system was poorly controlled and chaotic for a number of years after the surrender. The black market thrived, and in February 1946, the government introduced a system of "compulsory deliveries" of rice and other foodstuffs, which was enforced by the police. However, the question of donations later came under close scrutiny by the police and journalists, and a number of rumors surfaced accusing the group of fraud and extortion.

On 23 February 1946 Jiu moved to a spacious residence in Tokyo's Suginami ward, where they stayed until November 1946.[15] On 6 March, Jiu members made their first major move to make direct contact with the imperial family. A number of them marched solemnly around the imperial palace, Yasukuni Shrine, and Meiji Shrine with flags bearing the characters for the prayer *tenji shōmyō* (天璽照妙), which the members chanted as they marched around the grounds of the palace and the shrines. This activity yielded no results, and by the beginning of April the oracles began to order the members to make direct contact with the emperor. However, despite their efforts to communicate by circling the imperial palace, the group failed to reach him.[16]

The situation presented Jiu with a potential crisis that questioned the authority of Jikōson and the oracles. Fortunately for the group, an oracle on 1 May 1946 alleviated the pressure of the situation substantially. In declaring that a new era called Reiju (霊寿) had begun, the oracle effectively placed Jikōson on an equal position to the emperor. Another oracle on 8 May stated that while the emperor should rule because of his direct connection to the imperial line, in times of great crisis someone who was not necessarily a direct imperial descendant but actually held the same spiritual authority as the emperor could take his place. Furthermore, the oracle held that Jiu itself was the true imperial palace that housed the emperor's children and it called for the establishment of the headquarters of the new imperial palace at the foot of Mount Fuji. Given these circumstances, Jikōson could legitimately assume leadership in the task of world renewal. This oracle articulated another radical shift in doctrine for Jiu.

Jiu's situation is similar to that of Aum Shinrikyō in the 1980s and 1990s in terms of doctrinal shifts. Aum altered its doctrines at the same time as the surrounding social environment changed. Among growing internal tensions, Aum faced pressure from journalists, citizens' groups, and lawyers from the late 1980s, and after its shambolic attempt to enter into politics in 1990. The extent to which these pressures were the cause of the doctrinal changes or just one factor among others that influenced them, such as shifting power balances with the group, is debatable. Aum also created a kind of internal government structure, and as occurred with Jikōson, Asahara's followers reacted with trepidation whenever he seemed ill, fearing that it was a dire message of future occurrences. But while certain parallels can be drawn, caution must be exercised when attempting to draw comparisons with new religions that appear in vastly different historical and social circumstances. Jiu first began in an era of strong religious control by the state and then began to operate and attempt to expand just as the new era of ostensible religious freedom began. Although the Japanese authorities had the prewar powers of religious control removed by the Occupation and religious groups were allowed to operate with far more freedom than before, the Jiu case provides strong evidence that suggests that the police and other organs of government maintained a deep suspicion toward new religions in the immediate postwar period. They were controlled in their actions but not their thoughts on new religions by the Occupation authorities. Aum, however, developed in an environment in which the authorities had, as Shimada Hiromi put it, an "allergy toward new religions."[17] In other words, they used a strategy of avoidance concerning new religions, not wishing to get involved too closely in their activities. One factor in this may have been the readiness of new religions in the postwar period to claim that the authorities sometimes tried to revert to prewar tactics of control. But in the immediate postwar period, new religions were in a relatively weaker position, especially ones like Jiu that had been under investigation before the end of the war.

Although Jiu appeared to have failed in its initial quest to inform imperial family members of its mission, they did not completely abandon their efforts. From June 1946, members of Jiu began going to the palace to make offerings of white rice. On these occasions, they asked the palace guards to arrange meetings with the crown prince. Although a meeting never took place, Jiu felt an increasing sense of confidence that the initial stages of their plans had been successful.[18] Despite their apparent failure to reach the emperor or the imperial family, Jiu's efforts were certainly not ignored. The police recorded Jiu's movements around the imperial grounds and other areas of the city, with one report noting that although the group was denied a meeting with the crown prince, it was allowed to pass through part of the imperial grounds.[19]

THE MACARTHUR INCIDENT

The uncertainty and anxiety experienced by Jiu immediately after the war ended was replaced by a newfound confidence within the members that their mission would succeed. Rather than feeling intimidated by the police surveillance, the members launched a rather audacious plan to promote Jikōson's vision. While there are some extraordinary stories of the lengths some Japanese people went to try and contact MacArthur, Jiu's efforts, which culminated in the so-called MacArthur incident, must rank as among the most audacious. MacArthur relished the attention that was bestowed upon him as commander in chief. He enjoyed the effusive (and occasionally obsequious) praise heaped on him by many adoring Japanese citizens.[20] Although he received many letters and gifts that occasionally came with offers of support or requests for his help, he had little direct physical contact with ordinary Japanese people during his stay in Japan (30 August 1945 to 16 April 1951). Yet

Jiu members claimed that they managed to directly contact MacArthur and alert him to their mission. However, there is little indication in the records of the Religions Division to substantiate the claim that they contacted him directly, apart from the statements of Jiu members. Whether the contact occurred or not, it is clear that the Japanese police stepped up surveillance of the group after the incidents occurred.

While McArthur's name first appeared in an oracle on 5 May 1946, one recorded on 13 May was more significant. When the medium was speaking in the voice of the deity she suddenly shouted, "You must go to MacArthur!" All those present, including Jikōson, were completely overwhelmed at the enormity of the task commanded by the *kami*.[21] Go's wife, Kazuko, wrote down a message that was to be delivered to MacArthur. This message ordered the general to visit "the imperial palace of Jiu."

The details of Jiu's contact with MacArthur are found in the recollections of Jikōson, Go, and Katsuki, although their versions vary somewhat. In an interview with Religions Division staff on 20 September 1946, Jikōson claimed that of the three attempts that were made, two were successful.[22] On the other hand, Go states that only two attempts were made. Both accounts agree that on one occasion Go's wife and her sister stopped MacArthur's car outside the US embassy. According to Katsuki, MacArthur shook their hands, thanked them, and instructed the Japanese policemen standing outside the embassy to escort them back home by car. Go states that the police detained his wife and sister-in-law overnight, releasing them the following day with a warning. Apparently the police warned the group and told them that "because there are mad people like you around, we're always having a hard time."[23] Go and Katsuki claim that the contact with MacArthur resulted in the police taking decisive action against Jiu, a group that they had been watching prior to the Occupation.[24]

According to a Religions Division report, after the police arrested Jikōson on suspicions of lèse majesté in February 1945 they continued to keep a watch on Jiu's movements.[25] Katsuki claimed that the police continually harassed members wherever they moved and that they were intent on crushing Jiu. Jiu escaped prosecution and conviction during the war and so the police looked for any opportunity to arrest them or pin trumped-up charges on them.[26] While Katsuki placed himself as a victim, the police actions may suggest that they did maintain an unreconstructed attitude relating to social control toward new religions that carried over from the prewar years. When Jikōson was first arrested in early 1945, the police investigated groups suspected of violating the tenets of State Shinto and promoting practices and ideas not officially condoned by the state. While the police could no longer investigate groups on religious grounds after the Occupation began, they were required by the Occupation to maintain surveillance over any groups they suspected of disturbing the public peace or threatening public order. Under the provisions of a memorandum issued to the Japanese government relating to the abolition of certain political parties and organizations on 4 January 1946, the Japanese Home Ministry issued a directive to prefectural governors concerning the collection of information to "preserve public peace." A police officer was assigned in each station to be in charge of this area. Part of the officer's duties was to collect information concerning rumors or speech that might have a negative influence on the people and public safety.[27]

The centralized wartime system of police networks was still in operation during the initial years of the Occupation and remained so until the police force was reformed in 1948. The police were required to report to SCAP's Public Safety Division, which was part of G-2, the intelligence branch of the Occupation that became the most powerful agency within MacArthur's headquarters. They were required to inform them of "suspicious groups." The Public Safety Division's officers often relied on the judgment of the police, who were gathering information on the ground. Given that those judgments were made by officers trained in prewar methods of control, it is likely that they put extra pressure on Jiu given its history.

The police contacted SCAP's Public Safety Division after accumulating evidence about Jiu's activities. The report indicated that Jiu might present a threat to public safety and that the doctrines were problematic. Jiu's ideas contained strong elements of emperor-centered beliefs and were radical enough to be considered ultranationalistic. It is ironic that Jiu was targeted for these ideas in the prewar era of emperor-centered nationalism and the postwar era of imposed democracy. Nevertheless, Jikōson was also predicting that natural calamities would occur if people did not engage in world renewal. The police, therefore, presented these ideas of the group as potentially injurious to public safety. In response to the information supplied by the police, Brigadier General C. S. Ferrin of the Provost Marshall, which was connected to the Public Safety Division, agreed with their assessment and issued an order on 19 June 1946, which officially sanctioned the Japanese police to carry out surveillance on the group.[28] This order was issued approximately one month after the contact with MacArthur, which suggests that SCAP's intelligence network became involved as a result of information from the police.

Despite this, the group was unrepentant. On 22 and 23 June, messages for the superintendent-general of the Tokyo Metropolitan Police and the head of the local police precinct in Suginami appeared through oracles. The content was clear and provocative: they demanded that the police should visit Jikōson and show more respect to her and Jiu. A Jiu member went to the Metropolitan Police headquarters to deliver the message to the superintendent-general personally but was unable to meet him.[29] Jiu was therefore directly provoking the police.

Katsuki's claims of victimization should be considered within the context of claims that other new religions made during the immediate Occupation period regarding police attitudes and actions against them. Concerns over the involvement of the police and other organs of the Japanese government were constantly on the minds of SCAP's Religions Division officials. In 1951, the division received a number of complaints from representatives of new religions who complained that they were being investigated by the police in a manner reminiscent of the prewar years. The division issued a statement indicating that religious leaders felt that the prewar Special Higher Police was being revived. There were other rumors that the Special Investigations Bureau of the Attorney General's Office was engaged in investigations of religious organizations. Although these rumors were denied by SCAP's Government Section, SCAP's Religions Division had information to the contrary. In any case, no official action was taken due to lack of evidence.[30]

The relationship between Jiu and the authorities became more problematic after the incident involving MacArthur yet Jiu considered this mission to be a resounding success. Filled with a sense of accomplishment, they decided to take even bolder actions. The events concerning MacArthur, however, triggered the notorious incident in Kanazawa a few months later, which led to the group's spectacular downfall.[31]

THE PRESS TAKES INTEREST

Spurred on by what they considered to be a highly successful mission, Jiu members conducted more ceremonies at the "palace" in Suginami, opening its doors to the public. These incidents were duly noted in official police reports to the Home Ministry.[32] They also coincided with the first media reports on Jiu. Katsuki notes that a number of journalists appeared during the June ceremonies and short articles on Jiu were also published in some papers.[33] The media attention did not go unnoticed by Religions Division officials. Part of their task was to scan the papers and magazines meticulously, looking for references to religion, and then produce monthly summaries that often contained detailed translations. In another indication of Jiu's increasing confidence in spreading Jikōson's message to the outside world, at the behest of Jikōson Go Seigen visited the office of SCAP's Religions Division, located in the Radio Tokyo building, on 16 September 1946. Hiyane Antei, a professor at Tokyo Union Theological Seminary and advisor to the division on Japanese religions, indicated in a report that he had read about Go's world renewal beliefs in a newspaper. He sat in on the interview with Go because he felt the Jiu case would "furnish the most practical and modern way of knowing what kind of new religions are in Japan today."[34] Go announced that Christ had come to Earth on 6 September 1946, that calamities would soon strike worldwide, and that this information needed to be passed on to MacArthur.[35] Again, there is no mention of any possible contact with MacArthur prior to the visit but this does show that the General was not far from their thoughts.

Following this, Hiyane and other Religions Division staff members conducted another interview with Go and his wife the next day, and then paid a visit on 20 September to Jiu's "palace" in Suginami, which was a large, old house with spacious gardens.[36] Go Seigen showed them the main altar, which contained various paper amulets with the names of Buddhist and Shinto deities as well as Christ. The author of the report indicates some concern regarding the reference to Christ because it seemed to indicate that the group was trying to curry favor with the Occupation authorities by appealing to "the religion of the occupiers." Approximately thirty people were "attending" Jikōson, and they appeared to hold the "firm if not fanatical conviction that she is all or more than she claims to be, [and] all of them appear happy in their self-imposed and complete subjection to her will." In addition, "some hundred people, young and old, male and female, carrying national flags passed out of the gate. The procession was carried out in the utmost silence." The report indicates that it was later discovered from police sources that this group prayed outside the gates of the crown prince's palace, entered the grounds without the permission of the Imperial Household Agency, and made an offering of rice cakes.

After repeatedly petitioning Go, the Religions Division staff members managed to speak to Jikōson, who is described in the report as elegant and polite.[37] The conversation, however, revealed little about the group's doctrines. She claimed to have the ability to see and communicate with the "supreme deity" (Amaterasu Ōmikami) and the souls of all deceased persons, including Buddha, Jesus, Kannon, and the emperors Jimmu and Meiji. She also elaborated on her millennial visions, stating that the world had degenerated with the "dust" of evil and uncleanliness and would soon be destroyed. Only those good people who decided to follow the commands of the "supreme deity" would survive the forthcoming calamities and be qualified to undertake world renewal. In addition to the interviews, the researchers took careful note of the rituals of the group, which involved recitation of Buddhist and Shinto texts and chanting *tenji shōmyō*. However, despite concerns over Jiu's opportunism concerning blatant references to Christianity, there is no mention in the report about Jiu having any ultranationalistic connections or posing a potential threat to the public. The report reveals the researchers' bemusement rather than anxiety.

The Religions Division report is a rather dry account of the visit to "the palace" that does not reflect what often occurred when outsiders visited Jiu headquarters. Usually one of the mediums would communicate with their spirit and start to speak in the voice of that spirit. Even if the person was ostensibly friendly to the group, the voice of the spirit would announce that although it had come as a visitor, its real intention was to kill Jikōson or destroy Jiu.[38] Jikōson would sometimes fall violently ill, adding to the climate of anxiety and fear within the group. The combination of external pressure from the police, landlords, or the media and internal pressure from the alarming messages announcing that devilish functions were at work contributed to the feelings of fear and isolation.

Based on the growing interest in the group from the Japanese authorities and the occasional mention in the press, the Religions Division decided to continue investigations into the group and its activities. By this stage Jiu had become bolder in terms of its efforts to inform the public and society in general of world renewal. It had developed from a very insular group toward the end of the war into a highly motivated and self-confident unit with a well-defined mission.

A REPORT ON "QUESTIONABLE ECCENTRICITIES"

A Religions Division report noted that the number of newspaper and magazine articles about Jiu began to increase during September 1946.[39] Much of this attention focused on Go Seigen. In July 1946 he resumed his playing career. He had not played in a few years and his imminent return naturally stirred up interest. The *Yomiuri Shinbun* ran a series on the ten-game contest he played (and eventually won). When he began the contest, he stated to a newspaper that he would "play according to the will of the *kami*," thus making public his personal convictions and association with Jikōson.[40] But while Go's involvement was a significant factor in this initial press interest, the police were also leaking information to the media.

On 29 September 1946, the *Mainichi Shinbun* published an article based on information from "police sources" and translated by SCAP's Allied Translator and Interpreter Service as "Quiet Inquiry Concerning a Certain Religious Organization":[41]

> A certain religious organization is being investigated. Now that freedom of speech and assembly has been permitted, the authorities are at a loss concerning what to do with some eccentric religious organizations. The Metropolitan Police Board has started a quiet inquiry of a certain religious organization in Suginami ward, to which questionable eccentricities have been attributed. The leader claims to be a deity and has a considerable number of followers, including a certain celebrated go player. It is rumored that they claim if one contributes an amount of rice now, one will gather twice that amount next year. They are thus encouraging people to contribute rice to the deity instead of selling it to the government. Because of such doubtful eccentricities the authorities have launched inquiries, but as there is no law to apply to this case at present, they are studying the problem while investigating the actual state of affairs.

The article indicates the somewhat conflicting positions the press faced concerning the nature of authority in the immediate postwar period. As noted in previous chapters, in the prewar years—including the mid-1930s in the cases of new religions like Ōmoto and Hito no Michi—elements of the press criticized the groups for irrational beliefs and anti-state sentiments but also reprimanded the authorities for not doing enough. In terms of their identity in relation to authority, the print media could be seen as serving the nation (that is, playing a "servant" role) by supporting the crackdown on recalcitrant groups that grew too large for the authorities to handle. At the same time they also kept an eye on the authorities (that is, a "watchdog" role), thus claiming to protect the public from bureaucratic abuses or negligence. But in the immediate postwar period when the balance of power ostensibly changed from the Japanese to the Occupation authorities, the situation was quite different. The *Mainichi* article suggests that with the new legal framework in place, the authorities were struggling to come to terms with new religions, particularly those that operated outside normative behavior. "The authorities" mentioned in the article refers to Japanese authorities such as the police and the Home Ministry. The press was not allowed to directly refer to the Occupation or its policies during the time of censorship. Jiu's previous brush with the law before the surrender included a charge of lèse majesté, but under the new regime, the police could not use this as grounds for arrest. This suggests that their hands were effectively tied due to freedom of speech and assembly because legal restrictions on "eccentric organizations" did not exist. Thus, the article may be seen as covert criticism of the policies because it indicates that the law left the Japanese police with few options.

This suggests that the *Mainichi* was supporting the authorities by indicating the constraints they faced—in other words, the legal technicalities that held them back from dealing with "eccentric religious organizations." But the paper also appears to be acting as a watchdog, although the target is not the police but rather the "questionable eccentricities" committed by Jiu and the limits of the law. These eccentricities are clearly linked in the article with illegal activities, namely the improper distribution of rice. The reference to rumors relating to food law violations appears as a justification for police investigation and possible reprisals against the group. There is a clear link established within the report between this "eccentricity" and illegality.

The article did not refer to prewar police surveillance of new religions or make reference to the new laws relating to freedom of religion and the removal of government powers in that respect. It also did not consider the previous investigations into Jiu the police had conducted in early 1945. The information for the article came from the police, and by raising such issues the newspaper would have compromised its source or offended the authorities. By the time the news of the "quiet inquiry" filtered through the police and a print media organ—the *Mainichi Shinbun* in this case—Jiu's story had become public news.

While the police continued to watch the group, SCAP's Religions Division staff members were observing the police. A SCAP report translated from Japanese noted that the police had accumulated data on Jiu, including the group's attempts to contact MacArthur: "The Japanese public authorities are perplexed, not knowing how to handle the members of Jiu when they seek access to the General in extraordinary ways. It is believed the above authorities are in possession of an amount of data concerning the visits of the Jiu members to the General."[42] In response to a rumor that Jikōson had been arrested on November 4 1946, Watanabe Masao, an assistant police inspector of the Metropolitan Police Board, visited the Religions Division office to answer questions surrounding the Jiu investigation. He stated that while the rumor of her arrest was groundless, police officers were continuing surveillance on the group in accordance with the Public Safety Division's directive of 19 June 1946. Watanabe indicated that Jikōson ordered her followers not to deliver the required rice quota to the authorities, nor to "believe in the value of the currency." He added that he was apprehensive about Jikōson and her group because they might disturb the public peace.[43]

THE *ASAHI* INVESTIGATES

A month after the *Mainichi Shinbun* article was published press interest in Jiu began to pick up. This interest presented Jiu with the dilemma that is faced by new religions on the cusp of fame (or notoriety) that receive media attention. On the one hand, media interest provides an opportunity for groups to promote their message to a wide audience. Jiu was certainly interested in promoting Jikōson's vision at this point. On the other hand, given that they are generally unable to control and manipulate their image to their advantage, allowing closer scrutiny by the media presents great risks for them.

Two journalists from the *Asahi Shinbun* made direct contact with Jiu. They appeared at the front gate of Jiu's "palace" in Suginami on 25 October 1946 requesting an interview with Jikōson.[44] Although Katsuki claimed that Jiu were aware of the potential problems the media attention might bring them, the journalists were allowed into the house.[45] As it turned out, the journalists had a clear vision of the story they were going to write.

Although the journalists wanted to interview Jikōson, Katsuki first lectured them on her teachings. After they persisted, they were granted their request of an interview and were led into a room where Jikōson was praying in front of an altar. Although they had received specific instructions not to photograph her, they broke this rule immediately, surprising her with a camera flash. Katsuki immediately regretted allowing them into the house, suspecting they would write a negative article.[46] Despite this affront, Jikōson decided to continue the interview.

Katsuki's suspicions proved correct. The journalists left with a negative impression of the group. They later confided to colleagues that Jikōson's simplistic teachings placed a far greater value on material

Jikōson (Nagaoka Yoshiko), is taken by surprise by a photographer from the *Asahi Shinbun*. The image was later published in the magazine *Asahi Gurafu* just before Jiu was arrested in Kanazawa.

goods than on human life, and that the stocks of food the group had received were ill-gotten gains from naïve people who had been duped by a swindler. They felt that the religion could cause great problems if its beliefs were spread widely among the populace, particularly considering Jikōson's predictions of calamities if people did not follow her teachings and make offerings.[47] When the article was finally published on 15 January, just before Jiu members were arrested in Kanazawa, it placed Jiu in a negative light and represented Jikōson as a problematic living god. The title was "the god who got kicked out" (from her residence). The article ran over a few pages and contained an unauthorized photo of Jikōson and some of the other members. Most notable though was the rather damning description of Jikōson, which certainly upset the group.[48]

Meanwhile, the *Mainichi* had started a series of articles investigating new religions. In a story published on 15 December 1946, Jiu and other new religions were reported as being able to prosper while not being registered under the Religious Corporations Ordinance. The implication was that official "recognition" under the law was required in order for the group to be considered a proper "religion." The story warned readers that "nothing is more harmful than superstition. The more mysterious and strange [a religion] appears, the more it appeals to the credulous, ignorant population. Disease, disaster, and difficulties of living lead people to unwholesome religions." The article then listed a series of complaints about the groups, including false representation, rumors of sexual deviance, and allegations of money swindling. This raised again the issue of official government recognition as a standard for determining the legitimacy of a religious group. The implication was that groups that were not registered were somehow illegitimate, followed superstitions, and were potentially damaging to the public. Clearly this report recalls patterns of reporting that occurred in the Meiji period and beyond in terms of new religions.

Perhaps tired of the attention Jiu was getting, their landlord demanded that they vacate the property.[49] For a time they thought that they would be able to move back to their former lodgings but this plan fell through.[50] Jiu once again consulted the oracles for a solution, and the members were instructed by the *kami* to move north. Although they knew nobody north of Tokyo, they felt bound to follow the commands of the oracles. It was at this critical juncture that Futabayama, the famous sumo wrestler, appeared at their doorstep on the evening of 27 November 1946.

A SUMO CELEBRITY

Futabayama Sadaji (1912–1968) was one of the greatest sumo wrestlers of the twentieth century. He is still a household name in Japan. He entered the ring at fifteen years of age in 1927, and became the thirty-fifth *yokozuna* (grand champion) at twenty-five. His record of sixty-nine consecutive winning bouts over the course of seven tournaments remains unequalled. This remarkable winning streak, which occurred from January 1936 until January 1939, coincided with a new and successful phase of Japan's military push into China. Futabayama thus came to be "symbolically identified with the 'invincible' imperial army."[51] He did not merely represent greatness in the ring; he represented hope, power, and national pride. It was this image that many people clung to during the wartime years.

Futabayama no Sato, his birthplace, is located in Usa City and houses a museum in Ōita Prefecture. It contains an impressive array of objects celebrating his achievements, including photographs of victories, *keshō mawashi* (ceremonial silk belts worn by higher-ranked wrestlers), and a variety of trophies. A continuous video loop shows his career highlights and the crowds of adoring fans waving flags as he is shunted down the street in yet another victory parade. The footage provides a sense of his superstar status in his heyday. Eager fans are shown gathered around radios to listen to stark NHK broadcasts that discuss his brilliant moves in hushed, reverent tones. But in addition to this kind of media that hailed his greatness, the museum displays mass-produced items like stamps, badges, playing cards, and posters that show the champion happily munching on caramels or chugging down beer. The 1930s representations of Futabayama as a mighty conqueror of foes or a fun-loving, dapper dresser were powerful promotional tools for companies that could afford it.

Futabayama was an ardent nationalist during the war who worshipped the emperor, and he was said to be devastated by Japan's defeat. At the same time he sensed that his professional career was coming to an end during 1946. Although he participated in competitions that year, he was unable to make a significant impact and according to one commentator it was as if he had lost the will to fight. "The age of Futabayama" ended when he retired from active competition on 19 November 1946.[52] Retirement, however, had little effect on his celebrity and the impact he continued to have on the public. He was widely expected to remain involved in sumo after his retirement. There were concrete plans for him to begin training around sixty young disciples in Kyushu. He was not only a jewel in the crown of the Japan Sumo Association. There was much at stake for those interested in maintaining the positive aspects of his celebrity. The path he immediately chose came as a completely unexpected shock for the powerful Sumo Association, his fans, and his associates in the media.

How did this major celebrity become involved in Jiu, and what immediate impact did his participation have for him and for the group? Futabayama's brief association with Jikōson and Jiu, which began just

Futabayama's *danpatsushiki* (retirement ceremony) signalling the end of his career as a professional wrestler on 19 November 1946. Just days later he met Jikōson for the first time and took up her teachings.

after his retirement and barely lasted two months, is recorded in most accounts of his life as a somewhat amusing lapse into temporary madness in an otherwise unblemished and stellar career. His involvement in Jiu had a remarkable impact on his public image, which degenerated rapidly in the press from great sporting hero to deluded religious fanatic, and on the group itself. Jiu never recovered from the press criticism it sustained after his involvement was publicized.

THE WRESTLER AND THE JOURNALIST

In claiming that celebrities are cultural fabrications whose impact on the public may appear to be intimate and spontaneous, Chris Rojek argues that "celebrities are carefully mediated through what might be termed chains of attraction." People cannot become celebrities without the assistance of what he terms "cultural intermediaries," which can include journalists (as well as publicists, agents, photographers, and promoters). The key function of cultural intermediaries is to present celebrity personalities in a way that will result in their enduring appeal for fans. This term also holds for the public presentation of notorious celebrities.[53]

Futabayama was very important for his immediate circle of "cultural intermediaries," the Japan Sumo Association (the body that operates and controls professional sumo wrestling)[54] and journalists who had access to him and fed the public tidbits of information on his training and progress. A key figure in the story of Futabayama and Jiu is Fujii Tsuneo, an *Asahi Shinbun* journalist who was connected to the social affairs section and belonged to the Imperial Household Agency press club.[55] His reporting of Futabayama's decline after the wrestler joined Jiu and became a follower of Jikōson had a significant effect on other press reports and, according to his claim, the police investigation. Fujii had known Futabayama since 1936. After Futabayama retired from competition, Fujii assumed that his next move would naturally be to take up the position of full-time trainer proposed by the Sumo Association.[56] Instead, Futabayama struggled with spiritual questions that had been plaguing him for some time, and it was during this crucial time that he first came in contact with Jikōson's teachings and changed the direction of his life radically.

There are two conflicting positions concerning how Futabayama initially met Jikōson—Fujii of the *Asahi Shinbun* and Katsuki of Jiu. After he left Jiu, Futabayama never mentioned his association with Jikōson or the group publicly again. Fujii claims that when his *Asahi Shinbun* colleagues went to visit Jiu "headquarters" in October 1946, Katsuki asked for the name of the *Asahi* journalist responsible for reporting on the imperial family. When they told him it was Fujii, Katsuki became more interested because he had heard that Fujii was associated with Futabayama. Katsuki then proclaimed that Futabayama would soon join Jiu. Fujii contends that Jiu wanted to gain the support of the *Asahi* organization for two reasons. First, they wanted to exploit Fujii's connection to Futabayama so that they could draw the wrestler into the group and thus promote their movement by using his celebrity status to attract more followers. Second, they hoped that Fujii's connections to the Imperial Household Agency might gain them access to the imperial family, who could then be informed of their role in world renewal.[57]

Katsuki completely denies Fujii's claims and argues that no one in Jiu had heard of Fujii until he suddenly appeared at their door in Kanazawa some four months later.[58] According to Katsuki, a follower of Jikōson first approached Futabayama while he was on a tour of regional areas. After hearing of this person's experiences with Jikōson and Jiu's plans for world renewal, Futabayama visited the follower's home the next day to learn more. He was told that Japan could be rebuilt if people developed a love for the country and planted the seeds of "true religion." This message had a profound effect on him. Attracted to the ideas of world renewal and the reconstruction of Japan, Futabayama decided to visit Jikōson. After he returned to Tokyo, Go Seigen contacted him at the hotel where he was staying and told the wrestler more about Jikōson and her powers. A few days after the meeting with Go, Futabayama visited Jikōson.[59]

Fujii claims that he was present when Go met Futabayama at the hotel. Go suddenly appeared uninvited at the hotel door and began talking about Jikōson, who Futabayama had not heard of until then. Nevertheless, Go was also a famous celebrity in his own right. Therefore, the story goes, Futabayama allowed him inside. The two stars went into a separate room and had a discussion. After Go left the hotel room, Futabayama told Fujii about their conversation about Jikōson and world renewal. He then asked Fujii, "Is this gold or mud?"[60] In this version, Go plays a central role in the story although Go himself makes no mention of Katsuki's involvement in his own memoirs.[61] Fujii also holds that Katsuki had a kind of grand strategy to exploit the gullible public, disrupt society, and eventually create a new "government" that he would control. Part of this plan concerned moving to Kanazawa and was revealed by Katsuki to the *Asahi* journalists in October 1946.[62] But according to Katsuki, Jiu had no plans to move away from Tokyo until the police and their landlords forced them to do so.[63] Also, the records of oracles delivered in October do not reveal any plan to leave Tokyo, nor do they mention Kanazawa.[64] It could be inferred that Jiu tried to exploit the situation to suit their plans of promoting themselves. However, the idea that these activities were part of a grand scheme is somewhat far-fetched, given the ad hoc nature of their movements. This did suit Fujii's aim of developing a story that painted Jiu in the worst possible light.

Futabayama visited Jiu's headquarters on 27 November 1946, eight days after his retirement from active sumo competition. Although Jikōson rarely met people the first time they appeared, Futabayama was a special exception. Upon seeing her, he became "touched by spirits" (*setsurei* 接霊) and fell into a violent fit while praying with Jikōson in front of the altar. This experience convinced him that she had special powers, and he asked if he could bring his wife and child to meet her. Jikōson agreed and he left for Kyushu that night, returning with his family on 30 November, the day Jiu left for Kanazawa.[65] He returned to Tokyo with his family in tow just as Jiu members were desperately packing up their belongings and preparing to leave the "palace." The entire party went to the Ueno train station late in the afternoon, which was so crowded it was almost impossible to move. However, Futabayama cut through the crowd and reached the stationmaster's office. He managed to secure special treatment and he acquired tickets for the group. He was fully prepared to travel with them but Katsuki and the others advised him to return home for the time being. They assured him that once things had settled down for them in Kanazawa, he would be welcome to join them. He agreed to return home temporarily and left the group, promising to meet up with them in Kanazawa. They did not expect to see him again.[66]

LIFE IN KANAZAWA

When the group finally arrived in Kanazawa, a supporter offered them temporary accommodations. They were forced to move again by the middle of December. The strain of constant travel and the increasingly severe predictions in the oracles took a heavy toll on Jikōson. Physically weak, she suffered fevers and blackouts, and developed an extremely painful toothache. The members believed that Jikōson's problems reflected the dangers faced by the nation, which served to increase tension within the group. She had a number of frightening visions relating to the predicted calamities, and other people in the group also went through unusual experiences at that time.[67] At the same time, the circumstances served to strengthen their bonds to each other because they felt they would be protected.

To the group's amazement, Futabayama kept his promise and turned up on their doorstep in Kanazawa in mid-December. He had left his family in Kyushu. He was quite emotional but also excited about the prospect of working for world renewal. Jikōson reassured him by saying, "The children of the *kami* have no need to suffer. This is the headquarters of world renewal." Futabayama remained with Jiu for a period of thirty-eight days from 15 December 1946 until 22 January 1947.[68] A female relative of Futabayama's visited from Kyushu, bringing a message from his wife asking him to return home. Nevertheless, Futabayama was unmoved and told the woman that he would not return home.[69]

Once he rejoined the group, he was given a great deal of responsibility, and he was immediately elevated to Jiu's higher circle of leaders. Press reports later claimed that Futabayama was given the position of minister of health as part of the "celebrity cabinet," thus reflecting not only his status within Jiu but also his profession. Whether this was true or not, Futabayama evidently took his new beliefs very seriously. The others in the house realized his level of commitment and devotion to Jikōson when they discovered him early one morning pouring cold water over his body and chanting *tenji shōmyō*. Impressed by his actions, the others followed suit. He also made a deep impression on the group on one occasion when he became possessed by the spirit of a famous sumo wrestler, Tama no Umi.[70]

Life in Kanazawa for Jiu was quite hectic. According to Katsuki, "we had no time to write down memos, and we couldn't even deal with our luggage. We would simply follow the oracles, which appeared one after the other, and march up and down the streets with banners bearing the characters for *tenji shōmyō*. We visited local shrines and prayed there."[71] Go also recalls that the world renewal activities in Kanazawa were extremely draining. They would get up at five in the morning, pray, chant, march, and then finally go to sleep at one the next morning. Go's main task was to preach to those who had come to show respect to Jikōson.[72] They marched around trying to inform the townspeople of the impending disasters Jikōson had predicted, urging them to save themselves by following her. They called on people to make offerings to Jikōson. Futabayama often led the group through the streets, marching alongside Go and exhorting people to place their faith in Jikōson.

The sight of two major celebrities, and particularly Futabayama, leading the marching had an immediate impact. It was unusual for a new religion to appear in a conservative and traditional town like Kanazawa, where there were many adherents of the Pure Land Buddhist sect.[73] News of Jikōson's predictions of natural disasters spread quickly, the first being a major earthquake that would strike Tokyo on 15 January

Jiu members in Kanazawa. Futabayama is second from the left,
Go Seigen is fourth from the left.

1947. A devastating earthquake had occurred in Fukui prefecture just before Jiu reached Kanazawa, and for some people this occurrence lent credence to Jiu's claims. When the rumors surrounding Jikōson's predictions reached a climax on 19 January 1947, they were so widespread that the Kanazawa weather bureau actually issued a statement that the likelihood of an earthquake in the area was very slim.[74]

A SCAP INVESTIGATION

SCAP's Religions Division continued to monitor the circumstances surrounding Jiu. It was receiving reports from people claiming to have been duped into donating rice and other precious goods to Jikōson. Some letters demanded that the authorities act to control Jiu. One unsigned letter translated by the Religions Division and dated 29 November stated that Jikōson and her "parasites force devotees to offer vast amounts of cereals and clothing as tributes. They cheat devotees by making preposterous and irrational prophecies. I think they are a group of imposters [who target] the agrarian class that has a comparatively low standard of knowledge, and want to rid them of their foodstuffs and new yen. This problem was once submitted to the investigation of the police and appeared in a newspaper, but I have heard nothing about it since then. Please investigate Jikōson and [this] wicked religion."[75] Another letter, undated and written by "a democrat," demanded that the Religions Division take immediate steps to dissolve Jiu on the grounds that the group was "ultranationalistic, anti-democratic, and contrary to Occupation policy." It ended with a warning that the group had recently moved to Kanazawa in order to extort property from locals.[76]

Although the Religions Division received information about Jiu from various sources, including the police, the media, and members of the public, its staff did not play a direct role in the events leading up to the arrests in Kanazawa.[77] On the other hand, the Public Safety Division, which had sanctioned police surveillance of Jiu in June 1946, was closely involved in the events in Kanazawa. Dr. Akimoto Haruo, a young psychologist from Kanazawa Medical University, was approached in early December 1946 by the commanding officer of SCAP's regional Counter Intelligence Corps (CIC) unit, which was part of the G-2 military intelligence structure. He was asked to investigate the psychological condition of Jikōson and other members of the group.[78] Akimoto had a professional interest in pursuing the Jiu case because of his belief that the rational and scientific methods of psychology were needed in the postwar age where spiritual confusion reigned. By lending his expertise in this area, he believed he was helping to dispel irrational superstitions promoted by new religions like Jiu. His findings concerning Jiu, Jikōson, and the psychological dangers of new religions were used to justify the actions of the authorities.

The results of Akimoto's study, which was conducted between 27 December 1946 and 6 January 1947, found that "this group is a socio-pathological phenomenon centered on a person presumed to have certain pathological tendencies." His report stated that in times of social turmoil groups such as Jiu could easily attract intelligent, educated people. He recommended that a full psychological examination be made and the result publicized in order to avoid further confusion within the local community. Akimoto later claimed that SCAP's CIC unit in Kanazawa recognized that Jiu's activities could pose some problems during a time of social upheaval. The CIC commander felt that conducting a psychological profile of the central figure and making an official announcement would be sufficient to halt Jiu's progress and quell any unwanted hysteria.[79]

At this stage, apart from her supporters and followers, Jikōson was known only to a relatively small yet influential group of people, including some journalists, police, and SCAP officials. She had yet to make a significant mark on the public consciousness but this was about to change. Through the reporting in a number of major publications, she became a notorious "celebrity god" whose image was forged through collective mocking, vilification, and rumor.

THE PRESS MOVES IN

Jiu's arrival in Kanazawa attracted the interest of reporters from various publications. Katsuki claims that while most journalists were seeking to expose the group and profit through writing sensationalized stories, some were genuinely interested in seeking salvation.[80] One journalist, Wakasaki Hideo, who worked for a small publication called *Shōgyō Keizai Minpō*, earned the group's trust. Although the members were initially cautious toward him, he was extremely persistent and eventually persuaded them to allow him inside the house. He spoke at length with Go and Futabayama and left a favorable impression on them, and he was soon granted an audience with Jikōson. He fell into a kind of trance and began to speak in the manner of a samurai, surprising everyone who was in the room. Jikōson declared that Wakasaki was Itō Hirobumi, the first prime minister during the Meiji Era, in a previous life.[81] On 1 January 1947, *Shōgyō Keizai Minpō* published an article that set out the aims and beliefs of Jiu as propounded by Jikōson.

The *Asahi Shinbun*'s Fujii Tsuneo began his association with Jiu at around this time. Futabayama went to Tokyo on 13 January 1947 and met with Fujii at a hotel. When Futabayama warned him of the calamities predicted in the oracles, Fujii claims to have become immediately suspicious of Jikōson's motives. He states that Futabayama's distraught young wife pleaded with him to intervene and help get her husband back to his family and back on a proper career track.[82] On the other hand, Katsuki argues that although Fujii was acquainted with Futabayama's wife, his motives for being involved were not spurred by sympathy for the wayward wrestler's family. Rather, he claimed that Fujii was contacted directly by the Sumo Association. This organization balked at the possibility that one of its star performers would be lost to a new religion with an increasingly troubled relationship with the authorities. Thus it was prepared to go to any lengths to take him away from the influence of Jikōson and send him back to the training center in Kyushu. The main point of Katsuki's theory is that the Sumo Association hoped that the wrestler could be brought back in line by using the journalist Fujii, who had some influence on Futabayama, to apply pressure on the group.[83]

According to Katsuki, Fujii appeared at Jiu's temporary residence in mid-January and announced himself as an *Asahi* journalist and Futabayama's friend. Although Futabayama assured everyone that Fujii could be trusted, Katsuki claims that he was suspicious of him from the start. After all, Fujii's *Asahi* colleagues had ignored specific instructions not to take Jikōson's photograph when they interviewed her in October 1946. Nevertheless, as Futabayama had become a key member of the group, some concession had to be made for this. Fujii spent three days with the group in total.

THE "EMPEROR'S HORSE" AND THE POLICE CHIEF

Katsuki's suspicions about Fujii proved to be well-founded. As the writer of the *Asahi*'s short "blue pencil" (*ao enpitsu*) social affairs column, Fujii published a brief missive in mid-January about Futabayama and Jiu. He mentioned that Futabayama's friends were becoming concerned over his "strange conduct." The English-language *Nippon Times* acknowledged this column on 16 January, reporting on how Futabayama "has become a fanatical devotee of 'Jikō-sama', sun goddess deity." Fujii's experiences in the group were highlighted in a number of *Asahi Shinbun* articles published from 20 through 26 January.

The second article contained details of life inside Jiu's "palace" and a description of Jikōson's purported ability to look into past lives. Apparently she declared that the spirit of the Meiji emperor had descended into Futabayama and that the intrepid Fujii was possessed by "the emperor's horse." The article reached an obvious conclusion: the situation was a "tragedy for Futabayama" because he was being duped by clever tricksters who used his name to bring them fame. Fujii's final wish was that Futabayama return to being a human being, rather than "the child of a *kami*." The details of Fujii's story appeared in other articles published in the *Yomiuri Shinbun* and the *Mainichi Shinbun* in the following days.

Fujii claims that he went to the local police station to file a report on the situation inside the house. He met with a top police official from Tokyo, Hirooka Ken'ichi, soon to be appointed Tokyo Metropolitan Police chief. Hirooka was in town to oversee an investigation into the potential public safety issues surrounding Jiu's case. Fujii gave Hirooka a brief history lesson about how German society became a breeding ground for false religions immediately after the First World War when unscrupulous swindlers fooled many suffering people. Japan, Fujii lectured, now faced a similar situation and groups like Jiu were simply intent on cheating gullible individuals. The police chief, after listening to Fujii's story, asked him what possible violations the group was committing. The reporter listed a number of possible areas of illegality, including the issue of Jikōson and her followers promising protection from forthcoming calamities to those who donated rice and other goods to the group. Fujii argued that this action constituted a violation of the food laws, as did the stockpiling of rice. Furthermore, he knew that one of the members owned a military sword, which violated the ban on holding weapons. Based on his information, Fujii claims, the police began their operations to halt Jiu's activities.[84]

There are elements of Fujii's story, such as the timing of the subsequent police raids on Jiu's headquarters, which do not match Katsuki's chronology of events. Perhaps the most revealing aspect of his story concerns his relations with the police chief, which is worth considering in light of claims regarding collusion between the print media and the authorities in the cases of new religions during the prewar period. The media for the most part effectively endorsed the notion that new religions were dangerous and needed to be controlled.

In Jiu's case, however, the roles of the police and journalists changed somewhat. The police needed to treat the case cautiously. Although they continued to investigate Jiu, they were bound by the freedom of religion laws and could not arrest them on suspicion of promoting dangerous philosophies, as their prewar counterparts had done. But they could gather information regarding disturbances of the public peace and make inquiries based on information they received.

Fujii was not the only journalist who claimed to act as a police informant. Myōgan Gaijirō, the publisher of the *Shōgyō Keizai Minpō* and the boss of the journalist Wakasaki who had joined Jiu in Kanazawa, wrote years later that the local police asked him to spy on the group.[85] According to his story, the police chief, a friend of his, asked him to find out more about Jiu. He obtained information from a believer who complained that the substantial donations he offered did not result in the promised rewards. After hearing this story, Myōgan then passed this information on to the police who then made preparations to charge Jikōson and her henchmen with fraud. Tsushima points out that this story contains a number of factual inconsistencies.[86]

SUBDUING THE "MAN MOUNTAIN"

By 18 January 1947 the *Asahi Shinbun* reported that the local police, acting on an order from the prefectural level of the police department, raided Jiu's "palace." They ran identity checks on Katsuki and others and searched through the belongings of believers. Jikōson, however, refused to meet with them. On 21 January the police issued an order for her to appear at the police station in Tamagawa that day warning her that she would be arrested if she did not comply. They also arranged to have Dr. Akimoto carry out psychological tests on Jikōson and other Jiu leaders. This was merely a formality, a show for the media staged to provide concrete medical evidence of Jikōson's insanity. Akimoto had already presented his conclusions to the CIC branch commander. Although Jikōson did not appear, Go's wife, her sister, and others were examined.[87]

Later that night, around twenty officers raided the headquarters and arrested the remaining leaders, including Futabayama. Journalists and cameramen were on hand to record the dramatic scenes at the house as the police marched into the house demanding Jikōson's appearance. She came down the stairs and walked to the doorway with Futabayama by her side. Officers tried to take her by the arm but he blocked them and refused to step aside. Suddenly he tussled with the commanding police officer, who was a martial arts expert. Other officers joined in the fray, pinning Futabayama down and eventually dragging him outside. During the fracas, Futabayama bit an officer's hands. Meanwhile, the police bundled Jikōson into a separate vehicle and took her to the station. Jiu members outside the house called for the police to stop manhandling Jikōson. Some of them fell to the ground, screaming that the predicted calamities had begun. The commotion was over in minutes, but the effect of the images of the wrestler and the police lasted for years.[88]

The 23 January article in the *Stars and Stripes*, the English-language paper for the Occupation forces, embellished the tale with a story that the police "found that 30 men, including a jujitsu expert, were barely enough to subdue the 'Man Mountain.' For two hours the 300-pound wrestler, armed with a thick stick, single-handedly held off his intending captors, finally succumbing to superior numbers." The same day's *Nippon Times* called the fight over in thirty minutes, concluding that "ex-sumo champ beats up police but fails to save 'sun goddess'."

Katsuki and two other Jiu members were arrested and taken to the station. Thirty minutes after he was locked in a cell, he heard Futa-

A dramatic image of Futabayama trying to protect Jikōson
by wrestling with a police officer in Kanazawa.

bayama being dragged inside another cell, still tussling and calling out
Jikōson's name. Katsuki then overheard a conversation in which the
reporter Fujii and a representative of the Sumo Association told Futabayama that Jikōson had cheated him, that Jiu was an evil religion, and
that he should give up his faith in Jikōson. Futabayama left the police
station with these two men early the next morning, and was released
without charge.[89]

An article in the *Yomiuri Shinbun* published on the day of the
arrests described the reasons why the police launched a full-scale raid

on Jiu's headquarters. First, they suspected that Jiu violated SCAP's prohibition on ultranationalism, and that it advocated world control centering on Japan; secondly, Jiu was creating a public nuisance because of the predictions of natural disasters causing the public to panic; and thirdly, they needed to investigate the rumors that Jiu was extorting money and goods from believers. Regarding the first point, the police chief of Ishikawa Prefecture stated, "we are free to believe any kind of religion, but strict control must be kept over any which may disturb the social order. Jiu aims to reorganize the world under the control of the emperor. This is against the Potsdam Declaration. That is why we started this investigation." Ironically, as noted in chapter 3, in the pre-war period the police investigated groups that promoted world renewal on the grounds that their teachings might conflict with the state-imposed ideals and appropriations of Shinto. In Jiu's case, the methods of control were similar but the reasons the police offered were different to those of the prewar period.

Fujii's article published in the *Asahi Shinbun* on 24 January reported a conversation between Futabayama and the police chief in which the wrestler asked why the arrests were made. The chief apologized for the trouble and recommended he return home and get some rest. Fujii's subsequent reports contained references to "a representative from the Sumo Association" joining him and Futabayama on the trip back to Kyushu. Other newspapers, such as the local *Hokuriku Mainichi*, the *Mainichi Shinbun*, and the *Yomiuri Shinbun* ran the story and reported the various movements of Futabayama, Fujii, and the Sumo Association representative. After leaving Kanazawa, this group went to another town and then on to a hot springs resort. On 25 January they held a press conference, during which Futabayama announced that he had left Jiu.[90]

Jikōson made efforts to bring Futabayama back to Jiu after hearing of his release. On the afternoon of 25 January, Go's wife received a message for Futabayama through an oracle. As Katsuki was still in detention, the task of passing the message onto Futabayama fell to Wakasaki, the journalist from the *Shōgyō Keizai Minpō*. Despite having placed their faith in Wakasaki, Jiu members found that he was completely unreliable. The message never reached Futabayama, but landed in the hands of Myōgan Gaijirō, Wakasaki's boss. According to Katsuki, Myōgan then took this to Fujii, who was staying with Futabayama at the resort. Fujii urged him not to show it to Futabayama or to publish its details in the *Shōgyō Keizai Minpō*.[91] Wakasaki, not surprisingly, never returned to Jiu headquarters. Although Katsuki and others attempted to contact Futabayama on a number of occasions after the "Kanazawa incident," he never became associated with Jiu again.[92]

As the Futabayama saga was unfolding, stories concerning the results of Dr. Akimoto's psychological examinations of Jiu members appeared in national newspapers. Akimoto's report was based on his previous study instigated by SCAP in late December 1946. On 22 January the *Yomiuri Shinbun* reported that "three hours of examination proved that the two mediums suffer from mental abnormalities. When they could not answer a question, they hypnotized themselves and fell into convulsions. Dr. Akimoto judged that from their actions, Jikōson must also be mentally abnormal." It also noted that he believed she did not present any physical danger to the public. Jikōson was released from police custody on the evening of 23 January. She was not charged with any offence. Although Katsuki and two others were held on suspicions of fraud and embezzlement, they were released on 30 January. Despite the remarkable publicity surrounding this incident and the police announcements of long investigations, all those arrested were released without being charged.

THEORIES ABOUT KANAZAWA

There are a number of different versions and theories concerning why the Kanazawa incident occurred. Katsuki Tokujirō blames the police and claims that they had grown increasingly angry with Jiu members because they had previously escaped prosecution and continued to act in a haughty manner toward the authorities.[93] Certainly police pressure intensified after Jiu made contact with MacArthur, and the oracles sent to the police could well have made matters worse in terms of how they perceived the group. While this is viewed from the perspective of someone who was pursued, questioned, and jailed by the authorities, it does indicate that the kinds of official practices carried out toward new religions in the prewar period continued into the postwar period in this case. But this does not take into account the involvement of SCAP or the influence of reporters in the decisions taken by the authorities.

The psychologist Akimoto's testimony and the records of SCAP's Religions Division provide some evidence of the extent of SCAP's involvement. Akimoto states that SCAP's CIC (Public Safety) unit in Kanazawa essentially agreed with the police in that it recognized that Jiu's activities could pose some problems in terms of social harmony and stability. The CIC commander felt that in order to quell any hysterical public reactions to Jiu's claims of forthcoming calamities, conducting a psychological profile of the central figure and releasing the results would be sufficient to halt Jiu's progress. Nevertheless, he realized that the actions the police were taking against the group could be interpreted as religious persecution. As such, by releasing Akimoto's findings, the CIC commander felt that the medical professional's opinion would substantially damage Jiu's reputation and stave off possible criticism over police actions. The tests could then stand alone as justification for launching investigations into Jiu and other actions of the authorities, including possible arrests. The results of Akimoto's tests were released in the media and publicized as per his original recommendations. This would seem to coincide with the idea that after the heavy-handed nature of the arrests, SCAP did play a hand in ensuring that the authorities would not be accused of religious persecution. SCAP's Public Safety Division was not opposed to weakening Jiu's potential influence, and neither was SCAP's Religions Division.[94]

The question of censoring newspapers with regard to the Kanazawa incident was raised within the Religions Division soon after the arrests. SCAP's Civil Censorship Division (CCD), which was in charge of newspaper and magazine censorship, contacted the Religions Division regarding its views on censoring some aspects of the press coverage, and in particular the police interrogation of Jikōson. The division was mainly concerned with whether the police actions constituted a violation of freedom of religion and whether the media reports were biased in favor of the official police line that Jiu needed to be controlled.

The CCD received a verbal communication from the Religions Division on 22 January indicating that it saw no problem with the reports being published as they were. The next day Bunce, the Religions Division chief, signed a statement confirming his division's position that censorship was unnecessary.[95] This suggests that the Religions Division agreed that Jiu presented a threat to public safety. This idea overrode their officers' previous concerns over police persecution and suggests that Bunce accepted the police position in Kanazawa.[96] The division did not make any recommendations at the time to halt the actions of the Japanese police.

SCAP's *Religions in Japan* report stated that the Home Ministry ordered the dissolution of Jiu sometime in February 1947 on the basis that its doctrines were ultranationalistic and militaristic.[97] Furthermore, a Religions Division report in 1947 also claimed that the Japanese police actually dissolved Jiu in Kanazawa.[98] Both reports were mistaken.[99] While Jiu may have been the subject of investigations, it was never officially forced to disband by SCAP or the Japanese authorities. In fact, the misinformation circulated by the Religions Division may indicate a lack of communication between SCAP agencies in this case.

Myōgan Gaijirō, the self-promoting "police spy," held that SCAP attempted to purge ultranationalism, used the police to carry out a campaign against Jiu, and effectively suppressed the group.[100] Jiu's doctrines of world renewal and attitudes toward the emperor did provoke SCAP's suspicions, and SCAP did investigate some religious groups suspected of ultranationalistic tendencies. For example, SCAP placed Tenri Honmichi under suspicion in 1950 but did not disband it, whereas Tentsūkyō was dissolved on the basis of its doctrines. Myōgan claims that MacArthur, greatly angered after being approached by Jiu members, ordered the group's dissolution. According to his story, the police approached Myōgan and asked him to infiltrate the group, gather information that might support the charges of ultranationalism as well as violations of food laws, and then report back to them. According to Murakami Shigeyoshi, the police used this method of gathering evidence so that they could avoid being accused of religious persecution but at the same time quell the activities of a group that troubled them.[101]

Myōgan's story is imaginative but problematic. The dates he provides do not match other records, but more to the point the likelihood that MacArthur was personally involved in suppressing the group is remote.[102] If this had been the case, no doubt SCAP authorities would have taken action after Jiu members supposedly approached him in May 1946. The weakness of this explanation is that neither SCAP nor Japanese authorities disbanded Jiu. The police continued to investigate Jiu after Kanazawa, but SCAP never abolished it. If SCAP intended to eradicate Jiu because of ultranationalism, it seems likely that the Religions Division would have been involved sometime before the group moved to Kanazawa. The records indicate that from around September 1946 staff members of the division were concerned that the Jiu case may have implications regarding freedom of religion. However, the division's position appears to have changed after Kanazawa. It is possible that the Religions Division was presented with police evidence concerning food law violations and Akimoto's reports. It seems clear that the SCAP authorities accepted the police line that Jiu presented a threat to public safety. One of the most influential factors concerning this was the involvement of Futabayama, the wrestling superstar and national hero.

Go Seigen's theory holds that the main purpose of the arrests and the media coverage was to "recapture Futabayama" from Jiu.[103] The key person in the affair was the *Asahi Shinbun*'s Fujii, who was committed to getting the former champion away from Jiu and back to normality. Go accepts Fujii's story that he approached the police in order to stir up publicity and gain public sympathy for the wrestler. Given that Futabayama was quickly released from custody under Fujii's care, Go assumes that Fujii must have made some prior arrangements with the police. If there had been no contact beforehand, Go reasons, it would have been difficult to secure an early release after the battle with the officers the night before. Most Jiu members were held in the station for at least a few days yet Futabayama disappeared the morning after his arrest. These facts lend some weight to this theory.

These theories taken together contribute different understandings to the story. The police provided information to SCAP's Public Safety Division well before Jiu moved to Kanazawa, and were keen to control the group because they viewed it as a public safety threat. The police inquiries up until the Kanazawa incident had not focused on Jiu's doctrines as such. Aware that they had to tread carefully because of freedom of religion laws, they concentrated their efforts on showing SCAP that Jiu posed a threat to public safety because of the predictions of calamities. The rumors about illegal procurement of food and coercion of followers added to the list of possible charges against the group. SCAP's Religions Division had been cautious about police involvement when Jiu first came to the attention of its officers, yet the police made sure to keep in contact with the division following the MacArthur incidents.

Nevertheless, Jiu's own actions and attitudes must also be taken into account. The incident clearly highlights a public relations issue that many religious groups face, particularly new ones that strive for social change by going public with their cause. Jiu vacillated between the two extremes of restricting access and blatant promotion through its famous celebrities. Thus, it exacerbated the situation in three ways: (1) it maintained an insular perspective at a time when the press and the authorities were showing the greatest amount of interest; (2) it ignored the changing circumstances of occupied Japan, including the roles of the various authorities; and (3) it attempted to cultivate high profile supporters whose image as celebrities and public favorites was extremely valuable to other interests.

Jikōson's position was unassailable as leader of the group but she was not open to outside scrutiny. She met staff of the Religions Division only after they repeatedly requested a meeting, she initially refused to meet with journalists from the *Asahi Shinbun*, and she did not deal directly with the police. From Jiu's perspective, her unwillingness to meet with outsiders was related to her tendency to become sick when "contaminated" by contact with the unclean, outside world. Jiu is not unusual among new religions that straddle a fine line between maintaining an image of their leader as being both beyond reproach and unapproachable on the one hand, and presenting their vision as a viable alternative to current social arrangements. But while contact with Jikōson was limited to most people, this did not apply to Futabayama. She met him almost as soon as he became involved in the group arousing the interests and the suspicions of journalists. While Futabayama was considered to be a fervent believer and was given responsibility in the group because of his faith in Jikōson, from the perspective of journalists, and Fujii Tsuneo in particular, Jiu was simply using his status to promote its movement. This was a significant theme in many of the print media reports, and this helped to brand Jiu as a self-serving and cynical group. Another problem for Jiu members was that they chose to goad the police into further action by sending letters demanding that various police chiefs visit "the palace."

THE PRESS COVERAGE

The *Asahi*, *Mainichi*, and *Yomiuri* papers all reported on the sensational arrests and the stories were repeated in local newspapers as well as English-language and international papers. The *Asahi* ran eight major articles on the so-called Kanazawa incident throughout January 1947. This was a significant amount of space given the severe paper shortages at the time. Most press reports mocked and ridiculed Jiu, but also warned readers of the dangers posed by new religions. The stories generally carried similar themes that included claims of ultranationalism, Jikōson's madness, food violations, and the involvement of Futabayama and Go. They were generally judged to be gullible and foolish because they had been duped by unscrupulous manipulators during a time of great social crisis.

In the *Asahi Shinbun* of 23 January, Fujii Tsuneo reported that the police arrested Jiu members because they promoted ultranationalism against SCAP directives and violated food laws. They claimed that Katsuki was Jiu's ringleader, and that not only did he take charge for the group's proselytization activities, he also introduced members of the army and air force to Jikōson during the war.[104] An article in the English-language *Nippon Times* of 25 January, which was based on a report from *Jiji Shinpō*, described how wartime military leaders turned to Jikōson for spiritual advice in the last months of the war. It carried titillating details of how Jikōson used to massage the troubled military men by "applying her nimble fingers to the bodies of her devotees." The references to ultranationalism and wartime leaders, and licentiousness contributed to the idea that Jiu was an odious group that had close connections with members of the discredited military regime.

The police stance changed soon after this. The charge of ultranationalism was extremely delicate because criticisms may have arisen concerning authoritarian control of a religious group. Such control had become accepted by the mid-1930s but the new regime of freedom of religion presented a different situation. On 6 February 1947, the *Jiji Shinpō* reported that the new chief of the Metropolitan Police, Hirooka Ken'ichi, asserted that Jikōson's arrest was definitely not a case of religious control but that the authorities were concerned that gullible people would believe Jikōson if she had been allowed to continue her activities. The purpose of publicizing the results of the psychological test was to establish her as a lunatic. The charge of spreading ultranationalistic thought effectively vanished and was replaced by another potent charge of lunacy and irrationality. Akimoto's findings justified the police operation.

The results of Akimoto's tests that Jikōson was delusional but did not pose a physical threat were published in many of the papers. The *Nippon Times* of 25 January stated that Jikōson was "generally queer with fanatic traits, and definitely a mental case." A noteworthy contribution to the journalistic chorus came from Satō Hachirō, a famous poet who had written the lyrics to a hugely successful song that year, "The Apple Song." In the *Tōkyō Taimuzu* on 22 January, he argued that Jikōson was quite mad, just like the former leader of Ōmoto, Deguchi Onisaburō. Satō claimed that Onisaburō was trying to get back into the "religions business" in the postwar period. The *Mainichi Shinbun* of 24 January neatly captured the general tone of the theme: Jikōson was "clearly nuts" (*akirakani kichigai*). The same day's *Los Angeles Times* announced that "'Sun Goddess Jiko' [was] Just a 'Japanese Crackpot.'" The paper titled a brief article the next day as "Jap Sun Goddess Balmy but Free by Police Order."

The theme of embezzlement was also taken up. The *Jiji Shinpō* reported on 18 January that Jikōson took advantage of the postwar confusion to acquire many believers, particularly farmers who had been duped into handing over their precious rice crops. As a result, the report held, approximately fifty members of the group were able to consume twice the allotted amount of rice rations each day. Jiu managed to accomplish this because the people were gripped with fear over the predictions of calamities.

On 21 January the *Yomiuri Shinbun* supplied details of the estimated monthly income of the group ("the huge sum of 250,000 yen per month") and the amount of rice ("six bales of rice and a large amount of vegetables and other foods"). The article also told the story of a businessman in Kanazawa who was told through one of the oracles that he should offer the sum of thirty million yen to Jiu. Apparently, when he requested that the sum be reduced to ten million yen, he was banished from the group.

The *Asahi Shinbun* of 23 January reported that the police suspected Katsuki of violating the Food Control Act by swindling people, hoarding food, and hiding his ill-gotten gains from the authorities. It is unsurprising that Jiu's position was that people had donated food and other goods of their own free will. However, faced with strong police statements and a rising tide of press opinion, this viewpoint was virtually ignored, or simply dismissed as a lame excuse to cover up for nefarious activities.

FUTABAYAMA'S REDEMPTION

Futabayama's involvement in the group and the collision of his pre-Jiu celebrity and the group's increasing notoriety had a major impact on Jiu's fate. After he was released from the police station, Fujii travelled with him and filed reports on his condition and gradual recovery from his brief and turbulent time with a living god. On 26 January, his *Asahi Shinbun* article entitled "Eyes Awakened to False Predictions" reported that while Futabayama had not completely recovered from his traumatic experience, he had at least recognized he had been deceived. The article explored the reasons why Futabayama had set off on a spiritual path, listing his intense desire for reconstruction of the country after the devastation caused by war as his primary motivation. He felt that "the *kami* and buddhas had deserted the country" and that this reflected some fault in his own faith. Jikōson's teachings were therefore very attractive and he essentially lost all self-control. Finally, Fujii stated that Futabayama left the group because Jikōson's predictions had not come true. The gist of this article was that although Futabayama had made a tragic mistake, he had finally come to his senses. His brief foray with Jiu was described as a kind of temporary insanity.

Other papers soon added their perspectives. In an interview published in the *Mainichi Shinbun* on the same day, Futabayama apologized for causing a fuss. The article joked about how he had reverted back to being human (*ningen ni kaetta Futabayama*) and carried a photo of him looking somewhat sheepish. Borrowing a phrase from sumo, the article's subhead notes that the wrestler had been caught in a nightmare but was now laughing because he managed to perform a successful backward pivot throw (*ucchari*). This is a move that allows a wrestler to turn imminent defeat into victory. In his wrestling heyday, Futabayama used this move consistently, prompting the nickname *ucchari* Futabayama.[105] Thus, the use of *ucchari* in the article effectively reclaims the former victorious image of Futabayama. The accompanying photo of him laughing emphasizes the point and reduces a potential public relations disaster into a joke.

Futabayama's actions constitute celebrity redemption, "the ritualized attempt by a fallen celebrity to re-acquire positive celebrity status through confession and the request for public absolution."[106] Through this request to his fans for forgiveness, Futabayama acknowledged that his behavior contrasted with his idealized image and requested understanding for his human failings. Given his value as a cultural commodity, this request also focused attention on what drove him to this temporary descent into madness: Jikōson, whose image of a deceiving, irrational lunatic gained more traction in contrast to the purity of the vulnerable Futabayama. His public redemption served to elevate and emphasize her notorious status.

"EVIL CULTS," "SUPERSTITIONS," AND "TRUE RELIGIONS"

After the Kanazawa incident, there was a veritable flood of newspaper articles lambasting Jiu and new religions in general.[107] According to a Religions Division report that surveyed the print media reports at the time, the Jiu case "attracted considerable attention and aroused thoughtful speculation over the causes for the growth of freak religious movements."[108] But rather than just concentrating on new religions, some reports used the Kanazawa incident to highlight the challenges faced by established religions. An *Asahi Shinbun* editorial of 27 January 1947 entitled "The stagnation of established religions and the outbreak of evil cults" declared that the causes for the incident lay in Japan's defeat:

> After war, evil cults [*jakyō*] inevitably thrive. In particular, the spiritual confusion and trying living circumstances caused by Japan's defeat weaken the public's spirit so that society becomes a hotbed from which evil cults emerge.... As the essence of religion lies in the metaphysical realm of faith, which is a concept that is difficult to explain logically, any religion or sect may be said to be unscientific and superstitious. From that perspective, close investigation reveals that the difference between true religion and evil cults is paper-thin.

The editorial then argued that while established religions initially began to label "newly arisen religions" as evil cults in order to protect themselves, established religions were also persecuted at some stage in the past. *Shin Yūkan*, a Tokyo-based publication that was representative of the new papers (*shinkōshi*) of the postwar period, ran a series of articles about new religions from 6 to 12 February 1947. The stated purpose of the series was "to call for the appearance of righteous religions" while at the same time exposing the bad ones. The first article in the series stated that the oracles of Jikōson were very similar to those of Deguchi Nao, and that both Jiu and Ōmoto were run by "brains trusts," suggesting that these leaders were merely figureheads. The article offered the eye-catching suggestion that "it is highly likely that religion and sex are inseparable." This idea appeared in another article featuring Renmonkyō, which began with an explanation that suspicious "religions" such as Ōmoto and Jiu had been founded by uneducated women of limited intelligence. Although Renmonkyō's female founder was similarly encumbered, the article held, there had been a widespread rumor that she once had sexual intercourse with an aged fox.

The English language *Nippon Times* published an editorial column entitled "Religion or Superstition" on 14 February 1947. Quoting Bunce, the chief of the Religions Division who made a statement on superstitions in May 1946, it argued:

> It is undeniable that religious freedom means, as Dr. Bunce clearly pointed out, no one is competent to judge the question of whether a religion is good or bad or whether it is truly a religion or merely a superstition for any person but himself.... However, adequate protection offered under the criminal laws securing public health, welfare and safety must be constantly provided through an alert police administration....

While the [present postwar] situation does not limit spiritual assistance to only the old, established sects, it is equally clear that people must be protected against any sort of fanaticism or superstition utilized by persons for selfish or dangerous purposes…. When medical experts reach the decision that the leader of this sect is mentally unbalanced and when the disciple Futabayama goes so far as to resist physically police action, it is time for not only the people but also the public authorities to take steps to prevent the unlimited propagation of unsound and unwholesome beliefs…. It is the right of the people to judge for themselves the worthiness of any ideology. Yet, adequate protection must be offered them against fraud, medical malpractice or any other offence that may seriously affect public welfare.

Notably the article does not discuss the initial reasons given by the police for the raid—violations of food laws—but rather raises the question of true and false religion. Despite the fact that laws did exist to protect the public "against fraud, medical malpractice or any other offence which might seriously affect public welfare," the involvement of the authorities in determining the effect of superstitions was regarded as an essential and necessary requirement in postwar society.

AFTER KANAZAWA

Woodard of SCAP's Religions Division referred to Jiu in this following manner: "When it was learned that an organization whose followers had approached MacArthur was under police investigation, an inquiry was instituted in order to be sure that the religious freedom of the group was not being restricted by the government."[109] Although the Religions Division had been willing to accept the position of the local CIC branch that Jiu was a threat to public safety during the Kanazawa incident—a position that was informed by police reports of Jiu's activities from months earlier—after hearing the collective complaints of other new religions, it seems that the Religions Division once again changed its position regarding Jiu. Previously the division appeared to agree tacitly with the notion that Jiu posed a threat to public safety. However, once the stories of other new religions began to filter into the division regarding persecution by the police and other authorities, the division began to warn of the potential for reversion to the prewar situation of state control over religions. While Woodard's comments might suggest that the division had been vigilant in protecting Jiu's freedom, they actually obfuscate the confusion that occurred in Kanazawa and misrepresent what happened there.

Jikōson, shrouded in white, leaves Kanazawa with her supporters
trying to shield her with luggage.

Although the remaining members of Jiu did not leave Kanazawa immediately, they faced a number of problems. They stayed on in the same house that was raided until 15 March 1947, and then moved to another house that had been offered to them by a supporter. Katsuki claims that the police and various newspaper reporters continued to harass them, and the group was forced to leave Kanazawa on 20 May.[110] Their eviction was reported on 22 May 1947 in the *Yomiuri Shinbun*, which stated that around thirty armed policemen went to the house to order the group to leave. A SCAP report noted that "the wandering of Jiu ... was recorded by the Kanazawa Broadcasting Station and will be reproduced for national broadcasting from the station at 0:30 PM, 26 May." Over the next few months, Jiu moved to different areas, including Yokohama and Tokyo, with reporters continually chasing them for stories. She became labelled "god on the run" at this stage.[111]

Around this time, Jiu members suddenly appeared in Numazu outside the imperial villa of Prince Chichibu, the brother of the emperor, chanting and performing various "world renewal ceremonies." An article in the *Yomiuri Shinbun* on 22 July described how Jikōson and her party had informed the prince's household agency that Jikōson's headquarters would be moved there "by divine order." The police were called in but no arrests were made. The group camped outside the grounds all day and night but did not meet the prince. The paper stated that if they took Jikōson's picture, their souls would desert them. This ended without further incident. The group returned to Tokyo and in the summer moved into a house by Lake Yamanaka, which was owned by an acquaintance of Go's, but before year's end the group was forced to leave. Katsuki claims that wherever they travelled, members of the public would throw things at them and tell everyone in the town, "that evil cult is coming, don't be fooled by them."[112]

Around the beginning of 1948 Jiu settled into a house in Hakone, where they stayed for around six months. By this stage, the number of members had dwindled significantly, leaving only Jikōson, Katsuki, and a couple of other leaders. Jiu's approach to its activities changed substantially. Although it did not abandon its world renewal philosophies, it took a less confrontational approach to the outside world. Rather than attempting to effect change in society, Jiu took a more introspective view, seeking to purify itself through admissions of misdeeds, reformation, and repentance by Jiu members.[113] This eventually led to Go Seigen's departure from the group.

Although media attention concerning Jiu was now dwindling and other new religions became the focus of attention, Go Seigen's decision to play go while remaining with Jikōson was reported in some papers. In July 1947, he recommenced a ten-game go tournament sponsored by the *Yomiuri Shinbun*. He was leading the match four games to one, but temporarily stopped competing while he concentrated on his activities with Jiu. In an interview published in the *Mainichi Shinbun* of 8 July 1947, he said, "to play go and reform the world serve the same purpose … [This is] to improve Sino-Japanese relations." The *Yomiuri Shinbun* on 11 July 1947 also published his comments on the powers of Jikōson, saying that she "has the power to call down spirits whenever she wishes to do so. I have met many religious people, both Chinese and Japanese, but she was the first one who really satisfied me. I am conscious of another world, the world that is beyond our reach. She teaches us that we are subject to the control of the *kami*."

But while Go's professional career was picking up, his role in Jiu was in decline. In an article published in the *Chūō Kōron* magazine in October 1948 entitled "World Renewal Go" (*Yonaoshi Go*), Go Seigen expounded on his professional and spiritual progress. In this document, Go claims that the strength of his faith is why he is unbeatable at the game of *go* (he was enjoying a remarkable winning streak in newspaper-sponsored tournaments). But he also states that Jiu's troubles with the police in Kanazawa and other areas were the result of "a Freemason plot" in which he and his wife played a key role.

This pronouncement amounts to a public confession that they were acting to block Jiu's progress. Then, Go's wife suddenly left Jiu on 11 November 1948. She left a notebook that was discovered five months later. It contained a statement that amounted to an admission that she had attempted to block the path to world renewal. Her sister also left the group. Go stayed on for a brief period but then left. Their departure was considered by the remaining Jiu members to be an act of treachery.[114]

Once Go Seigen left, the group essentially lost much of its news value, and the media began to focus on other groups, particularly Tenshō Kōtai Jingū Kyō toward the middle of 1947. Jiu moved to a house that belonged to a believer in Yokohama, where they lived a relatively quiet existence, at least from the outside.

Jikōson continued to send messages to a number of influential and famous people, including former silent movie voiceover star and radio personality Tokugawa Musei, and the president of the Heibonsha publishing company, Shimonaka Yasaburō, as mentioned above. Some became Jiu's supporters and benefactors. Nevertheless, from then on the main coverage Jiu received was related to retrospectives on Futabayama, Go Seigen, or occasionally postwar new religions. It was limited predominantly to weekly magazines (*shūkanshi*) and not newspapers.

From the perspective of the media and the public, Jikōson and Jiu led a relatively quiet existence from the mid-1950s. Yamada Senta, who met Jikōson in 1957, moved to London in the early 1960s and established an Aikidō school. When in Japan, Yamada lived with the group in Yokohama. He believed that Jikōson was a living god and made efforts to introduce some of his students and other overseas contacts to her.

When Jikōson passed away in 1984, Katsuki Tokujirō took over as leader of Jiu, but he had no interest in promoting her memory or her teachings.[115] Yamada left Yokohama after a rift with Katsuki surfaced. He continued to talk about Jikōson to various people until his own death. However, for much of the public, the name Jikōson has become a minor historical footnote that may appear in the context of memories of the great wrestler Futabayama.

JIKŌSON AS "CELEBRITY GOD"

There are a number of factors that led Jikōson to become Japan's first postwar celebrity god, including the leaking of information to the press by the police and Futabayama's participation. The press reports before and during the incident in Kanazawa show similarities to themes relating to new religions that had developed in media reports since the Meiji period. Superstition and suspect doctrines, fraud, mental instability, and the fear of social disturbance were all part of this general picture. The particular conditions of the prewar period, with its emphasis on loyalty to the emperor and nation, were replaced by the newly imposed democratic ideals. Yet the representation of new religions was relatively unchanged. While much of the press promoted these themes, Jiu's own actions engendered suspicions to a certain extent. The members' attitudes toward the police invited further trouble. Jikōson's reticence to deal with outsiders attracted suspicion, as did her willingness to allow Futabayama to assume a position of responsibility in the group. The group made some fatal miscalculations that led to the development of Jikōson's highly negative image. Yet the promotional value of Futabayama to the Sumo Association and his public standing were factors far beyond the group's control.

After the "Kanazawa incident," the newsprint had barely dried on the papers before the next celebrity god, Kitamura Sayo, better known in the press as *odoru kamisama* ("the dancing god"), made her appearance on the national stage. Although she was placed in a similar category to Jikōson in print media reports, her reaction to the media was entirely different.

6

Kitamura Sayo
Celebrity in the Maggot World

FROM the beginning of the Occupation, Kitamura Sayo, who was eventually labeled "the dancing god" in the press, was openly confrontational toward the Japanese authorities and those who opposed her. In her millennial vision, Japan's surrender was merely a temporary pause in hostilities between the "maggot world," which included the imperial line, the bureaucracy, intellectuals, and established religions. In contrast to Jiu's refusal to accept Japan's defeat and the Occupation, Kitamura welcomed the changes to Japanese society and declared MacArthur to be a divine messenger who dispensed harsh justice to the selfish leaders of the wartime government. The intensity of her convictions, evidenced by her willingness to confront rigidly established social institutions without holding back, stood in stark contrast to the isolationism that characterized Jiu in its initial stages. However, she was not openly critical of SCAP. This suggests that while she acknowledged that a new regime was in place, she revealed a flexibility that allowed her to work with the authorities who she thought might be able to help her cause.[1] Her highly idiosyncratic approach belied a keen political astuteness of the changing conditions Japan faced at the end of the war.

Kitamura's forthright and critical approach had a significant effect on representations of her in the press. While she was vilified in some press reports, she was also an appealing figure to the media because of the different variations of the story of "the dancing god" that were contrived. After Jikōson, she became the most recognizable "celebrity god" in the immediate postwar period.

Kitamura's reputation in the local area of Tabuse developed largely through word-of-mouth. The number of people who testified to miraculous recoveries from illness after hearing her preach grew. Kitamura used her farmhouse as a preaching hall and often held three preaching sessions each day, with some of the sessions lasting up to three hours. This cracking pace continued until 1958, when she slowed down to two sessions per day.[2] She had a commanding physical presence, seemingly tireless enthusiasm, and a deep confidence in the righteousness of her message. To those who came to her seeking cures or improvements to their lives, Kitamura's message was simple: they would have to determine to sacrifice themselves for the sake of the new earthly paradise. She promised them that once they had done this, she would cut off their evil karma, thus allowing them to be cured, provided that they followed the instructions she received from the "absolute god of the universe."[3]

Tenshō Kōtai Jingū Kyō's official history, *Seisho*, paints a picture of an inspiring leader whose uncompromising attitude of converting everyone she met spurred others to follow her example. New followers would stop passersby in the streets and tell them of the benefits they had received since meeting Kitamura. Like her, they denounced those who mocked them. Food rations were extremely scarce around the Tabuse region, as was the case throughout the country. Corruption and black market operations were rife, and rumors circulated about illegal activities involving officials and townspeople in Tabuse. One normally timid individual who joined the group attended a town meeting to discuss rationing. He issued a stern warning to the gathering that he would personally pursue anyone who committed a crime or caused the people to suffer. The audience was reportedly amazed at his remarkable transformation of character.[4]

Kitamura's son Yoshito returned home from the battlefront in early November 1945. He was initially skeptical of his mother's newfound convictions, which was not surprising given that upon welcoming him home she told him she had gone insane. As time passed, however, his doubts began to dissolve, and he became convinced of her powers in early 1946 when she became possessed with the spirit of one of his army subordinates who had been killed in battle and began writhing on the ground as the young soldier had. From that point, he began to pray together with her in earnest.[5]

Kitamura declared that the beginning of 1946 marked a new era of equality for all those who cleansed themselves and abandoned all attachments to the "world of maggots." She believed the strongest and most insidious attachments people held were their connections to traditional, established religions. Intolerant of all other religions, she reserved harsh judgment for "professional religionists" of any persuasion who made money from people without showing them how to overcome their suffering. While this stance gained her some converts, it naturally invited opposition from established religions. Her criticisms of other religions continued throughout her career.

According to a SCAP report based on an interview with Kitamura, her first target was "Pure Land Buddhism," which was the traditional faith of her family and the sect that claimed more adherents than any other religion in her area. Her first public sermons contained criticisms of the faith and the organization of the sect. She declared that Buddhism and other religions were impotent in the new age, and that her followers should get rid of all religious paraphernalia. As for her own group, Kitamura declared that "we do not believe in having objects of worship. The universe alone is god."[6] She considered Buddhist icons to be merely empty vessels, and argued that offerings of food would bring no benefit to the donor. But the Pure Land sect was not her only target. In February 1946 two followers of the Nichiren tradition appeared at Kitamura's farm and told her that they had come to worship. She confronted them over their beliefs and launched a scathing attack on established religions, stating that even though the Absolute God of the Universe existed, people continued to carry out ineffectual practices of the maggot world, such as praying at altars and toward stone statues. According to *Seisho*, after two days of listening to her sermons, they became keen followers.[7]

Another target was the imperial institution and the emperor himself. Although various movements in the area claimed special allegiance to the imperial family,[8] Kitamura went in a different direction entirely. She attacked the emperor for not recognizing his mission and duty toward the people, for allowing the government to fall into disarray, and for allowing himself to be used by militarists. In her sermons, she often mentioned how the emperor had let down the people and was no more than a puppet.[9] Although Sodei Rinjirō notes that it was difficult for most Japanese to openly attack the imperial system even after the war, there were instances of public criticism. John Dower shows that the emperor became the butt of jokes and a source of rumors and conjecture by the end of the war and in the months that ensued.[10] Kitamura was still openly protesting the emperor and the imperial system in an interview recorded on 25 November 1950 with William Bunce of SCAP's Religions Division. She declared that the entire imperial palace should be burned down apart from one building and that the emperor should be nailed to its ceiling because he had neglected the people.[11]

Kitamura's relations with the police and the authorities were entirely different to Jikōson's. Before the end of the war, she was not targeted by the police. She actively sought opportunities to engage with anyone, including police, journalists, and members of the public whereas Jikōson and her close followers were extremely selective in their approach to people outside their circle. Although *Seisho* is the main source of information related to the immediate postwar period, such as the incident with the police and the district office described above, some of Kitamura's later dealings with police and SCAP officials are recorded in SCAP documents. These do show her confrontational approach, but they also reveal her awareness and sensitivities to the authorities of the day.

During the first few months after the surrender, the local police were somewhat confused about how to deal with Kitamura. Under Kitamura's command, her "comrades" would gather at the local train station and other public areas to listen to her sermons and preach to the townspeople. One day in mid-February 1946, a group of around three hundred people led by Kitamura marched to the police station in the nearby town of Hirao where they began praying in the street. A policeman came out and asked them to stop the noise. Kitamura went inside the station with some supporters and told the officers that any attempt to halt their activities would result in divine punishment. As she would soon become famous, she said, it might be embarrassing for them if they did not know of her activities.[12]

On the way home, the group passed by the district administrative office, which was responsible for controlling local economic matters. Kitamura called out that it was a "nest" for beggars who were financially incompetent and also morally decrepit.[13] Although this outburst did not have any immediate ramifications, a few months later she was arrested and spent time in prison. This event had significant ramifications for the group in terms of its self-identity and its relationship to the authorities and the press.

TAKING THE MESSAGE TO TOKYO

On 8 March 1946 Kitamura set out by train on her first trip to Tokyo with some *dōshi*. She began preaching on the train and continued to sermonize to the "maggots" of Tokyo after her arrival there.[14] She spent a total of twenty-five days in Tokyo and gave sermons in a rented house. On 17 March she went to the headquarters of the new religion Seichō no Ie whose leader, Taniguchi Masaharu, was giving a talk. Kitamura interrupted his introductory speech and launched into a singing sermon.[15] She took over the stage for the whole morning.

After completing her tour of Tokyo, Kitamura's next stop was Yotsukaidō in Chiba prefecture where she had been invited to give sermons. She started during the daytime, preaching to mothers and their children while the men worked in the fields.[16] Although *Seisho* records that she impressed her daytime audiences with her keen insights into human nature and understanding about daily living, she received an entirely different reaction when she preached in the evenings to the men. Most of them had been high-ranking army officers who were forced to take up manual labor after the surrender. They were singularly unimpressed with Kitamura because she refused to show any deference to them, and she also launched into a typically withering assault on the institution of the emperor, the wartime government, the military, and established religions. She argued that the militarists had duped the nation and that the "holy war" was "a maggot's war" and a lie. The war they now faced was between the "true god" and the devil.[17] She also pointed out that the emperor, to whom they had all dedicated their

Kitamura Sayo preaching before a crowd in 1948.

lives, had recently declared he was not a "superhuman being" but a common human.

In her speech she evoked two banned wartime slogans, *shinshū fumetsu* (神州不滅, "the indestructible nation of *kami*") and *hakkō ichiu* (八紘一宇, "the whole world under one roof"). In fact, Kitamura later ran into some trouble with SCAP officials over the use of these terms but in Yotsukaidō she was still unknown to the Occupation authorities. Her audience was familiar with these slogans and concepts, and she used these phrases to present her own teachings in the same manner as she appropriated other well-known terms. She explained that the characters for *shinshū fumetsu* should be changed to 神衆不滅, meaning "the people who believe in god are indestructible." And in "god's kingdom," she stated, the characters for *hakkō ichiu* (八光一宇) will mean "the light of god pervades the universe."[18]

Although the former army officers in the audience became quite aggressive, particularly after hearing her comments on the emperor, she remained unperturbed. A few days passed and the person who had arranged for Kitamura to appear in the first place pleaded with her to omit comments about the emperor. At the next meeting Kitamura ignored this request and faced the hostile crowd with more harsh words about the emperor. This time she received a death threat from a heckler and a scuffle broke out. Chaos ensued but Kitamura apparently remained unmoved and continued preaching, declaring that it was truly wonderful that "god" had provided a law concerning freedom of speech and then sent her out to preach. Although she may not have had too many in the crowd agree with her on that occasion, she nevertheless remained in the area until 13 April, when she returned to Tabuse.

NO RICE FOR "MAGGOT BEGGARS"

Seisho records that in the spring of 1945 Kitamura received a command from the god in her stomach to go to prison. She fulfilled this order in April 1946. After the defeat, demoralized farmers around the local area were doing little work in the fields, and she demanded that they not comply with the compulsory rice quota requirements. At harvest time Kitamura and the *dōshi* did not submit any rice. Upon her return from Tokyo, she rejected the authorities' demands on the grounds that she had no rice to waste on "maggot beggars."

When she refused to comply with a court order, the police and district clerks seized the rice and took her to the police station.[19] She taunted her jailers, preached sermons, and sang songs to the *dōshi* who had gathered outside through the bars of her cell. Kitamura spent a total of thirty-five days under incarceration. She considered this incident to be a test and a necessary trial she needed to pass in order to teach the world about the "kingdom of god." This incident became one of the defining moments for Kitamura and her group.

The trial was held at the Yamaguchi District Court. Kitamura was not a model prisoner, and she was certainly an unusual defendant. Before Watanabe Tomekichi, the young district attorney assigned to the case, could make his opening remarks, Kitamura described his faults to the court. She declared defiantly that the prosecution's accusation that she had instructed ten people not to hand over the rice quota was completely false. Instead, she countered, the actual figure was more like ten thousand. Given this situation, she demanded that the court apply the maximum penalty. Although Watanabe pressed on with the case, she often disrupted the proceedings by breaking into song and dancing. *Seisho* reports that over time Watanabe became more impressed with her words and attitude.[20]

These descriptions from *Seisho* about the image of Kitamura are useful because of the way it tries to represent the leader. She appears to be strong, unyielding, and unwilling to bend to any authority. But she was also quite astute when it came to dealing with the press, in contrast to Jikōson.

THE PRESS BEGINS

The trial generated some minor interest from the local press. The first print media reports about Tenshō Kōtai Jingū Kyō appeared in a small paper, the *Bōchō Shinbun*. The first article appeared on 22 April 1946, followed by one on 25 April, and then another on 16 May. The trial was not a major story, and the articles were squeezed in between other news. The *Bōchō Shinbun* made no attempt to address Kitamura's teachings but rather described her as a madwoman. The articles concentrated more on her refusal to submit the rice quota and willingness to encourage others to break the law as well. They also contained a number of inaccuracies, such as the claim that it was Kitamura's husband who actually refused to hand over the rice and that her object of faith was Inari, the god of the harvest.

On 22 May, a large group of supporters gathered inside the courthouse together with other curious onlookers and members of the press to hear the court's decision. Kitamura launched into a sermon, and at one point during the proceedings marched over to the desk where journalists were seated, slammed her fist on the table, and demanded that they print a picture of her angry face and spread the news throughout the world. This episode is a good example of how Kitamura saw the press as a potential instrument for proselytization. In a sense she was trying to strike a bargain with the press by demanding publicity yet giving them what they could use—a highly unusual story of courtroom drama and theatrics. Despite this performance, it took some months before the story of the trial was publicized in the national papers.

Bōchō Shinbun, which started to report the details of the case with more accuracy toward the end of the trial, published an article entitled "Eight Months Imprisonment Sought for God" on 23 May. Kitamura was placed on probation for three years. Before she was released, the prosecutor Watanabe visited her and listened to her sermons. Her presence and teachings evidently had a profound effect on him and he became a fervent *dōshi* around six months after the trial,[21] eventually becoming a central figure for the group in Tokyo.

Although his involvement was highly significant for the group, the participation of people from an intellectual background became an important theme in subsequent press reports. During the Meiji period, new religions like Renmonkyō and Tenrikyō had been derided in the press for attracting and influencing people of little education from rural communities. Critics of new religions argued that the groups targeted followers who were not able to discern "true" religions from "false" ones. But Ōmoto and other groups had attracted intellectuals of some renown by the late-Taishō and early-Shōwa periods, and these people were criticized because their education did not cover the field of psychology, hence their acceptance of "irrationalities." In the postwar period these ideas continued, and journalists, psychologists, and academics considered the participation of intellectuals to be indicative of irrational thought that pervaded the postwar malaise. The notions that educated people were being drawn into new religions as a result of the postwar chaos became an important part of the media discourse during the postwar period.

THE "WHIP OF LOVE"

During Kitamura's period of incarceration, some people had given up the practice, apparently feeling that practicing faith ("going to god") had not protected Kitamura from imprisonment. The majority of *dōshi* were waiting for her "as children yearn for their mother." However, Kitamura treated them sternly and trained them with the "whip of love" by saying, "I do not provide answers to questions, cure illness, or tell fortunes. I give favors to no one. I am simply teaching you the correct way to live through revealing two paths—one that leads to a living hell, the other to [a] heaven."[22] After receiving this guidance, the remaining *dōshi* stepped up their proselytizing efforts. She ordered them to ignore all other religions and insisted that they abandon idol worship and sever relations with their former temples and churches.

She also instructed them on how meetings should be conducted and how the community of comrades should be organized. She decreed that there would be no professional clerics or committees, and no discrimination between the *dōshi* on grounds of seniority. She made it clear that while there were to be leaders, such as Watanabe, relationships between the *dōshi* were not hierarchical as they were all part of the "maggot world." Initially Kitamura had declared that no halls or worship would be built, but this policy changed when it became apparent that the number of people coming from other parts of the country was rapidly increasing. She allowed dormitories to be built on her property, thus paving the way for the construction of meeting halls.

Within a few short months, Kitamura distinguished herself as a strong critic of any traditions or customs that did not fit into her vision of the kingdom of god. Seemingly unafraid to attack established institutions or authorities, she built a reputation in local and surrounding areas as a woman not to be trifled with. In the process of accumulating local fans through her charisma and predictions, the media began to formulate an image of her as a celebrity god.

While the incidents leading up to her court trial reveal some aspects of her personality, it was during the trial that she demonstrated her understanding of the power of the media. As time passed she became more conscious of the media's role and its potential to pass on her message. Soon the farmer's wife from Tabuse would be transformed into the "dancing god," a role she was to play through national and international media until her death in 1967. An important factor in this transformation was her ability to work with, or against, the postwar authorities. Although she was highly critical of the Japanese authorities, she was far less critical, at least in public, of the Occupation authorities and their activities.

OFFICIAL RECOGNITION FROM THE MAGGOT WORLD

In contrast to the representations of Kitamura in her group's texts as someone who refused to compromise for the sake of the "maggot world," her attitude toward the SCAP authorities appears to have been markedly different. The records of SCAP's Religions Division show that not only was she very sensitive with regard to her public image, she also went to some lengths to ensure that Occupation officials would have a favorable impression of her and the group. It seems clear that she recognized that SCAP held vast authority within Japanese society from the beginning of the Occupation, and she made consistent efforts to develop relationships with SCAP officers.

In December 1946, Kitamura received a message from the god within her to officially register the group as a religion.[23] Following this, on 11 January 1947 Kitamura's son registered Tenshō Kōtai Jingū Kyō under the Religious Corporations Ordinance with a set of rules that were, according to *Seisho*, designed to not compromise the group with the "ways of maggots." Although *Seisho* seems to imply that registration was a legal necessity, in fact religious groups were not under any obligation to register under the ordinance.

As with the case of Jikōson and Jiu, SCAP's Religions Division initially became aware of Kitamura's activities from press reports and via information supplied by the Religious Affairs Section of the Ministry of Education. Kitamura headed to Tokyo for the second time on 14 January 1947 to hold a series of public sermons and rallies. A journalist from the *Mainichi Shinbun* attended one rally and wrote a brief article describing the rally and the group's recent visit to the Ministry of Education office for the purposes of incorporation. Religions Division staff knew of her impending visit to Tokyo and representatives attended some of the rallies held in the city. A Religions Division report dated April 1947 noted that journalists were present at some of the rallies the group held in parks and public areas of the city.[24] On those occasions she also met with Religions Division officials and explained her teachings to them. Over the next few years Kitamura kept in contact with Religions Division staff, informing them of her activities and giving them advance notice of her sermons. But she would also occasionally visit the Religious Affairs Section of the Ministry of Education. On one occasion on 24 September 1947, a group of scholars from various fields had met to discuss conducting a study on "superstitions." She was welcomed by the scholar Watanabe Baiyū, a sometime advisor to the Ministry of Education who had visited the headquarters in Tabuse the previous spring. The gathering of experts included psychiatrists, religious studies scholars, linguists, philosophers, and students from the University of Tokyo.[25]

NUMERICAL DIFFERENCES

It is not unusual for Japanese new religions to claim membership figures that may not necessarily be accurate. Number inflation may be used by the group to demonstrate its influence. On the other hand, the press can also overestimate or exaggerate figures for the sake of a good story, thus resulting in a distorted picture of the group's actual influence. Religions that incorporated under the Religious Corporations Ordinance were required to present certain details, including the address of their head-quarters and other facilities, and membership statistics. Nevertheless, Kitamura argued that keeping statistics indicated the deterioration of a true religion, and she felt they spelled trouble for the group.[26] While this is how her views are presented by the group, clearly it was keen to show that the increasing numbers reflected its effect on society. On occasions when Religions Division officials attended the sermons and rallies she held, primarily from mid-1947 until 1951, Kitamura or other representatives of the group invariably raised the issue of increasing numbers of believers.[27] These claims are not matched by the records of the Religions Division, but this is not to say that the Division's reports were always accurate.

A staff member of the Religions Division visited Tabuse on 8 April 1947 and conducted interviews with Kitamura and her son to gather information on the group. In his report he noted that the Ministry of Education's Religious Affairs Section recorded membership figures of 21,187 at that time. In 1949, a SCAP report recorded her claim that the membership had risen to 350,000 people by that year.[28] This amounts to an increase of 329,000 people in two years. In any case, this does indicate that Kitamura and her representatives wanted to present the group as an active, growing movement. And while Religions Division reports did not reflect such dramatic increases in numbers, Kitamura did attempt to provide answers for the discrepancies.

On 8 November 1948, a Religions Division staff member observed a rally in Tokyo and noted that the group "drew a large crowd of curious passersby, none of whom joined in the ecstatic dancing except for one GI. The proceedings were broadcast by NHK and numerous newsmen were in attendance." Kitamura explained to the officer who wrote the report that "the poor turnout of dancers was due to the fact that most of her Tokyo 'comrades,' who are students, were attending classes."[29]

In April 1949, Kotani Tan'un filed a Religions Division report on "the dancing religion" that was somewhat critical, and mentioned the significant difference between the claims of the group and the actual numbers that attended a well-publicized rally and sermon in Tokyo. The rally was "an utter failure. [Kitamura gave] her usual stereotyped sermon intermingled with songs."[30] Kotani spoke to Kitamura afterward and he found the excuses she offered for the poor turnout, such as bad weather and the large number of student followers who were attending classes at the time, to be rather lame and unconvincing. Although most Religions Division reports in the SCAP records are rather dry accounts of meetings with little or no commentary on the perceived outcomes, the tone of Kotani's reports suggest that he was more than a disinterested observer. In the dedication to William P. Woodard's book, he was one of two "esteemed friends and colleagues" mentioned, and he acted as Woodard's associate and advisor during and after the Occupation. His somewhat harsh stance may have been influenced by his own stance as a "devout layman of True Pure Land Buddhism."[31] Kitamura consistently attacked the beliefs of the Pure Land sect and it is possible that this was one factor influencing Kotani's perspective on her and the group.

A Religions Division advisor (who is not named in the report) attended a meeting in July 1950 that was held in Tokyo's Hibiya Hall. The report noted that there were only two hundred followers present but that Kitamura claimed in her sermon that their numbers had reached 420,000, and that she "boasted of not being a financial burden to her followers." After inviting some of her followers to dance on the stage, "apparently leaving them to the indwelling God to have their self-less selves purged during this period of ecstasy," Kitamura spoke to him about her healthy condition and the fact that her followers had given her so many gifts there was hardly any room to move in her house. "She was profuse in her thanks to the advisor for attending."[32]

Despite the occasional disparaging comments in these reports, clearly Kitamura made particular efforts in keeping SCAP officials aware of her movements. So although certain sources do provide the impression that she simply denounced everyone who did not follow her or renounce their own beliefs, Kitamura seems to have been quite deferential toward SCAP officials. On occasion, however, these methods did backfire.

RELATIONS WITH SCAP

If Kitamura did harbor negative feelings toward Religions Division staff or the Occupation administration, these do not appear anywhere in the records. She made more frequent visits to Tokyo by 1948, and on these occasions she visited the Religions Division office at the Radio Tokyo building or met with staff at a designated place where she was due to give a sermon. She often gave prior notice to the division regarding her preaching engagements through invitations, greeting cards, and notes that were sent to the Religions Division chief and staff.[33] But it is not surprising that Kitamura and the *dōshi* tried to elicit as much support as possible from SCAP because by that stage the group had become the subject of substantial press criticism.

One SCAP official who appears to have been relatively sympathetic was Walter Nichols. Born and raised in Japan, Nichols was the son of the Episcopal bishop of Kyoto.[34] Nichols was educated at Harvard University, and he became a field officer for the Religions Division who eventually developed connections with the leaders and founders of a number of new religions, including Tenshō Kōtai Jingū Kyō and Sekai Kyūsei Kyō. Nichols was a religious advisor with the Religions Division from July 1949 and then became deputy chief of the division from January 1950. After returning to Tabuse from a trip to Tokyo in November 1948, Kitamura sent him a card thanking him for his kind favors and wishing they could meet again in the near future.

Nichols later worked for the American embassy after the Occupation, and he maintained contact with Kitamura.[35] Occasionally she would praise Occupation officials as part of her efforts to improve relations with the division staff. For example, during a visit to the Religions Division in February 1949, Kitamura met William Bunce. She followed this visit up with a personal letter that told him of her intention to return to Tokyo. She added that she felt it was fortunate that the Religions Division had someone like him working there.[36] Kitamura also treated Bunce to a personal sermon at the Religions Division office on 25 November 1950.[37]

It appears that the Religions Division officials were, for the most part, courteous toward her, although Kitamura did test their patience on a number of occasions. On a visit to Tokyo in May 1947, she asserted during a public sermon that SCAP officially "approved" her movement and supported it. The Religions Division went to some lengths to ensure that no religion, Christian or otherwise, was shown any favor over others by the Occupation.[38] The Japanese police questioned Kita-mura after her sermon. She told them she had received "GHQ approval" for her movement during conversations with a SCAP official who "alleg-edly recommended the new religion to the Japanese people. [The SCAP official] denied giving any such approval but admitted that he had talked with Kitamura in his office and had attended one of her services." When a representative of the Japanese Government's Central Liaison Office (CLO) reported this claim to the Religions Division on 7 May 1947, he was instructed by a Religions Division official to advise her to cease immediately her allegations of SCAP support and approval of her movements.[39] This exchange does suggest that she was prepared, on occasion, to display certain survival skills while attempting to promote her movement.

Although Walter Nichols seems to have been relatively supportive of Kitamura, other officers of the Religions Division were less open. On 3 February 1949 she arrived in Tokyo and visited the division to report on her recent activities. She also made arrangements for Religions Divi-sion staff members to visit the group's Tokyo headquarters to attend a sermon. The responsible officer (not named in the report) wrote that at the meeting she revealed nothing about her teachings that the division did not already know. Furthermore, the report stated that her teachings were ambiguous, inconsistent, and ultimately unconvincing because she "refuses to answer most questions except by implying that the questioner is an unbeliever and so cannot understand, or by calling him 'unbeliever' or 'maggot' outright."[40] The writer also found Kitamura's stance contradictory. On the one hand she sang songs implying that Amaterasu Ōmikami had definitely left the Grand Shrine of Ise and had descended into her own body, which represented a "strong Shintoist element." On the other hand, she launched into an intense session of chanting *na-myō-hō-renge-kyō*,[41] which the writer took to be a Nichiren Buddhist element.

When Kitamura returned to Tokyo in late April 1949, she contacted the division's office on 30 April concerning "the use of certain phrases." Kitamura had been claiming that the deity in her body was telling her to use the slogans *hakkō ichiu* and *shinshū fumetsu* to spread the mes-sage of "god's kingdom." Watanabe Baiyū visited Tabuse sometime in 1948. He warned her about the problem of using the phrases because of SCAP's concern about words reminiscent of Japan's ultranationalistic and militaristic past. Although Kitamura told him that she did not use the phrases in the same manner as the wartime slogans, he advised her against using them in case her speeches might be misinterpreted.[42] She ignored this recommendation and continued to use them in her sermons.

She was, however, concerned about possible repercussions and so she raised the question about their use with the division's staff. Although she did not receive an answer immediately, on 3 May 1949 Nichols attended a rally she held in Tokyo and he told her that there was "technically no objection to her use of such terms provided it is made clear to her listeners that her usage of the slogans has no militaristic or ultranationalistic connotation. The difficulty of making her audiences understand such distinctions was pointed out, and she was advised to amplify her remarks along such lines instead of using slogans that are almost certain to have undesirable connotations in the minds of listeners." Kitamura responded by promising that "she would do her best to forestall misunderstanding by making her meaning in using the above terms quite clear."[43] On the one hand she ignored the advice of Watanabe of the Japanese Education Ministry while following the recommendations of SCAP officials.

After a few years, Tenshō Kōtai Jingū Kyō was represented in Tokyo by Kitamura and other prominent individuals. Although Watanabe Tomekichi, the former prosecutor at her trial in 1946, eventually assumed a position of responsibility in Tokyo, a young woman named Nakajima Zuiko was also active in the group. Nakajima was an official in the Kindergarten Affairs Section within the Education Bureau of the Education Ministry, and a Religions Division report of October 1949 stated that she was the head of the Tokyo branch of the group at the time.[44] Nakajima acted on Kitamura's behalf by presenting reports on the group's movements to the Religions Division. In July 1950 Nakajima went to the Religions Division and provided information about meetings and forthcoming events, including Kitamura's recent pronouncements. She claimed that around six thousand people, including followers from Tokyo, Aomori, and Kagoshima turned up to a meeting in Hiroshima in April 1949.

The Religions Division report noted that there were no remarkable changes to Kitamura's sermons although Nakajima emphasized to the division's officers that no money was collected either from the faithful or the curious. Kitamura refused to initiate membership fees for the group or insist on "donations."[45]

In an undated Religions Division report Walter Nichols writes, "An interesting feature of this religion is that no one is obliged to assist fellow human beings financially since Tenshō Kōtai Jingo [*sic*], the

Absolute God of the Universe, will provide all necessities in accordance with the individual merits or demerits of people. The foundress absolutely refuses to accept financial assistance from anyone."[46] Although Jiu urged people to make offerings to Jikōson and was roundly criticized in the press for this, Kitamura's policy gained her grudging recognition from journalists like Ōya Sōichi.

Nakajima also reported to SCAP on Kitamura's travels, which included a stopover at Zushi. Some Religions Division officials appear to have become somewhat cynical regarding the claims and teachings. The report of this exchange, which cannot have come directly from Nakajima herself, is somewhat ironic: "The founder harangued the pleasure-mad crowds on the beaches who were unaware that they were teetering deliriously on the edge of the end of the world."

The report noted that Nakajima was also proud to pronounce that the public opprobrium that had been directed at Tenshō Kōtai Jingū Kyō was gradually fading away. As evidence for this claim, Nakajima told the advisor of "the actions of a wizened eighty-year-old Japanese woman at the Zushi rally who, tremendously moved by the exhortations of Mrs. Kitamura, quietly crept up to the platform upon which the evangelist was bellowing and perspiring, and fanned the good lady from behind until she subsided."[47]

A PUBLIC NUISANCE

Despite Kitamura's attempts to portray her movement in a positive light to Religions Division officials, she did not receive favorable treatment when certain problems arose. According to a *Yomiuri Shinbun* article published 1 October 1951,[48] the police based at Tokyo's Meijiro ward received complaints from people living nearby Tenshō Kōtai Jingū Kyō's Tokyo branch regarding a public disturbance. When Kitamura visited the branch on September 22, a loud speaker was set up and the broadcasts apparently continued from morning until night. Kitamura was asked to present herself at the police station on September 28, where she was told to not use the loudspeaker or to turn down the noise. Although the speaker was moved from the second floor to the first floor, the noise was still a problem, even to police officers living in a station dormitory just behind the branch office.

The police are portrayed in the newspaper as being in a somewhat helpless position because a new religious group was acting in an anti-social manner. This reflects the *Mainichi Shinbun*'s characterization of the constraints the police faced when confronting Jiu's "questionable eccentricities" in May 1946, as mentioned in the previous chapter. In the Religions Division translation of the *Yomiuri* article, a police officer from Meijirō station is quoted as saying "The Light Offences Law can be applied. However, we are thinking of making the application later *in view of the certain accompanying circumstances*" (emphasis in the original). It is quite likely that the police were somewhat concerned with how SCAP and the Religions Division might react if there was a suggestion of police interference toward a religious group.

The Religions Division's reaction to this was clear. William Woodard, who was then acting as head of the Religions Research Unit, wrote a recommendation for the division chief on the translated document under the underlined words: "Note: If this means SCAP then I think we ought to encourage them to go ahead on the prosecution as a public nuisance."[49] Although the folder does not contain any further information about this incident, the documents reveal Religions Division officials did not object to the Japanese authorities using the normal legal powers that were available to them to warn the group and prosecute them if necessary.

The Religions Division was still concerned that the police did not revert to prewar tactics, and the police were keen to be seen as operating within the limits of their authority, and reaffirm the extent to which they could act in the case of religious groups that were causing trouble for the public. This is significant because the police and other Japanese authorities like the Special Investigations Branch of the Attorney General's Office had been accused by a number of new religions of violating their rights and freedoms. The Religions Division was concerned that a return to the prewar situation of religious control was possible after the Occupation ended. Therefore, it began its own investigations into these claims. Woodard holds that the investigations did not bear any fruit.[50]

However, by October 1951, which was six months after the introduction of the Religious Corporations Law, religious groups had been granted a significant amount of organizational autonomy and their freedoms guaranteed in the constitution remained in place. Furthermore, with the introduction of legal changes, direct involvement in religious affairs, especially surveillance, became a difficult subject for the police and government officials to broach. This situation was to change radically after the extent of Aum Shinrikyō's crimes became apparent in 1995.

BATTLING ESTABLISHED RELIGIONS

While the Religions Division records reveal certain aspects of Kitamura's relationship with SCAP officials and the Japanese authorities, they also show her continuing battles with representatives from established religions. SCAP records show that 1949 was a particularly busy year for Kitamura and her group in this regard. Although individual priests and temples in various areas had locked horns with Kitamura, there had been no coordinated effort by established religious groups to deal with her until August 1949.[51] An editorial in the *Tokuyama Kōron* on 6 August 1949 stated that the Tokuyama Buddhist Association (Tokuyama Bukkyō Rengōkai), an organization comprised of representatives from the Nichiren and Pure Land sects in Yamaguchi prefecture, had declared that Tenshō Kōtai Jingū Kyō was a heretical religion with no doctrinal basis in Buddhism. Furthermore, the association threatened that any of its members who made contact with the "dancing religion" would be expelled. Although the editorial argued for the established religions in the area, this is not to say that all views expressed in the paper were necessarily in complete agreement with the association's position. On 10 September 1949 the *Tokuyama Kōron* published an article reporting on an interview with a follower. The attitude of the reporter was quite positive toward the believer, encouraging him and the group to dance vigorously in order to bring about peace as soon as possible.

Kitamura often attended, and occasionally disrupted, proceedings at various gatherings and conferences that were designed for "serious" discussions on religion by scholars and priests from various sects. During the immediate postwar period, there were regular conferences held among religious and social leaders discussing issues such as the war and collective responsibility. On such occasions the participants would often pass resolutions offering collective apologies and repentance (*zange*) for their inability to stop Japan's path to war and speak out against the government's militaristic agenda.[52]

During Kitamura's fourth trip to Tokyo, she attended an international roundtable conference on religion held at the Buddhist Tsukiji Honganji temple on 6 November 1948. The participants included representatives of established religious groups and religious studies scholars. Under the lights of news cameras, Kitamura rose up and delivered a sermon in song (*kamiuta*) that apparently shocked the chairman and other participants. Her sermon, not surprisingly, included a sharp message that admonished the participants to awaken to "god's kingdom" or else live forever in the beggar's world.[53]

Seisho reports of this event in somewhat triumphant terms, although it is probably safe to assume that not all participants were pleased with her performance. During her fifth trip to Tokyo, which began on 2 February 1949, she was involved in a whirlwind of similar events. She attended a roundtable conference sponsored by the literary magazine *Sekai Hyōron*, which was preparing a story about her that was eventually published in May 1949. The editors of the magazine invited her to attend and be questioned by other participants, including religious studies scholars, physicists, psychiatrists, and psychologists.

Kotani Tan'un, who prepared a summary of the entire trip for the Religions Division, wrote that during the proceedings Kitamura launched into a singing sermon that drew the ire of the other participants. A number of them "attempted to criticize her religious movement and expose her deity as a bogus one."[54] On 4 February she participated in a similar roundtable conference sponsored by an association in Ginza that was attended by "various intellectuals and journalists." She reported to Kotani that this conference also yielded victorious results for her group. The next day she attended "a study meeting on psychic science at Tokyo University sponsored by students." Although she claimed that she had defeated all the other religionists decisively in the *Sekai Hyōron* debate, Kotani noted that, "Mrs. Kitamura apparently does not gain many converts by engaging in such debates, but she gets invaluable publicity."[55] A few days after the *Sekai Hyōron* debate, he reported that Kitamura created a "mild sensation" by disturbing the proceedings of another religious conference, one which was focused on the need for religionists to offer repentance and collective apologies.[56] She "rose in the midst of the learned discussion and proceeded to chant a sermon at the assembled scholars and priests. Her action threw the assembly into an uproar, and it was some ten minutes or so before she could be persuaded to stop, after which she was escorted to a small private room where she continued her hypnotic chanting and dancing in comparative seclusion."[57]

She followed this up with a visit to SCAP's Religions Division three days later to protest against the way she and her followers had been ejected unceremoniously from the meeting room. She stated that action was more important than empty theorizing, and claimed that the other participants had made lofty resolutions that they could not possibly carry out. She argued unselfconsciously that most of them were only interested in gaining publicity for their own sects. Furthermore, they were charlatans posing as religious leaders because they had to rely on carefully prepared speeches whereas she, "with only 6 years of formal education but inspired by true religion, could have carried on for 5 hours extemporaneously in magnificent style." The ever-critical Kotani noted dryly that he had no doubts about her capacity "to carry on and on for hours."[58]

During her sixth trip to Tokyo, she attended a symposium on "religious problems" on 18 April 1949 that included researchers on religion. However, this meeting was again taken over by Kitamura.[59] The prime minister's official residence was also the site of another similar fracas in October 1949. The *Naigai Taimuzu* reported a disturbance at a conference scheduled to discuss "ways and means to contribute to a spiritual uplift of the Japanese for the rebuilding of the country through the power of religion." Forty-six representatives of various denominations of religion, including Shinto, Buddhism, and Christianity attended the conference. However, proceedings were interrupted when Kitamura and some of her followers suddenly appeared. They were angry that they had not been invited and demanded to be allowed in. "Following an argument, the enthusiasm of the followers of the dancing cult won and they were allowed to sit as spectators. The promoters of the conference, however, were apprehensive all the time lest the members of the 'dancing religion' should begin dancing in the middle of serious discussions."[60] Apart from the distinction made in the newspaper between the "serious discussions" in juxtaposition to the implied frivolous behavior of the "dancing religion," the report does reveal that other groups saw Kitamura as a force to be reckoned with at the time.

THE "DANCING GOD" BECOMES A CELEBRITY

The national publicity that surrounded Tenshō Kōtai Jingū Kyō from early 1947 was arguably the most intense of all the new religions of the immediate postwar period. The initial coverage tried to draw connections to Jikōson but eventually Kitamura's own identity developed through the media representations. From 1948 to 1950, the phrases "dancing religion" and "dancing god" were widely used in the press, and according to a Religions Division report, during 1948 Tenshō Kōtai Jingū Kyō received the most publicity of all the new religions that had been reported on since the end of the war.[61]

In some ways, Kitamura's approach to handling the press could be considered successful compared to Jikōson's. As opposed to Jikōson's inaccessibility, Kitamura was open and expressed her teachings in clear, forthright terms. Jiu wavered from insularity to using very bold and rash moves to promote their cause. While the group attempted to use Futabayama's fame to attract attention to its cause, Kitamura did not co-opt celebrities. Rather, she built up relationships with Religions Division officials. While it is unlikely these relationships influenced the way the press reported on the group, her efforts to ensure that the division officials knew her movements played a role in the group's progress.

Kitamura and the *dōshi* received scant attention from the press during most of 1946. The *Bōchō Shinbun* published a series of articles on the rice quota trial in early 1946, but it was not until early 1947 when reports of Kitamura appeared in the national newspapers that her media presence began to develop. After the Kanazawa incident involving Jiu, Jikōson, and Futabayama in January 1947, media interest in postwar religion and society was at a peak. Articles, editorials, and opinion pieces relating to the incident and new religions appeared in national and local newspapers, and less popular scientific and religious publications. Kitamura was labeled, variously, as "the second Jikōson" (*daini no Jikōson*), "the new Jikōson" (*shin Jikōson*), and "the northern Kyushu version of Jikōson" (*Jikōson Kita Kyūshū ban*).[62] Certainly it appeared that Jikōson and Kitamura shared a number of traits. From the media's perspective, this was a relatively easy story to frame. Both women lead new religious groups that appeared at around the same time, and they advocated radical transformation and revolution in society through their particular spiritual paths. But the comparisons were generally superficial and the media did not go into any details of the doctrines or histories of the groups.

Kitamura eventually became recognized as a celebrity god in her own right in media reports without direct references to Jikōson. Her second visit to Tokyo in January 1947 and rallies conducted by *dōshi* were briefly mentioned in the *Mainichi Shinbun*. On 7 July, six staff members from the Hiroshima central branch of the national broadcaster NHK visited the headquarters in Tabuse to make recordings of the proceedings. On 22 July, the anniversary of Kitamura's first sermon, her speech was broadcast "to the ears of the nation."[63]

While it is difficult to quantify the impact of this broadcast on the public, it certainly had an effect on her standing with the press because it announced to the media community that there was a story about this woman to be told. When she visited Tokyo for the third time on 22 September 1947, her arrival at Tokyo station was covered by journalists from the *Asahi Shinbun*. *Seisho* reports that a press pack, including a news film crew, was waiting at the station. She launched into a sermon after a microphone was thrust in her face. The train then went to Meijirō station where a news truck with a camera mounted on top was waiting. The film crew asked her to perform the "dance of ecstasy" and she obliged them.[64] The next day, Kitamura and some *dōshi* gathered outside Shibuya train station for a sermon and they were filmed by the Shin Sekai Nyūzu (New World News) company. In March 1948 this company produced a news film that was shown to cinema audiences nationally. The screening of the film *Odoru shūkyō* ("The dancing religion") at numerous cinemas around the country triggered off more publicity and announced the name of the group given by the press.[65] Thus, widespread national reporting of "the dancing religion" began in earnest, and "the dancing god" and "the dancing religion" assumed significant media value.

WARNINGS AND AWAKENINGS

According to Fujii Takeshi, while most of the print media reporting about Kitamura and Tenshō Kōtai Jingū Kyō was critical, the press reports can be divided into two general categories.[66] The first category includes articles that blatantly mocked Kitamura and the *dōshi*. Reporters made no attempt to consider her teachings, but focused on disparaging the group's appearance and mannerisms. Kitamura made statements such as "Tokyo is a nest for maggot beggars," which was perfect headline material. A review of the news film shown in cinemas appeared in the *Tōkyō Shinbun* on 30 April 1948. None too complimentary, the review described Kitamura as being crafty and cunning with "the face of a fox," and her followers as appearing completely besotted with her as they madly danced to her tune. An article published on 31 January 1948 in the *Mainichi Shinbun* published a photograph of Kitamura sitting cross-legged, and quoting her somewhat masculine speech. Clearly, the comparisons between Kitamura and Jikōson were still dominant at that stage, with Kitamura herself declaring in the same article that Jikōson was also "like a fox." Eventually, the stories comparing Jikōson with Kitamura faded as she achieved fame and notoriety as the "dancing god."

The second category of media reports carried stark warnings of the possible negative effects of the faith and practices of the group on ordinary, unsuspecting people. These reports were damaging because rather than simply portraying the founder and the group's members as mentally unstable, they hinted at deep-seated social problems that could arise if too many people were attracted to the founder. Some articles demanded that the (Japanese) authorities clamp down on the activities of the "dancing religion."

On 29 September 1948 a *Yomiuri Shinbun* writer warned readers in the following manner: "The fact that some people dance fanatically in the streets in broad daylight in defiance of scientific rationality is an absolute disgrace to the nation's politicians, and I urge them to take heed of this phenomenon." *Tōkyō Minpō* published a similar report the previous day that urged the nation's lawmakers to recognize their role in realizing "a society in which people can take pleasure in working rather than dancing in this manner."[67] Criticisms and derisive comments appeared in the first reports of this kind about the group, but when it was revealed that educated people with some degree of social standing were participating in the singing and dancing, the press warnings took on a more ominous tone. Although initial reports announcing the prosecutor Watanabe's decision to become a *dōshi*, such as a *Nishi Nippon Shinbun* article of 2 February 1947, were not particularly critical, warnings of the dangers of intellectuals being involved in the group became more pronounced later. The writer of an article in the English-language *Mainichi* on 27 October 1949 hoped the group would quickly disappear and be forgotten, and wrote of concerns over the participation of intelligentsia. Tenshō Kōtai Jingū Kyō "came into being as an outstanding by-product of the postbellum spiritual instability and moral degeneration…. No new religion has been subjected to more ridicule and made more a laughing stock than this 'dancing religion' since its foundation. Yet, the continued popularity of this all-too-nonsensical religion [bothers some] psychologists." These kinds of stories mirrored those warning of social unease in the wake of the Kanazawa incident involving Jiu.

A significant difference between Jiu and Tenshō Kōtai Jingū Kyō was that Jiu leaders had been arrested. Furthermore, Futabayama's celebrity proved to be a significant problem for Jiu, as did the accusations of fraud. Tenshō Kōtai Jingū Kyō was not accused of any crimes, and apart from Kitamura's court trial early in her postwar career there were no significant legal clashes. Nevertheless, the group was still viewed as one that promoted irrational ideas that were inconsistent with Japan's modern democracy. Thus, the stories of Jiu and Tenshō Kōtai Jingū Kyō shared a consistent theme: postwar new religions required some kind of official intervention by the authorities, and qualified experts agreed that these groups had the potential to cause danger to society. This question of religious freedom versus public safety and the role of the authorities is one that continues to affect post-Aum-era Japanese society.

But not all media reports about the "dancing religion" were entirely negative or completely dismissive of Kitamura's ideas. The attitudes of some journalists toward the group became more positive after they interviewed Kitamura and her supporters. The articles they published added a new dimension to the representations of Kitamura within the media. Rather than simply criticizing her, they presented different perspectives on her beliefs and her followers. Journalists from the Tokushima-based *Bōchō Shinbun*, the newspaper that first published articles about Kitamura, visited the headquarters on 11 August and asked for permission to produce a small booklet that would introduce the teachings of the group to the public. As a result, a special thirty-page booklet called "Odoru kamisama" was published in October 1947. The booklet contains extensive coverage of the group based on field trips to Tabuse. In addition to reprinting some of the more derogatory articles from other newspapers such as the *Tōkyō Shinbun*, it includes interviews with Kitamura as well as parts of her sermons and a discussion with believers, including some of their experiences. The publication recognized the influence of the group, at least in terms of the amount of media coverage it was received. The booklet noted that the group had survived through the initial difficult years of development. Clearly, the group was pleased with the result, claiming that "many people were saved" through this publication.[68] On 22 January 1949, the *Bōchō Shinbun* published an article that also contained the field trip notes of a reporter who showed some sympathy for Kitamura. Using a tone that appears conciliatory compared to that of other journalists, he wrote that she "is probably not a bogus teacher but merely a fanatic. Even reporters feel comfortable sitting beside her."[69]

The magazine *Sekai Hyōron* published a long interview with Kitamura that sought to understand the religious significance and details of the group.[70] Although these articles did not report any particular incident or occurrence, the style of reporting was relatively positive. In addition, there was a greater degree of accuracy to the reportage because they included interviews with Kitamura and the believers themselves. As the reports touched on the actual contents of the faith itself, the descriptions are detailed to a certain extent. Rather than emphasizing one particular unusual aspect of the practice, the reports tended to attempt to clarify the reasons behind the movement from a religious perspective.

Some of the articles, while not necessarily condoning the dancing and sermons Kitamura gave, commended her for the stance she took with regard to money, donations, and professional clerics. One article in the *Yūkan Kyōto* on 20 December 1949 (subsequently republished in the religious publication *Chūgai Nippō* on 1 January 1950) stated that although the religion itself was primitive, established religions should take note of its example of advocating no idols, no offerings, and no professional priests as role models for followers. In other words, because these detailed and descriptive articles presented Kitamura and her teachings in a specific manner, they contributed to her "news persona" as not simply a female founder of a brash new religion, but the "dancing god" whose mannerisms, attitudes, and beliefs set her apart from others.

Nevertheless, these positive appraisals generally appeared in smaller or local publications, such as the *Bōchō Shinbun*, which had cultivated relatively close connections to the group. The articles that sought to delve deeper into the group and not simply criticize the founder or her followers were rare. The texts did little to challenge the general tone of print media reports that Tenshō Kōtai Jingū Kyō was a danger to society because of the purportedly negative psychological effects the faith could have on believers.

"GOD'S STRATEGY"

Kitamura declared the media to be part of "god's strategy" in that she felt they could become part of the promotion process for the establishment of "god's kingdom." The hagiographical descriptions in *Seisho* present one view of Kitamura's attitude toward journalists during the rice quota trial. In demanding that the press print her picture, this source gives the impression that she was prepared to be reported in any way so long as the message of her teaching spread. For the most part she was open to investigation, encouraged journalists to report on her activities, and considered bad publicity to be better than no publicity at all. *Seisho* describes her meeting with journalists from the western regional headquarters of the *Mainichi Shinbun* in Tabuse on 26 January 1948. She told them that rather than seeking their praise, she did not mind if

Kitamura being interviewed by a journalist, 1949. She was remarkably adept at self-promotion, and rarely missed an opportunity to appear in the press.

they portrayed her in a bad light. She stated that any media reporting was promotion in any case, and that as journalists should report things correctly, they should feel free to look around and report things as they saw them.[71] She also actively encouraged journalists to visit the group's headquarters in Tabuse, such as when the Yamaguchi bureau chief of *Jiji Tsūshin* appeared on 29 January 1948. She agreed to have them accompany her on trips away from Tabuse, like the trip in early April that year in which newsmen from the western regional headquarters of the *Asahi Shinbun* accompanied Kitamura to Kita Kyushu.[72]

Nevertheless, her relationships with members of the press were complex and her stance with respect to the media was, not surprisingly, more nuanced than these sources suggest. Religions Division records also show that she was sensitive to the potential impact of negative media reports, particularly because they may have had an effect on how the division staff perceived her. When visiting the Religions Division on 5 November 1948, a few months after the news film was shown in cinemas, she told officials the reason why she had come was because she feared that the rising number of "derogatory newspaper articles would lead the Occupation authorities to believe that Tenshō Kōtai Jingū Kyō is one of the less desirable new religions flourishing in Japan."[73] She then explained her teachings to the officers present in order to clear up any misunderstandings.

She maintained regular contact with Religions Division officials, sometimes pointing out where press reports were adversely affecting her group's progress. Thus her numerous visits to and communications with the Religions Division between the years 1947 to 1951 can be considered to be part of her strategy to combat the potential negative effects of the media criticism. Nevertheless, other than to occasionally attempting to encourage balanced reporting, Religions Division officials did not try to influence the negative reporting of Tenshō Kōtai Jingū Kyō and new religions in general. But in considering the application of "god's strategy" in more detail, it is worth examining Kitamura's dealings with two media figures in particular, the journalist and critic Ōya Sōichi, and Tokugawa Musei, a radio personality who was involved in a variety of media in the postwar period.

THE VETERAN JOURNALIST AND THE DANCING GOD

Ōya Sōichi's prewar journalism work was familiar to many readers in the postwar period, and these were significant factors, it has been claimed, in the resurrection of his career.[74] Ōya earned the respect of his colleagues and the public alike for his often compromising stance on postwar social issues, including those concerning new religions. Many journalists believed that he deserved his reputation for impartiality and non-adherence to any particular ideology.[75] He wrote a famous article for *Chūō Kōron* in 1955 entitled "Mushisōjin sengen" ("Declaration of a non-ideologue"). It was directed at postwar intellectuals who he believed had traded their beliefs for the sake of expediency in the postwar period.

According to John Dower, "the sudden postsurrender appearance of intellectuals, politicians, and a host of other public figures spouting paeans to democracy and demilitarization smacked of hypocrisy and opportunism."[76] Many writers and intellectuals who were imprisoned in the prewar period after being tried under the 1925 Peace Preservation Law recanted their former beliefs, "contradicted their own conscience" at that time, and then claimed to promote peace in the postwar years.[77] Ōya criticized this tendency in 1957, writing that "it is highly problematic that scholars and intellectuals who threw their wholehearted support into the concept of the Greater East Asia Co-Prosperity Sphere[78] and cooperated in the so-called 'holy war' have, at some point during the postwar period, joined the Communist Party and become leaders of the 'peace movement'."[79] And he went further in another passage written in 1959, criticizing the active intellectuals of the day and accusing them of wartime complicity with the military regime.[80] Ōya's suggestion that he was "non-ideological" (and therefore balanced) harks back to the purported Meiji-period principles of journalism—"neutrality and fairness" and "without prejudice or bias."

Nevertheless, in the postwar period Ōya wrote little on his wartime career. Ōya had been arrested in 1933, and after that time some of his writings favored state policies such as the military advance into China. From 1937 he worked for the army and for the next six years he spent time on the Chinese mainland, Taiwan, and Java, among other areas. According to Matsuura, Ōya viewed the Japanese political situation as if he were "observing the weather" while carefully avoiding imprisonment.[81] He wrote about Japan's military advance into the Chinese mainland, and Matsuura argues that passages like "the advance into the continent has been a long-held dream of the Japanese race.... The flag of the Rising Sun has crossed the Great Wall and traversed the Yellow River.... We are conquering China,"[82] which was published in the first edition of the magazine *Tairiku* in June 1938, were used by his postwar critics as evidence of Ōya's hypocrisy. During the early 1940s Ōya traveled to a number of countries working as a war journalist and returned to Japan around the autumn of 1943. He gave up writing for a few years and worked quietly as a farmer.

By the time he began contributing articles to various newspapers and magazines in 1948, Tenshō Kōtai Jingū Kyō had developed a media persona as "the dancing religion" and Kitamura as "the dancing god." Among Japanese journalists, Ōya was a veteran in religion reporting who had accumulated a substantial portfolio. By the beginning of 1949, the topic of new religions appeared often in the press. Ōya's article on Tenshō Kōtai Jingū Kyō in the *Tōkyō Nichi Nichi Shinbun* on 9 January 1949, which was his contribution to a series of articles on the sudden rise of new religions, was less a report on the group's recent activities than a general critique of society. He displayed his ironic sense of humor by linking the "dancing religion" to the postwar trend of social dancing clubs that were proliferating in the capital, describing the group as a dance club that did not require participants to buy tickets. He conceded that Kitamura and her group did not appear to be seeking to profit financially from its activities. Groups like this, he claimed, comprised of either a fraudulent leader or a sinister group of string-pullers who stole the possessions of the people they swindled. On a more serious note, Ōya argued that it was an "irony of modern culture" that "a barbarous peasant woman" led the group. Although the "dancing religion" did not have "the foulness of Kannonkyō and PL Kyōdan,"[83] his description of Kitamura was harsh, stating that she was "a filthy farmer" who was "like a cow." Although he stated that the "dancing religion" could claim to be different from other groups because it did not require material goods from followers, Ōya left his readers with a warning about not being complacent about the group. After all, he reasoned, it was quite ridiculous that rational people in the current democratic age were following this woman.

Ōya gradually built up a portfolio of critical reports on new religions throughout 1949, and through these he promoted the idea of "models" for new religions. He claimed that they fit into certain patterns, had irrational leaders with fanatical followers, broke social conventions, and caused trouble for society. He wrote a series of articles on "newly arisen religions" including Jiu, Kannonkyō, PL Kyōdan, and Tenshō Kōtai Jingū Kyō for the *Shūkan Asahi* magazine. In an article for the March 1949 issue focusing on "postwar versions of newly arisen religions" ("Shinkō shūkyō sengo ban"), Ōya labeled Tenshō Kōtai Jingū Kyō a "newly arisen Potsdam religion," referring to the treaty signed at Potsdam in July 1945 where the seeds of religious freedom for Japan were sown. In noting that the group did not have professional preachers or leaders, and did not require membership fees, he nevertheless warned that the public had no guarantee that the group would not make the change from being an "amateur religion" into a professional one, just as an amateur sportsman might turn professional. He argued that even if the founder was opposed to such a move, social problems may occur if her supporters started to demand money, causing it to "turn professional." Ōya thus used one noted aspect of the group, Kitamura's steadfast refusal to accept membership fees, to suggest that one day it might do what other "newly arisen religions" were doing—prise money from gullible, ignorant people.

Ōya then turned his criticism onto Kitamura's followers by claiming that the driving forces behind "newly arisen religions such as these are unemployed journalists, failed writers, and mad teachers." Kitamura was described as an ignorant woman possessed by some spirit who babbled nonsense, stole phrases from established religions and claimed them as her own, and tried to attract former military officers, bureaucrats, artists, and others who had some social standing.

> As I have written before, these types of religions are quite clearly out to swindle people. In times of social unrest, they play on ignorance and emotional instability, and engage in the most insidious type of exploitation by trying to remove the money from people's wallets. Rather than actually helping people, intellectuals who are mobilized to contribute to these swindles are criminals together with the founders, and are very often the main instigators.

Ōya ended his critique with a prediction that despite a number of young people and intellectuals joining the group, Tenshō Kōtai Jingū Kyō and other "newly arisen religions" would be judged as mere aberrations and would disappear in time.[84]

In November 1949 he wrote another article for the *Tōkyō Nichi Nichi Shinbun* about Tenshō Kōtai Jingū Kyō in which he called Kitamura the "newest face" in the world of living gods (*ikigami sama no sekai*). "When I look at the 'dancing god,'" he wrote, "I am reminded of the recently deceased Deguchi Onisaburō from Ōmoto." He asserted that a common link between Japanese newly- arisen religions was that they "used rather lame jokes and sophistry." He compared Deguchi's use of idiosyncratic terms combined with common expressions with Kitamura's, arguing that it was apparent that founders of new religions used commonly understood terms in order to draw in uneducated followers. As such, he claimed, it was surprising whenever people of substantial education joined new religions. As if to drive his point home to his readers that they needed to exercise extreme caution with "newly arisen religions," Ōya claimed that Hitler used similar methods to capture people's hearts.

Ōya's writings on the group appeared in a number of different newspapers, including the *Asahi Shinbun*, the *Mainichi Shinbun*, and the *Yomiuri Shinbun*, as well as a variety of magazines. Criticisms from a writer of his stature and experience presented a significant problem for the new religions he targeted. Despite Kitamura's assertions that media attention was part of "god's strategy," his acerbic criticisms definitely had an effect on Kitamura and the group.

Kitamura refused to let these criticisms go unchallenged. She began speaking out against him in her sermons. Spurred by her example, some *dōshi* sent Ōya letters protesting his reports. Furthermore, two new converts who were students from the economics department of the University of Tokyo went around to his house to confront him. They attempted to arrange a meeting between Ōya and Kitamura. Writing about these experiences in the April 1949 edition of the magazine *Seinen Bunka*, Ōya compared their actions with those of Hito no Michi adherents in the mid-1930s. After he published a critical report of Hito no Michi before it was suppressed by the religions police, some members approached him and demanded that he take a less harsh stance, saying that they were prepared to offer their lives for their faith in the religion. Ōya attributed this kind of action to military fascism that had permeated the minds of young Japanese in particular.[85] Ōya was, however, impressed by their zeal and enthusiasm, if not their beliefs.

MEETINGS BETWEEN GODS

Kitamura never forgot Ōya's attacks on her, and nearly eleven years after the Occupation began they actually met. Ōya was used to meeting his subjects: he had faced Ōmoto's Onisaburō Deguchi and other leaders of new religions in the past. In Tenshō Kōtai Jingū Kyō's version of this story, it was another famous media figure, Tokugawa Musei (1894–1971), who facilitated the meeting between Ōya and Kitamura. According to this source Tokugawa told Ōya that while he had personally met many living gods during his long career, Kitamura was "the real deal."[86]

Tokugawa Musei was a famous voice-over star and actor of the silent screen during the late-Taishō and early-Shōwa periods, and was one of the top vocal artists in Japan from 1920 to 1960. He was also a prolific writer who published close to one hundred books. In the 1950s he became a radio talk show host and interviewed a wide range of people. Tokugawa had an ongoing interest in spiritualism and religion, and he met with Jikōson in early 1956. Although the details of how he came to meet Kitamura are unclear, his interview with her was published in the *Shūkan Asahi* magazine on 15 February 1956.[87] Furthermore, Tokugawa had arranged a rather remarkable meeting between Kitamura and Jikōson, which occurred in Yokohama on 28 February 1957. Naturally Kitamura knew of Jikōson and even discussed her in response to a question from a *dōshi* in Tokyo in the early years of the group. She declared that Jikōson was merely a toy of an "evil god."[88] The meeting in Yokohama was apparently not a pleasant occasion. Katsuki Tokujirō of Jiu recalled that Kitamura was extremely loud and crass, whereas Kitamura's followers recall that she scolded Jikōson and yelled at her: "You call yourself a living god? You're pathetic. Pull yourself together."[89] There are no other records of them meeting after this.

Tokugawa was relatively sympathetic toward Kitamura, who had met his daughter in Los Angeles. During their interview Tokugawa praised Kitamura's stance over not requiring that people pay money to participate.[90] Their dialogue covered a number of subjects relating to her vision of the "kingdom of god," "beggar religionists," and her travels overseas. In their conversation, she also referred to her journalistic nemesis, Ōya Sōichi, as "a maggot beggar" who wrote terrible things about her.[91] The published dialogue with Tokugawa appears quite lighthearted, and while he asked her if she could point out his own faults, she was quite reserved in her judgments that were printed.[92]

Although Ōya had attended rallies in the past and listened to Kitamura's sermons at the group's Tokyo branch in Meijiro, he had never published a full interview with her. She had called him a "maggot beggar" to his face on at least one occasion; after that experience, Ōkuma Hideo writes, Ōya longed for the opportunity to meet with her.[93] His chance came when the magazine *Bungei Shunjū* commissioned him to write a series of articles based on his travels within Japan (Tokugawa's name is not mentioned in this account). He arranged to meet her in Tabuse and travelled there with a photographer.

When the two met on 18 May 1956 in Tabuse, Kitamura exclaimed that Ōya probably had the "worst mouth in Japan" and that she would definitely defeat him in this "contest."[94] Ōya mentioned that Tokugawa had given her a positive assessment, but if he thought this might mollify her, he was mistaken. She criticized him for not opening his heart to her teachings,[95] and launched into a sermon complete with songs. Ōkuma writes that she challenged Ōya to ask her anything, demanding that if he "lost" the battle he must become a follower. He ventured forth cautiously, asking "If a god did reside in your stomach, when you went to America, surely you would have been able to communicate in English?" Instantly Kitamura struck back: "But I did speak English. When I went shopping, I spoke English and didn't need any help. There's your proof."[96]

This exchange, which is not recorded in Tenshō Kōtai Jingū Kyō's account, indicated to Ōya that his inquiries would not take him much further and that he would not be able to "win" the contest.[97] Obviously Tenshō Kōtai Jingū Kyō's account hands Kitamura a clear "victory." She criticized Ōya for misinterpreting the sermons he had heard in the past and admonished him for letting his ego influence his judgment.

Kitamura Sayo and Ōya Sōichi, photographed during
Ōya's visit to Tabuse in May 1956.

She sealed her "victory" with one of her famous word plays: "So, your
name is Ōya Sōichi—what a joke! If you think you've lost this debate,
and I declare that you have, from now on you should be known as Koya
Soichi [小屋粗一, "rough little shack"]."[98]

Bungei Shunjū eventually published Ōya's account of the meeting in
a book. Ōkuma claims that Kitamura flew into a rage after reading the
article and threatened to sue Ōya. He holds that her rage subsided and
nothing came of the incident after Ōya wrote her a letter stating that
he had never heard of a living god who had sued an ordinary human
being.[99] The meetings between the celebrity Tokugawa, Ōya, and the
living gods did not develop any further. Ōya continued to write about
new religions, however, eventually turning his attention to the rapidly
growing Sōka Gakkai. More of Ōya's legacy in terms of the reporting of
new religions in the postwar period is discussed in the next chapter.

NEWS VALUE GRADUALLY FADES

The intense media attention on Kitamura and Tenshō Kōtai Jingū Kyō
began to fade slightly by the early 1950s. The group itself solidified its
own base in Japan and began to expand overseas. When Kitamura made
trips to Hawai'i in 1952 and 1954, the local press covered the story, and
these reports filtered through to Japan. She also travelled to other parts
of the United States including Boston, New York, and Los Angeles,

and presented lectures and seminars at prestigious universities including Harvard and Columbia. The purpose of her trips was to encourage followers who lived there and build up her overseas following.

A number of articles had appeared in different media organs that included detailed interviews with Kitamura, personal testimonies of people who claimed to have been cured of illness, and explanations of the doctrines. Such articles demystified the group to a certain extent, thus contributing to a weakening of the shock value that had characterized earlier reports.[100] Another factor to consider was the reporting of other new religions in Japan, including Kōdō Chikyō, Sekai Kyūsei Kyō, Reiyūkai, and Risshō Kōseikai. These groups were associated with various scandals in the late 1940s and 1950s, as was the Sōka Gakkai, particularly from the mid-1950s.

Kitamura and Tenshō Kōtai Jingū Kyō had become well-known as a result of her own flair for self-promotion and enthusiasm for the cause. This ability, however, may have contributed to a general loss of media interest in the group. SCAP reports noted that Kitamura used events sponsored by media companies to gain publicity. It is possible that her reputation for self-promotion spread around media circles, and journalists had become somewhat jaded. While the story of Kitamura bursting into various meetings and disrupting proceedings may have been initially attractive to the press, after a few occasions these actions may have been seen as publicity stunts. Kitamura and the group were never associated with the kinds of scandal involving money or drugs, such as those that plagued Sekai Kyūsei Kyō and Reiyūkai at the time. Furthermore, the group did not experience the rapid growth it claimed. Overseas trips and meetings with major figures aside, had the group expanded significantly in Japan, journalists may have been more inclined to pursue the story.

The next wave of major publicity for the group came when Kitamura passed away in 1967. Her seventeen-year-old granddaughter, Kiyokazu (1950–2006), who was known to followers as Himegamisama, took over as the leader. Although press attention was not as intense as when the group first appeared, the "dancing religion" briefly made news again, with attention focused on the succession of Kitamura's granddaughter. Some weekly magazines ran stories, but after a brief flurry of attention, the news value of this story quickly faded.

In the mid-1970s there was a brief resurgence of media interest. In 1975, the magazine *Ōru Yomimono* ran an article about Kitamura Sayo in its series chronicling postwar personalities. This contained detailed descriptions of the group, its practices, and, of course, the founder. In the same year, the *Bōchō Shinbun*, the first newspaper to report on Tenshō Kōtai Jingū Kyō some thirty years earlier, published a special edition. In an interview, Kitamura Kiyokazu stated that for the most part the press basically ignored Tenshō Kōtai Jingū Kyō for many years. Although some local journalists did request interviews with her at the time of the Aum Shinrikyō incident in 1995, she refused to do so because Aum had nothing to do with her group.[101] Her own passing in June 2006 was followed by her father's in July 2007. These events barely registered on the news cycle, so remote were they from those of the postwar activities of Kitamura Sayo.

DIFFERENT APPROACHES OF "CELEBRITY GODS"

The relationships between Kitamura and her followers, the authorities, and the media were complex, and they changed as the group developed. Although Kitamura viewed the secular realm as the "world of maggots," and the group's official history depicts her as uncompromisingly critical in her dealings with Japanese authorities, she was still keen to have her religion recognized as "legitimate" by registering it as a religious corporation. The SCAP records also show that she attempted to gain approval for her movement and promote it as a genuine religion as opposed to others that were appearing at the time. Thus, Kitamura's relationship with the authorities is one of the major differences between her and Jikōson.

During wartime Jikōson had been under investigation and in the postwar period the police continued their inquiries into her activities and those of her followers. Jikōson's followers, Katsuki and Go, claimed the police may have considered Jiu's attitude toward them to be an affront to their authority thereby inviting official investigations. Rumors that Jiu was extorting money and food from people had been rife from the early part of the Occupation. Jiu's insular nature was certainly a factor in raising suspicions, and it served to fan rumors because members of the press could only guess as to Jiu's motives. Kitamura, on the other hand, was quite clear with regard to her intentions to establish the "kingdom of god" and convert "maggot beggars" to her teachings. She also refused to accept donations. There was no suggestion that her teachings were ultranationalistic. She went to great lengths to denigrate the emperor and the wartime regime. Her stance against authority attracted a number of followers.

Kitamura's relationship with the Japanese media changed as the group developed and as some journalists gained a more detailed insight into the group over the years. Stories included issues related to mental illness and the vulnerability and gullibility of people after the surrender, the inability of traditional religions to reach the hearts of the people, the weakening power of intellectuals to judge their own actions, and the ineffectiveness of the authorities to deal with strange groups that cause social problems. Some reports sought to explain Tenshō Kōtai Jingū Kyō in terms of the phenomenon of postwar new religions, and even provided positive, albeit muted, comments about Kitamura. In general, however, the print media reports were quite negative and, in some cases, abusive. However, unlike Jikōson, Kitamura proved to be adept at manipulating the press for her own benefit to a certain extent. Whereas Jikōson avoided contact with the press, Kitamura appeared to relish the opportunity to get publicity. The visions and beliefs of Kitamura were different from those of Jikōson, despite initial media reports to the contrary, and they shared little in terms of personality. Yet understanding these differences does help to explain, to a large extent, what happened during the careers of the two women and their followers.

7

New Religions and Critics
in the Immediate Postwar Press

THE APPEARANCE of Jikōson and Kitamura Sayo in the press as "celebrity gods" coincided with the beginning of the so-called "rush hour of the gods." As the new laws liberated religious groups and individuals and allowed them unprecedented freedoms, the staff of SCAP's Religions Division and the Ministry of Education's Religious Affairs Section attempted to deal with the impact of the new policies. Yet while the term "rush hour" developed from the media, it was not only journalists who focused on new religions. Academics and intellectual elites also contributed to media texts that became part of the reconstituted images of new religions that drew from prewar representations and notions of superstitions and irrationality. New religions became a focal point for discussions about beliefs in the postwar period. The cases of Jiu and Tenshō Kōtai Jingū Kyō demonstrate that although their reputations were damaged by the predominantly critical negative media reporting, there were other important factors that affected their eventual trajectories, such as their reactions to the coverage and their awareness of postwar conditions.

The leaders of new religions like Sekai Kyūsei Kyō, Reiyūkai, Seichō no Ie, and Makoto Kyōdan (later Shinnyo-en) also came under critical press scrutiny. But as the Occupation began to draw to a close toward the 1950s, the negative coverage inspired some new religions to join together and form an organization that could present a united front in the religious world. One view is that the participating new religions that were "once held in contempt, acquired, at least in form, citizenship in the Japanese religious world."[1] At the same time, some journalists and commentators attempted to examine the role of religion more broadly within the context of postwar democracy. This chapter will examine examples of criticism, counterattack, and defense surrounding the subject of religion and new religions in particular during this period. It focuses on published work related to new religions and established groups, considering the motives of the interlocutors and their claims to holding a legitimate voice in the conversations related to spirituality and society in the immediate postwar period.

RELIGION UNDER ATTACK

Although new religions and their various unique leaders came under press scrutiny in the postwar period, the problems affecting established religions were also publicized. A SCAP report from the Religions Division analyzing publications that were written just after the Kanazawa incident of January 1947 involving Jiu noted that "there seems to be no lack of freedom of religious criticism in Japanese publications, and both Buddhism and Shintoism are severely treated in a number of instances."[2] An article published in the *Asahi Shinbun* on 17 October 1949 claimed that Buddhism and other religions had "lost face" as a result of the appearance of the new religions that were gaining adherents from the established groups.

Many established groups in the postwar period continued to advocate stricter controls over new religions as they had in the past to protect the public from their "dangers." However, as Takagi Hiroo notes, Buddhist groups were unable to launch a successful campaign of criticism against new religions as they had done in the Meiji period.[3] A combination of internal disputes and continued press criticisms of their own social standing effectively weakened their attacks on new religions. Buddhist and Shinto groups struggled with a variety of internal problems, not least of which was a widespread perception that they had colluded with the wartime government and had abandoned the spiritual needs of the people. No longer constrained by the wartime government policies that forced them to merge together in the late 1930s, many Buddhist groups established themselves as independent religious organizations under the Religious Corporations Ordinance of 1945. However, internal quarrels that had existed for some time resurfaced and financial scandals emerged.

Eventually representatives of established religions published or contributed chapters to books that criticized the new groups and their leaders who were gaining significant attention at the time. The struggles established groups faced in the Occupation period were related to their inability to effectively attack new religions. This inability reflected not only the criticism they faced from commentators in the press but also their own internal issues. On 3 November 1947 an article in the *Mainichi Shinbun* argued that established religions were responsible for the masses going toward "superstitions," Christianity lacked capable leaders, while Buddhist sects were occupied in sectarian disputes. The article concluded that "there will be no end to superstitions until the masses are awakened to true religion and established religions exert themselves to discharge their duties."

Many Shinto groups struggled to overcome associations to their wartime past. On 2 February 1946 the Association of Shinto Shrines (Jinja Honchō) was established, and this group attempted to answer its press critics. Significantly, in its attempt to reassert a social legitimacy, the category of new religions was once again used as a benchmark for unacceptable social behavior. On 26 April 1948 an editorial in the *Jinja Shinpō*, the organ newspaper of the Association of Shinto Shrines, attacked the major daily newspapers "which make unwarranted and sustained attacks on all religions." At the same time the paper argued for fairness in religious reporting with respect to those religions that contributed to "the welfare of the nation." The article demanded that the press concentrate their attacks on the new religions, all of which caused trouble for society.

Disputes with Christianity were also aired in the press. In late October 1949, on the occasion of the celebration of the four-hundredth anniversary of the arrival of St. Francis Xavier to Japan, a relic of the priest had been flown into Tokyo. This generated substantial interest in the press yet the reporting was not critical of Catholicism. It focused more on the historical significance and Japan's initial connections to Christianity.[4] But a different kind of reaction to the press reporting of this event appeared in the Press Society Newsletter (*Shinbun Kyōkaihō*) on 3 November 1949. The writer, Abe Kōzō, a pastor with the Church of Christ in Japan (Nihon Kirisuto Kyōdan), congratulated journalists for exposing what he called the unscrupulous activities of leaders of new religions like Jikōson and Ohikari-sama (another name for the leader of Sekai Kyūsei Kyō, Okada Mokichi). He advocated more stringent government controls on new religions. While praising journalists for acting as "watchdogs" in dealing with new religions, he simultaneously condemned them for their inability to attack the Catholic Church over its irrational practice of relic veneration. Abe argued that journalists were hypocritical because on the one hand they attacked new religions yet on the other they bowed to the great power of the Catholic Church. He held that because of this inconsistency, Japanese journalism was like "the stupidity of an idiot who is offended by plain insult but charmed by a cleverly designed one." Abe's stance assumed that new religions were a common enemy society faced because of "superstitions" and "illegal activities." But he was also attempting to strike a blow against another religious rival, the Catholic Church.

Established religions lost public support, land, suffered from internal dissent, and received criticism in the media. Although they held conferences to offer penance for not doing enough to stop the military government during wartime, these were not particularly well received by the public. In order to combat the negative perceptions, established religions attempted to draw clear lines between themselves and new religions, emphasizing distinctions between genuine religions and fakes.

EXPLOITATIONS AND REPERCUSSIONS

During 1949 the image of new religions deteriorated as a result of media representation. Around this time, rumors of money laundering, drug use, and sex scandals began to circulate in press reports about Sekai Kyūsei Kyō, Risshō Kōseikai, and Reiyūkai. While there were different claims concerning their negative impact on society, the cases of two groups in particular that exploited the somewhat lax conditions of the Religious Corporations Ordinance had significant repercussions for other new religions. The ordinance offered tax concessions to incorporated groups, and the leaders of Denshinkyō and Kōdō Chikyō, mentioned in chapter 4, took full advantage of the poor controls and the confusion over religious administration. The reporting on these groups contributed substantially to the discourse of new religions as primarily business concerns that abused the postwar freedom of religion and the uneducated public's reliance on superstitions for the personal profit of the founders.

The press began to report on Denshinkyō in early 1949, and coverage of Kōdō Chikyō soon followed. As the extent of Kōdō Chikyō's activities was quite widespread, the reports concentrated on this group. Most articles followed a similar pattern: Kōdō Chikyō had taken advantage of the postwar conditions in an attempt to fool the authorities and the public, just as Jiu (among other new religions) had done. In July 1949 the *Asahi Shinbun* ran a series on "bogus" religions with Kōdō Chikyō as its main focus. Although it introduced new religions with the cases of Jiu and Tenshō Kōtai Jingū Kyō, thus acknowledging and reaffirming the impact on the public consciousness of these groups, the *Asahi* portrayed Kōdō Chikyō as the worst possible new religion. Kōdō Chikyō, it charged, promoted spurious superstitions, fooled many people, and obtained huge amounts of money illegally by manipulating a lax and poorly controlled system that protected the group and allowed it to flourish. The *Asahi* claimed that the laws needed to be changed to take into account the large number of swindlers who were taking advantage of the postwar system of slack administration of religions. With a clear case of abuse like Kōdō Chikyō, this would have seemed reasonable to many people. These kinds of arguments were also made during 1995 in the wake of the Aum affair.

On 3 July 1949 the *Tōkyō Taimuzu* published three articles by different writers that reflected central concerns that were triggered by the Kōdō Chikyō incident and addressed the question of new religions in general. Kaneko Junji, a professor of the Shōwa Medical University, argued that although established religions seemed to be losing popularity, the public was still inclined toward seeking solace through religion. However, he argued, many people were suffering from postwar distress and mental anguish, which allowed new religions to take advantage of them. This argument reflects the general opinion expressed by psychologists about new religions and their effects on society.

A bureaucrat working in the Ministry of Education's Religious Affairs Section argued in another article that the spirit of Article 12 of the Constitution, which is related to maintaining public welfare, should be the guiding principle concerning how religions should behave in society.[5] Stating that this should be a standard for whether a religion was "just or unjust," the writer made a case for a stronger role for the Religious Affairs Section in determining these issues.

The Ministry of Education had planned to revise the Religious Corporations Ordinance into a new law almost from the time of its inception in 28 December 1945. It lobbied SCAP many times throughout the first years of the Occupation to do so based on two main points: firstly, large Buddhist and Shinto sects had suffered damage due to the secessions that had occurred after freedom of religion was granted, and secondly, there was severe public criticism (channeled through media reports and letters of complaint to the ministry) regarding new religions that were blatantly abusing the law and flouting the rules in order to receive financial gain. By hoping to revise the law, the ministry was advocating more government control. Education Ministry officials first suggested drafting a new law sometime in 1947 but the head of SCAP's Religions Division, William Bunce, was not interested; he argued that a new law was not necessary.[6]

The final article in the *Tōkyō Taimuzu* series was by a critic, Matsunami Shinzaburō, who argued against introducing more government controls. He asserted vaguely that understanding the difference between a "genuine" religion and a "superstitious" religion requires a special knack (which he did not elaborate on). In response to the growing discourse on "superstitions" and their dangers to society, Matsunami argued that not all "newly arisen religions" should be labeled "superstitions" and therefore unworthy of the name religion. By the same token, he continued, not all established religions could be held to be free from superstition. Although it was undeniable, he stated, that there were many religions purely out for profit, as long as religions did not break any laws they should not be controlled without good reason. Ultimately, he said, people would make a final judgment on whether a religion would continue, and the religion could then "reap what it sowed." He asserted that the majority of Japanese were hardly stupid enough to believe in insane superstitions.

MEDICAL PROFESSIONALS COMBATING "RELIGIOUS DELUSIONS"

The exploitative methods employed by Denshinkyō and Kōdō Chikyō generated discussions in the print media over the propriety of new religions. While these cases gave established religions grounds for stepping up their attacks on new religions, psychologists and religious studies scholars were also using the media to present their views. While their predecessors in the 1920s had begun to publish work on the dangers new religions posed in terms of "scientific" arguments and rationality, the postwar situation provided a younger generation of academics and psychologists with more material. These intellectuals invariably directed their attacks toward the "irrationality" of new religions, as well as superstitions and anti-modernity.[7] While these opinions generally opted for more education of the people, the tone of the arguments varied somewhat.

Akimoto Haruo, the psychologist who diagnosed Jikōson and her followers in Kanazawa, was among the first prominent figures to discuss new religions in the postwar press. Nakamura Kokyō, whose strong views on new religions of the 1920s and 1930s influenced the actions of the authorities at the time, was Akimoto's mentor. Akimoto argued in the *Mainichi Shinbun* of 26 January 1947 that people believed in Jikōson because they were suffering from "religious delusion" (*shūkyō mōsō*). Such a condition made it difficult for people to distinguish "superstitions" from "normal religions" (*seijō no shūkyō*) because religion itself contains mystical elements. However, he argued that doctors who used the modern techniques of medical psychology were able to determine the symptoms and conditions of this malady through scientific means. His conclusion was that the incident in Kanazawa occurred ultimately due to lack of intelligence and low cultural values. Akimoto's report of Jiu members featured prominently in newspaper articles on Jiu.

Akimoto's writings are mild compared with another psychologist, Minami Hiroshi, who wrote a strongly worded article in the January 1950 issue of the magazine *Mainichi Jōhō*.[8] While his main focus was Sekai Kyūseikyō, he criticized "heretical religions" in general. He offered three points that could be used to determine whether religions may be called heretical. First, the doctrines of such groups are fraudulent because they base their ideas on "worldly benefits," and many groups claim they are scientific, thus attempting to exploit the postwar interest in ideas of democracy and science. While not making an explicit declaration, Minami appeared to present himself as an example of democracy and scientific rationality. Second, he claimed that the founders of "heretical religions" led highly materialistic and luxurious lifestyles, building huge "palaces" at the same time as bilking their followers of goods and cash. In the wake of the Denshinkyō and Kōdō Chikyō incidents, this was an argument that must have resonated with some readers. Third, citing the case of Sekai Kyūsei Kyō as an example, he argued that "newly arisen evil cults" (*shinkō jakyō*) degraded politics by trying to attract influential politicians.

Minami held that the problem was not simply a question of psychologists diagnosing the founders as schizophrenics, or the fanatical followers as hysterical. Nor was it a question of dismissing the phenomenon of new religions as cases of "abnormal psychology." New religions were, in fact, a spiritual disease of the entire society. If people wanted to understand the seriousness of the problem, they needed to pay more attention to psychology, his own field of study, because it represented the "true" ideals of democracy. Minami concluded his criticism with the statement that, "heretical religions can only prosper in a society that allows them to do so."

Minami's views echo those of another psychologist, Inui Takashi. While Inui's writings appeared in both the *Asahi Shinbun* and the *Mainichi Shinbun* during the late 1940s, he also took up the issue of "newly arisen religions" in a book published in 1953 entitled *Nihon wa kurutteru* (Japan is Insane), which included a chapter entitled "The Rush

Hour of the Gods." Inui claimed that although SCAP aimed at Christianizing Japan,[9] people including students, teachers, bureaucrats, and businessmen were actually attracted to "newly arisen religions" because these groups often emit a sense of optimism and an escape from the desperation of postwar life. However, although such groups appeared to have a bright outlook or optimism, people should not misconstrue this behavior as anything "normal."[10] Inui held that spiritual possession (*kamigakari*) is a form of psychological illness, and that many "newly arisen religions" are barometers that indicate the serious disorder and chaos of the times.[11] They reflected the lifestyles and emotions of people from small towns and villages and were closely linked to the survival of traditional social structures. He claimed that the new religions could divert ordinary people away from the path of freedom. What is worse, new religions were preparing to lead people toward a path of fascism and war because they operate on undemocratic principles.[12] To emphasize his point, he expressed his concern that a former military officer may be able to pull the strings of such groups and draw people down a path of total disaster. Thus, in raising the possibility of a connection to Japan's dark wartime past with new religions, Inui was effectively warning his readers to be on their guard to protect their new freedoms.

Apart from Akimoto, who actually met with and conducted various tests on Jiu members, it is hard to tell whether Minami and Inui had direct contact with the groups they studied. Neither provides evidence of firsthand experiences with groups or individuals. Their writings reflect prevailing journalistic perceptions of new religions as pernicious, troublesome movements and are linked with the notions of democracy and freedom, as opposed to superstition, irrationality, and even the "fascism" of the past.

PERSPECTIVES OF RELIGIOUS STUDIES SCHOLARS

Another barometer that is useful in considering the position of new religions in Occupied Japan is the opinions of religious studies scholars. According to Ōishi Shūten, during the immediate postwar period religious studies scholars tended to regard new religions as "vulgar religions" that were unworthy of serious study. Ōishi, a priest from the Sōtō Zen tradition and a friend and colleague of William Woodard of the Religions Division, was an important figure who made a significant contribution to new religions in the postwar period.

Ōishi became the first executive director of the Union of New Religious Organizations of Japan (later named the Federation of New Religious Organizations of Japan; Jp: Shin Nihon Shūkyō Dantai Rengōkai, or simply Shinshūren). It is not surprising that representatives of some established religions, and particularly other Sōtō Zen priests, criticized Ōishi for his involvement with new religions. According to his account, he had been accused by some of receiving graft from some new religions for his involvement and support. He denies this charge by holding that his central concern was religious cooperation. The criticisms eventually faded away after Ōishi took up a position as executive director of the Japan Religions League.[13]

Ōishi argued that there were relatively few attempts by scholars to study new religions, and most of them were straightforward criticisms of their activities. Even though a number of new religions had made a significant impact on society by 1960, there were still few religious studies scholars seriously studying these groups. Ōishi offered two reasons for this: new religions were relatively recent phenomena and most had short histories, and the study of the groups was difficult and underdeveloped.[14] Two scholars, Saki Akio and Kotake Akira, each contributed chapters to a book produced in 1950 by Ōya Sōichi, *Shinkō shūkyō* (Newly arisen religions). In their work, new religions are presented as ecstatic movements that rely on superstition and magic, which they argued brings into question their legitimacy as religions per se.

Ōishi argued that as the new religions were subjected to widespread social criticism, much of which had been generated by the press, the founders of new religions often tended to isolate themselves from scholars and journalists.[15] This holds true in the case of Jiu, particularly in the wake of the "Kanazawa incident." The group was followed closely by journalists for some months after the incident but the subsequent reports show that the group granted no interviews to the press. The stories that appeared were essentially reminding readers of Jikōson and the famous incident.

The case of Jiu drew a notable comment from Kishimoto Hideo, the sometime SCAP advisor and professor of religious studies at Tokyo University. In arguing in the *Asahi Shinbun* on 27 January 1947 that Jiu promoted a "vulgar faith" which had caused problems for the group's famous adherents, Go Seigen and Futabayama, Kishimoto effectively warned Buddhist, Christian, and Shinto groups to take heed and act with a sense of social responsibility. Although Kishimoto's attitude toward this group may be indicative of how religious studies scholars viewed new religions at the time, the lack of academic publications concerning new religions from the beginning of the Occupation until the early 1960s may also indicate the difficulty scholars faced in trying to explain such groups.

Although the print media continued to report in a predominantly negative fashion, Ōishi claimed that around 1952, there was a slight change in the attitude of scholars and journalists toward new religions. Scholars who had once criticized new religions began to focus seriously on the issues surrounding these groups. Ōishi writes that Takagi Hiroo attempted to look closely at the new religions rather than simply despise and ridicule them.[16] Although Takagi still criticized new religions over doctrinal issues, arguing that they "contain very vulgar teachings and are backward and stagnant,"[17] he was one of the first to open up the path to serious academic study of new religions. Before his work started to appear in the mid-1950s, new religions received little consideration from the academic community.

The formation of other groups indicated a slight change in direction. Saki Akio, mentioned above, and another scholar, Matsushima Eiichi, formed the New Religions Research Group (Shinshūkyō Kenkyūkai) and another group formed at Waseda University and focused on the study of contemporary religions in Japan. It was through the activities of such groups that, Ōishi claims, religious scholars began to consider new religions without prejudice and attempted to understand and explain them for the first time in the postwar period. Although Ōishi finds that the results of their inquiries are not necessarily favorable to the new religions in question, when compared to the prejudice, hatred, and slander that new religions had experienced beforehand, this work is a positive step.[18]

By the 1950s it was apparent to scholars that some of the new religions had clearly established solid followings and could not simply be ignored. But most published works still tended to emphasize new religions in relation to the promotion of superstitions and "this-worldly benefits." And while religious scholars may have begun to examine new religions with different lenses, psychologists such as Inui were still extremely critical of new religions generally. In 1955 a book called *Kyōso: Shomin no kamigami* (Founders and leaders: Gods of the common people) combined the efforts of religious studies scholars and psychologists to describe founders and leaders from a historical to contemporary perspective.[19]

While intellectuals offered their own perspectives on new religions, what were the views concerning how the press dealt with the various issues? Kishimoto Hideo offered one notable characterization of print media reporting in arguing that new religions were "the plaything of journalism."[20] One of the major trends in postwar reporting of new religions in newspapers and magazines, he claimed, was to caricature them. He argued that one exception to this was NHK's "serious effort" to study the phenomena of new religions. Although he did not provide cases, one example of this might be the first installment in a television series, *Nihon no sugao* ("The bare face of Japan"), called "Shinkō shūkyō o miru" ("Focus on newly arisen religions"), which aired in November 1957.[21]

According to Kishimoto, journalists would generally take up a story with gusto if a new religion or its members could be characterized in a comical fashion, or if the group could be portrayed as breaking social conventions, or if the group was the subject of rumor or innuendo. He held that new religions were represented in three ways in the mainstream press. First, the leaders or followers of a new religion were often mocked and scorned in the press.[22] Second, journalists often characterized new religions as breaking social conventions.[23] Third, the press seized on a story if there was any suggestion or rumor that the group in question engaged in illegal activities.[24] The images promoted in many reports included the ideas that new religions were generally concerned with financial gain, that their founders were uneducated swindlers with shady pasts, and that the followers were often ignorant and besotted individuals trying to cling onto some type of salvation during the difficult period of postwar reconstruction.

Ōishi Shūten also argued that articles by journalists about new religions mainly took the form of aggressive attacks. Most journalists in the postwar period either loathed new religions or laughed at them, refusing to try to understand the circumstances or histories of new religions.[25] *Sengo shūkyō kaisō roku*, which was produced with the support of some groups that formed the Union (now Federation) of New Religious Organizations of Japan, unsurprisingly reveals no ambiguity in its characterization of the press. The book claimed that there was a deeply rooted tendency within many areas of Japanese society to regard all new religions as "immoral and heretical cults." Any new group was immediately cast as a superstitious and evil cult, and journalists, who made very little attempt to learn the real nature of the groups, led public opinion against new religions by conducting determined attacks.[26]

The Union of New Religious Organizations did attempt to promote the idea that its members were legitimate religions, and that not all new religions fit the negative image that had been shaped within print media reports. The strategy was not necessarily entirely successful. As Morioka notes, both Sekai Kyūsei Kyō and Risshō Kōseikai, members of the federation, were the subject of intense and highly critical media campaigns from the late 1940s.[27]

Akimoto Haruo, the psychologist in the Jiu case, expressed his own opinions about the press. He began to speak out about the press coverage soon after the Kanazawa incident, expressing some of his strongest statements in a scientific journal, *Kagaku Shushi*, in November 1947. He argued that by simply lampooning Jikōson and her followers, the media was acting irresponsibly and was not making any positive contribution toward educating the public in the value of rationality and medical science. He stated that Jikōson was a pitiful paranoiac who needed medical attention, and that what connected those who derided her and those who regarded her as a deity was their mutual disinterest in scientific views on the case. He felt that the Jikōson case provided a perfect opportunity to "expose the true nature of fake religions and dispel religious illusions through cooperation between the police authorities, the press, and scientists."

Although Akimoto's comments were published in a small journal, they did not escape the attention of Akai Masami, the editor of the *Asahi Gurafu* magazine and one of the journalists who visited Jiu's headquarters with a staff photographer in October 1946. Akai claimed that Jikōson assured him during their meeting that only the *Asahi* newspaper would survive the forthcoming calamities she predicted. This convinced him that Jikōson was a charlatan and that her group presented a grave danger to postwar democracy. People like Akimoto, he wrote, should be taken to task for only discussing the psychological aspects of the case and not recognizing that "anti-democratic" forces were at work. He argued that people should not listen to Akimoto, claiming that "the sanity of the doctor should be tested."[28]

DEMOCRACY AND "ANTI-DEMOCRACY"

Akai's argument about "anti-democratic" forces is representative of one of the dominant themes that appeared in both journalistic and academic discourse on the subject of new religions during the Occupation. While a common theme of prewar and postwar discussions of new religions centered on irrationality, superstition, and "true" religion, prewar notions of empire and state were replaced with postwar visions of democracy.

After the beginning of the Occupation, journalists often wrote in glowing terms of the democracy that had been bestowed upon the nation. This may have reflected a genuine sense of relief that the harsh government controls and demands placed on journalists during the prewar period had finally been lifted. On the other hand, recalling the enforced censorship of publications until 1948 by SCAP, in some cases the paeans to democracy may have been journalists' attempts to not upset the Allied conquerors. Nevertheless, the change in regimes did little to alter widespread perceptions in the media of the undesirability of new religions in society. Journalists in the new democratic environment were not inclined to favor religion in general.

In early November 1949, one of the country's most prominent media figures, Baba Tsunego, who was the editor of the *Yomiuri Shinbun* and president of the Japan Press Association, released a statement arguing that the chanting of Buddhist sutras and Shinto prayers had no meaning for the new democracy of Japan. Democracy, he held, could only be realized when individuals exert themselves to the utmost. In response to this, on 10 November 1949 the religious newspaper *Chūgai Nippō* reported that some religious leaders were deeply offended by his statements. The writer attacked some of the large religious collectives, such as the Japan Religions League (Nihon Shūkyō Renmei) and the Japan Buddhist Association (Nihon Bukkyō Rengōkai), for not immediately issuing rebuttals to Baba's statement. These organizations may have chosen not to draw attention to themselves by not responding and entering into public debate with the editor of one of the most powerful media organizations in the country. But Baba's criticism of Buddhism and Shinto is indicative of the public image problems faced by these groups. Eventually the *Yomiuri Shinbun* published some of the most strident attacks on new religions in the print media at that time, and Morioka Kiyomi holds that the paper became a specialist in new religions, and raised its circulation with a series of exposés on Ōmoto, Tenrikyō, Sekai Kyūsei Kyō, and the Reiyūkai.[29] Baba's comments indicate the powerful nature of representations of democracy, beliefs, and religions in the press.

According to John Dower, the magazine *Shinsei* (New Life) was among the new group of periodicals that appeared during the period that were calling for a "newborn Japan" while claiming to repudiate completely the country's political and social past.[30] The special issue of the magazine published in September 1947 promised to reveal the real story behind "the seamy underbelly of contemporary religion." While it covered various scandals involving established groups, it also investigated new religions. In an article focusing on the growth of "heretical cults," the writer, Masuda Jumpei, praised Japan's new democracy while launching a strong attack on all such groups, starting with the prewar Hito no Michi. He listed four conditions that "heretical cults" share: (1) they have a primitive and unscientific nature and invariably involve sex of a deviant nature; (2) the founders, such as Renmonkyō's Shimamura Mitsu, are "mostly illiterate old women or mental cases" and seldom are they of the intellectual stature of people like Christ, Buddha, or Mohammed; (3) they thrive according to geographical locations, and in the Kansai area of Japan, where people are "known for their inclinations toward commercial and worldly benefits," large numbers of groups flourish; and (4) without proper methods to develop and spread their teachings, they wither and die.

Tenrikyō's method of survival, which was to "urge its followers to follow the example set by the founder, who gave everything in her possession to save the indigent poor," apparently worked, according to Masuda, because the group grew from a "heretical cult" to a "full-fledged religion." Another group that successfully made this transition was Seichō no Ie. Masuda asserted that "heresy is defined simply as religions that disturb public peace and compromise public interests," and argues that many of the new religions that appeared in the postwar period, including Jiu and Tenshō Kōtai Jingū Kyō, were "heretical religions" because they disturbed the peace. "Heretical cults do no harm while they remain unknown but if they develop into the size of the 'Hito no Michi' cult, which once flourished, then they do incalculable harm to the public's mind and to the society." Although it may not have been his intention, Masuda inferred that the harm such groups cause was related to their public presence. If such groups remain unknown, he suggests, the damage they inflict on society is diminished.

Masuda's comments reflect arguments that had been made during the 1920s and 1930s in claiming that groups with "heretical tendencies" were generally unscientific and irrational and that the founders were mostly illiterate women or mentally unstable individuals. Furthermore, he argues that "postwar heretical cults," such as Seichō no Ie, tried to become involved in publishing, education, and social welfare programs, thus cultivating a pseudo-intellectualism that other postwar cults were trying to emulate. In attacking this group in particular, he not only focused on its postwar activities, but also its wartime associations with the ruling regime, implying that it was untrustworthy because it supported militarism and was therefore undemocratic.

These kinds of arguments appeared in other publications as well, such as the *Naigai Taimuzu*, a paper with a history dating back to the Meiji period that had been taken over by the *Yomiuri Shinbun* in June 1949. The paper established independence from the Yomiuri company in December of that year but continued to publish on new religions. On 27 August 1950, an article entitled "Don't Laugh at Fake Religions" characterized Futabayama's involvement with Jikōson and an alleged incident involving Makoto Kyōdan as "laughable." At the same time, the article questioned whether "postwar society" had the right to mock individuals who belonged to "fake religions" when Japan had attacked neighboring countries under the orders of foolish soldiers who claimed it was the will of the emperor just five years earlier.[31]

While this was hardly a ringing endorsement for new religions, it does demonstrate the willingness of some journalists to take a morally superior position at a time when the Japanese government and the occupying forces no longer controlled or censored articles. The *Yomiuri Shinbun* began to develop its significant portfolio concerning new religions in the late 1940s. An editorial of 27 September 1949 attacked "undesirable religions," claiming that postwar Japanese society was like "rotten soil" that breeds "poisonous bacteria" like new religions. Beginning with the "scandalous heresy expounded by Jikōson," thus placing her as a "model" of new religions, the article claimed that it was time to expose the "undesirable religions" that were afflicting Japanese society. These did not include Buddhist and Christian groups that were rich in tradition and history, but referred to the "diverse superstitious heresies" that claimed to be legitimate religions. The writer argued that most people lacked independence and suffered from spiritual weakness and therefore joined a new religion, or else they were fanatics who blindly believed in one truth and joined the Communist Party. Either way, the people were not masters of their own destiny. Urging the people to "tear away the masks of hypocritical living gods" who were duping them, the article called for more rational thinking on the part of the people, arguing that "the heretical religions are the enemy of democracy and the hindrance to progress."

The *Yomiuri* continued to chase down new religions with an article published on 6 March 1951, describing "fake" new religions like Reiyūkai and Makoto Kyōdan as being "driven by salacious lust and greed." The article contained claims of sex among the leaders of Reiyūkai, abuse of followers, and hidden caches of enormous amounts of jewelry and gold. It also claimed that the police were going to start investigating "questionable religions," a phrase that was duly underlined and noted by SCAP's Religions Division officers in the copy contained in the SCAP records.[32] These newspaper articles demonstrate that similar arguments were used against new religions in the immediate postwar period to those of the prewar period. Yet accusations of the anti-modern and irrational tendencies of new religions, in addition to shady financial dealings, questionable social mores, and psychological instability, were presented in a new light. In praising the new era of democracy, the press warned of potential dangers presented by pernicious groups who had been given too many freedoms. The clear implication was that if something was not done to control "these groups," the innocent public would be cruelly manipulated and cheated. With the large numbers of new groups that were appearing, and the opportunities the postwar freedoms allowed, journalists had a rich source of material they could tap in order to present titillating stories of greed, money, and madness.

ŌYA SŌICHI'S CRITIQUES OF POSTWAR NEW RELIGIONS

As mentioned in the previous chapter, Ōya Sōichi had revived his career by 1950 and had built up a new portfolio of work on groups like Jiu, Tenshō Kōtai Jingū Kyō, Sekai Kyūseikyō, and PL Kyōdan. For Ōya, these groups were the representative or "model" new religions in the postwar period. Ōya held onto his prewar beliefs that new religions promoted superstitions and were inherently dangerous to society. In an article on "newly arisen religions" published in the magazine *Seinen Bunka* in April 1949, he argued that his intention was neither to criticize all religions nor to claim that science had all the answers to difficult questions of human spirituality. His main concern was that some people were gullible enough to believe that the answers to these questions lay in miracles that could be performed by certain people with allegedly superhuman powers. Those who are fooled by the promoters of superstitions, he claimed, have a kind of "air pocket" in their brains, which renders them susceptible to all kinds of swindlers who cloak themselves with the trappings of religion and claim special powers.[33]

Ōya's *Shinkō shūkyō* (1950) provides a clear exposition of his ideas on new religions. The introduction serves both as a useful overview of his opinions and it reflects some of the significant arguments leveled at new religions by the press and intellectuals. In this work, he begins by expressing the concern that established religions are not only irrelevant and but also irrational in the context of postwar democracy. Ōya claimed that the "great inflation" of "newly arisen religions," such as Ōmoto, Hito no Michi, and Seichō no Ie that began from around 1930 occurred because there was nothing to replace Marxism after its exponents were oppressed during the 1930s. Therefore, he argued, there was a lack of spiritual leadership of the people. The reason why people turned to "newly arisen religions" during this period was because the established religions had lost their effectiveness and the medical system became driven by profit, meaning that people turned to religions that promised miraculous and mystical cures to their problems.[34]

Although he admitted that there are some minor differences between the "newly arisen religions," fundamentally they are all fake and potentially dangerous. He discussed the history of new religions from the Meiji period, noting that many "newly arisen religions" ran into trouble with the authorities at some stage. However, he argued that the immediate postwar period was a time of democratization for the "world of the gods" in which "the religious world flourishes like a street market." He claimed that the "newly arisen religions" such as Jiu, Tenshō Kōtai Jingū Kyō, and Sekai Kyūsei Kyō are different from the "systematized and ossified established religions" in that they directly reflect the character and cultural level of the times. Finally, he expressed concern that an increasing number of people with high levels of education joined "immoral and evil cults."

This kind of criticism reflects his prewar work on new religions. In 1936 he wrote an article entitled "Ruiji shūkyō to interi sō" ("Pseudo-religions and the intellectual class") that describes what he felt was the "disturbing" trend of educated individuals joining new religions.[35] His work reflected that of other critics of the early 1920s who had argued about the potential dangers posed by Ōmoto. Ōya's prewar and postwar critiques of intellectuals joining new religions or participating in their activities both argue that this trend was indicative of social breakdown and the degradation of rational scientific thought. He argued that Go Seigen and Futabayama who joined Jiu were not intellectuals, even though they achieved excellence in their respective fields. On the other hand, PL Kyōdan's prewar precursor, Hito no Michi, once claimed a number of intellectual heavyweights, which caused great confusion amongst the public.[36] The founders of postwar "newly arisen religions generally passed through the doors" of prewar groups, and that in order to learn the essence of the postwar "newly arisen religions," one must study their prewar predecessors. Most of the postwar "newly arisen religions," he claimed, were variations on old themes, holding that the original models for these groups included Butsuryūkō,[37] Tenrikyō, and Ōmoto.[38] For example, Butsuryūkō was the model for Buddhist-related "newly arisen religions" whereas Tenrikyō was the model for Shinto-based ones.[39] The fanatical characters of the adherents of the postwar "newly arisen religions" exactly mirrored those of Butsuryūkō. Butsuryūkō's founder was severely attacked by "professional religion-ists" (that is, representatives of established religions), thus making his group a strictly "non-professional" religious outfit.[40] This "non-pro tendency" (*non-puroteki keikō*) is something, Ōya held, that was shared by all "newly arisen religions." Although he claimed that most of the founders of "newly arisen religions" were "ignorant men and women," the founder of Seichō no Ie, Taniguchi Masaharu, had received a mod-ern education and had been a journalist.[41]

Ōya continued his analysis with a list of characteristics he claims are common to Japan's "newly arisen religions," including the use of lame jokes and far-fetched explanations of events. The master of these tech-niques was Ōmoto's Deguchi Onisaburō.[42] But he added that there are other recognizable traits that can be discerned. For example, once the founders have captured followers, they try to keep them and strengthen their relationship to the group. In order to do this they follow a few simple rules, such as criticizing other religions at the same time as tell-ing their followers their own groups are unique and special. Further-more, they try to encourage a kind of competition in which the believ-ers attempt to assert their own influence within the group.[43] He also criticized the way in which large groups such as Ōmoto and Tenrikyō set out with grand plans to expand their groups, coercing their follow-ers to make great personal sacrifices for the sake of their religion. Ōya holds that this particular method of capturing people's hearts is not lim-ited to "newly arisen religions." Elaborating on the potential dangers of "newly arisen religions," he argued that Hitler used similar methods, as did the fascist movement within Japan during the 1930s.[44]

Ōya added other characteristics to his list in order to help the reader recognize "newly arisen religions." The characters of founders of such groups, he claimed, are easily discerned because those who are women are generally ignorant, mentally unstable psychotics while the males are clever businessmen, prospectors, or peddlers. He warned that a great number of them had criminal pasts.[45] Another characteristic was that "newly arisen religions" invariably require "a famous face to work with ... there's no need to repeat the story of Futabayama and Go Seigen, the 'poster boys' for Jikōson."[46] Ōya ended his introduction with the following: "Comparing these groups in this way, I'd be pleased if just one person can realize how stupid it would be to believe that any one of these groups holds the absolute truth. If readers know of anyone who is currently obsessed with any of these religions, I hope they show them this book. If they still refuse to give up their faith, it's probably wise to cart them off to [hospital]."[47]

The strength of Ōya's writing on religion, and on new religions in particular, lies in the extent of his research, as well as his broad grasp of Japan's modern religious history. His sense of irony is sometimes palpable. His critiques of new religions were sometimes uncompromising and harsh, and there is no doubt that some of his publications harmed the reputations of some groups. But he was not an armchair critic by any means. He secured interviews with various leaders and followers of new religions and reported on many of them, including Ōmoto, Hito no Michi, Seichō no Ie, and Tenshō Kōtai Jingū Kyō. While it is clear that he was singularly unimpressed and highly suspicious of religion in general and new religions in particular, he was not a journalist who simply parroted or regurgitated the work of others.

A CRITIQUE OF ŌYA SŌICHI'S LEGACY

Ōya Sōichi was arguably one of the most influential journalists during the 1950s and 1960s, and his reputation is formidable among media workers. One of Ōya's protégés, Ōkuma Hideo, christened him "the emperor of the mass media" (*masukomi teiō*).[48] Matsuura Sōzō, one-time editor of the left-wing journal *Kaizō*, called his former colleague one of Japan's "standard bearers of the mass media."[49] Matsuura claimed that Ōya's students were members of an "Ōya religion."[50]

Despite these assessments and other references to Ōya Sōichi that continue to be published years after his death, there is one noteworthy criticism of Ōya and his legacy. Sociologist and media scholar Murakami

Naoyuki published his ideas on Ōya in the *Seikyō Shinbun*, the organ newspaper of the new religion Sōka Gakkai. During the 1960s Ōya was highly critical of Sōka Gakkai's political involvement, financial strength, and proselytization activities. Murakami's arguments are worth considering because he presents an alternative and challenging view not only of Ōya but of his influence on postwar media representation of religion in Japan in general.

In Murakami's second article published in the *Seikyō Shinbun* (1999), he argues that Japan's "secular religion" in the postwar period was the mass media and Ōya Sōichi its founder. He attempts to consider the relationship between religion and media in sociological terms, claiming that when there are campaigns "against religion" there is a kind of panic that exists within the consciousness of the people. He offers the case of the Ranters, a sect that was viewed as heretical by the established church of seventeenth-century England. According to Murakami, the group's opponents within the church distributed scandalous, erroneous news pamphlets in a campaign aimed at quelling the moral confusion that gripped the people at the time. The Ranters were the "necessary scapegoat" the religious authorities used to carry this out: the media of the time became the instrument of social control.

In connecting this tale of persecution by the press to his main point, Murakami argues that the media in Japan launched an "anti-religion campaign" from 1945, and that journalists who had cooperated with the authorities in the prewar and wartime periods waved "the flag of the democratization movement" during the chaotic immediate postwar period. These journalists held assumptions about the way Japanese civil society should operate, and religious organizations became the necessary scapegoats they required to define and to articulate their positions. Most Buddhist and Shinto groups were broadly seen as supporting the wartime regime and thus struggled to gain credibility in the postwar environment. Journalists, Murakami asserts, used this wartime connection initially to hail the opening of a new era of freedom and severely criticized established religions not only for their previous wartime associations but also because of alleged corruption and their perceived distance from the people and their real suffering.

The separation of church and state, one of the important reforms introduced by SCAP, was associated with the principles of democracy. But with the appearance of a number of new religions, journalists felt that the freedoms introduced and imposed by SCAP affected many areas of society in a negative manner. Not only were the freedoms limiting the Japanese authorities in terms of the range of possible measures they could use to curb the activities of groups that caused "problems," the new legal measures were also contributing to the degradation of social norms. New religions were attracting adherents who had substantial educational backgrounds, and journalists believed that this was one of the costs of freedom.

Murakami claims that Ōya's noteworthy contribution to the postwar media "campaign" was to draw attention to new religions and condemn them. He notes that Ōya's work alleging tales of financial extravagance by various *kyōso* left readers with the impression that all new religions were simply out to make money. This, he argues, is Ōya's sin (*tsumi*) because by characterizing new religions in this way, Ōya did these groups and the people of postwar Japan a great disservice. However, Murakami does acknowledge Ōya's positive point, which was to admit that all people must have a belief in something, and that it was extremely difficult to be "non-ideological" (as noted earlier, one of Ōya's famous works was his "non-ideological declaration," *mushisō sengen*). Murakami takes this position to mean that there is no one who does not hold a belief in what might be termed "religion" of some kind or another. He then proposes that the reason for the "hatred" that journalists of the modern period displayed toward religion was because they were "blind followers" of the "media religion." While acknowledging that criticizing Ōya is basically taboo within journalism today given his status, Murakami proposes that Ōya should be named "founder of Japan's mass media religion." Although this is a somewhat ironic characterization, it acknowledges Ōya's unchallenged status in the press and the almost blind loyalty his followers felt for him.

Murakami accurately pinpoints the tendency of journalists to focus on the imported and imposed notions of democracy as a discursive tool to attack new religions. His provocative reassessment of Ōya's legacy also provides a balance to the predominantly positive views of his colleagues and students. However, the connection he makes between Ōya's wartime activities and supposed "responsibility" and his reporting of new religions in the postwar period seems somewhat tenuous.

In claiming that Ōya is the "founder of Japan's mass media religion," Murakami overstates his case by criticizing Ōya without considering his prewar stance in detail. Although Ōya did work for the prewar government and reported favorably about the military advances into China, for example, he was also critical of the actions of the authorities in both prewar and postwar periods concerning their policies toward new religions. His reporting of new religions was reasonably consistent during the prewar and postwar periods in that he was highly critical of such groups. Murakami's idea of "mass media religion" is problematic in that it suggests a uniform set of beliefs that all journalists adhered to blindly. Ironically, while he criticizes journalists, and particularly Ōya, for characterizing religion and new religious groups in virtually the same way, Murakami paints a monochromatic picture of journalists and the postwar media. Ōya's work in the years immediately following the Occupation (from 1948 to 1951) is taken as the model that journalists follow; given that Ōya's position in the media industry essentially remains unchallenged today, Murakami assumes that what he wrote during that period might be taken as the gospel of the "mass media religion."

Another problem with Murakami's argument is that he mentions Tenshō Kōtai Jingū Kyō in connection to Ōya's work on new religions and money. Although Ōya did criticize the group harshly, it must be recalled that he also pointed out that this group was remarkable among the new religions he looked at because it was not concerned with making money. Although there are some problems with his criticisms, Murakami's position is important and worth considering because he raises issues about trends he sees within the media, using Ōya as his main example.

A JOURNALIST "SUPPORTS" THE NEW RELIGIONS

While Murakami's view that most journalists were critical of new religions during the immediate postwar period is supported by other commentators like Kishimoto and Ōishi, journalist Taki Taizō was one exception to the rule. He stated in 1956 that when he first began covering new religions, he followed a similar pattern as other journalists in that he initially refused to try and understand the groups on their own terms and simply engaged in unfair and highly critical attacks. According to his reflections, his attitude to new religions was encapsulated in a popular novel serialized in 1952 in the *Shūkan Asahi* by Niwa Fumio, a literary critic and author. Titled *Hebi to hato* (The Snake and the Dove), it concerned a fictional "newly arisen religion" established by an individual of dubious character with the intention of making money. The novel was praised by literary critic Nakajima Kenzō, who wrote that, "Niwa is not catering to the vulgar tastes of the masses but has approached his work seriously. In handling the difficult details and in drawing out his own individual writing style, the author has produced a work that can (and should be) widely read."[51] In 1953, Niwa won the seventh Noma Literature Prize, which was to become a prestigious award in the literary world, for his work. Although it was a work of fiction, his descriptions of "newly arisen" religions fitted closely with what the reading public (and the judges of the prize) had come to accept about new religions. Taki wrote that he once saw parallels with Niwa's work and his own uninformed ideas. He admitted that his impression of "newly arisen religions" was that the leaders were notorious cheats who schemed to make money from the sufferings of ordinary people. He imagined the world of such groups as being plagued by taxation problems, drugs, and sex scandals. In this sense, Niwa's novel supported his own prejudices.[52]

Around the late 1940s to early 1950s Taki was assigned to the Education Ministry's press club. He began to spend time in the ministry's Religious Affairs Section office which was located near the press club office. It was a busy time for this section, with representatives from various religious groups filing in and out of the office. He heard various conversations between bureaucrats and "living gods," including one involving a patriotic individual who tearfully declared that he had no choice but to stand up and declare that he had been anointed the savior of humanity. This man's conviction moved Taki to the extent that his attitude toward "newly arisen religions" changed dramatically.

Although he had once considered all "founders" to be mad psychotics, after meeting a number of them he decided that most were easy to talk to, that they had experienced enormous struggles, and that they were actually remarkable human beings. And he found that the followers were actually very normal people, such as housewives one might meet in a department store, for example. According to Taki, Niwa's linking of "founders" to "snakes" was far off the mark. He argued that Niwa's storyline of new religions as businesses was a convenient angle for journalists with little time or inclination to study the phenomenon of new religions. For this reason, new religions received unfair treatment from the media.[53]

In the book's preface, Ōishi Shūten named Taki as one of the first journalists to write about new religions who did not carry the prejudices of other media workers that had plagued many of the groups since the beginning of the Occupation. Taki's reports in the *Tōkyō Nichi Nichi Shinbun* and in the magazine *Yūkan Shinchō* presented the new religions in a straightforward manner that did not immediately criticize or judge them. Ōishi noted that while these two publications were not necessarily major media organs, Taki's reports took journalists' understandings of new religions to a new level. Therefore, all new religions should be grateful not only to the publications but to Taki himself.[54] Ōishi called Taki's book *Kamigami tabō* (The busy gods) a steppingstone toward serious research on new religions, arguing that Taki's new position represented a slight change in journalists' perceptions of new religions toward the end of the Occupation.[55]

Nevertheless, Taki's objectivity has been called into question. Sugata Masaaki argues that Taki's newfound respect for new religions apparently did not remain purely professional. He writes that Taki later became a leader of Risshō Kōseikai, one of the founding members of the Union of New Religious Organizations, and was the first editor of the group's organ newspaper *Kōsei Shinbun*.[56]

A SCAP OFFICIAL SPEAKS OUT

Representatives of SCAP's Religions Division rarely made comments that appeared to support particular religious organizations, individuals, or movements. It is noteworthy, therefore, that Walter Nichols, who was familiar with a number of new religions including Tenshō Kōtai Jingū Kyō published an article in the religious journal *Shūkyō Kōron* in late 1950 that discussed new religions and the press.[57] The article clearly states that Nichols is an official of CI&E. Some of the ideas in the article appeared in a longer essay written in English entitled "The New Religions" and dated 29 November 1950.[58] Unsurprisingly, his position indicates a staunch defense of SCAP's policy of freedom of religion. He also made a passionate effort to encourage fairness in terms of reporting about religion:[59]

> No other postwar religious development in Japan has received so much publicity as the appearance of numerous so-called "new religions" following the removal of restrictions on religious liberty. Unfortunately, however, and in spite of extensive treatment by both religious and secular journals, very little reliable information about the new cults is available to the public. Most of the articles printed about them are based merely on cursory investigation, on brief interviews with their leaders, or on nothing more than rumor or hearsay.

The main point of Nichols's argument is that Japanese religious and secular newspapers and journals at the time were severely biased against new religions and that this bias was reflected in the public's negative attitude toward them. He continued by stating that as religious journals were designed to serve sectarian purposes, their published attacks on new religions reflected established religions' attempts to protect themselves by pointing out the perceived faults of new religions. On the other hand, secular newspapers and journals were reporting only sensational incidents, and were mainly concerned with "unsavory aspects" of new religions. He claimed that the religious and secular press were largely responsible for the generally widespread (and, in his view, mistaken) opinion held by the public that the new religions were "nothing more than heretical doctrines or mystic cults of a voluptuous character foisted on a gullible public by religious psychopaths, fraudulent faith healers, or shrewd entrepreneurs."[60]

Nichols argued that new religions actually have deep historical roots within Japanese society that go back to the early part of the nineteenth century, insisting that they were only new in an organizational sense, and that they were able to develop and propagate openly only because of the freedom of religion guaranteed in the constitution. As such, the new religions should not be cast aside or denigrated as "illegitimate." In characterizing the public's general reaction to the new religions as unfortunate, Nichols also claimed there was reason to suspect that "they are in many ways more truly representative of modern Japanese culture than are the social refinements of the past (such as tea ceremonies and flower arranging)." In support of this, he noted Buddhist, Shinto, and Christian theological and philosophical concepts, as well as deities from ancient texts such as the *Kojiki* and *Nihon Shoki*, which are employed by a number of new religions. Nichols asserted that many founders of new religions had connections with one of the older religions and that in order to make the teachings intelligible the founder had to reinterpret them in such a way as to be understood by modern society. By making this claim, Nichols tried to directly confront the idea that new religions were somehow perversions of traditional beliefs, or that the founders of new religions abused gullible people by using concepts with which they had some familiarity. Nichols was not only attempting to address the issue of "newness" of these groups but their legitimacy in terms of their links to the past.

On the subject of new religions being labeled "superstitious cults," Nichols argued the Religions Division's basic position on the freedom of religion:[61]

In considering beliefs at variance with our own convictions we must, if we are to retain an objective point of view, recognize the fact that, however primitive or naive they may seem, they represent the personal beliefs and religious convictions of others. We cannot substitute our consciences for those of others. Religion obviously means different things to different people, and few anthropologists, for example, would agree with a theologian's definition of the terms "religion" and "superstition." One should not forget that all of the better-known religions, at least in the institutionalized forms, could be traced back to a point of origin in history at which time they were themselves considered superstitious or dangerous by the religions they later superseded.

Nichols clearly recognized that during the chaos of the first few postwar years a number of fraudulent individuals and groups had taken advantage of the hastily drafted laws concerning incorporation of religious groups. While acknowledging that groups who abused their status as religious corporations should be punished for their crimes, he stated that his real concern was that newspaper reporters were creating problems for all new religions by associating them with criminals. His essay seems to be an attempt to correct some of the inequalities he saw in Japanese society.

This article had little effect on the way journalists in general viewed new religions or considered their own reporting habits. The Japanese version appeared in a journal for religious specialists and was not republished in more mainstream print media publications. Nevertheless, what is important about the appearance of the piece is the timing and significance for new religions. It was printed in late 1950, which was a time of significant change for religious policy in Japan. This change had an immediate and major impact on all religious institutions, particularly new religions, and continues to affect religion in Japan today.

THE SHIFT IN RELIGIOUS ADMINISTRATION

When the case of Kōdō Chikyō became public knowledge, the calls from established religious groups, Japanese bureaucrats, and press commentators for significant changes to the structure of religious administration grew louder. There were three main issues at stake. First, the Religious Corporations Ordinance, which was introduced as a temporary measure when the SCAP regime took over in 1945, was due to expire when the Occupation ended. In order to prevent the possibility of around 200,000 incorporated religious bodies being forced to dissolve and then reincorporate, the ordinance either needed to be extended by the Diet or replaced by a new law. Second, there were fears within religious circles that if a specific law was not introduced, politicians in the first post-Occupation Diet would compromise the gains achieved with respect to religious freedom and the separation of church and state.[62] Third, representatives of established religions, who had lobbied for more stringent controls of "unwholesome" religions throughout the Occupation, stepped up their calls in light of the evidence about groups like Kōdō Chikyō that abused the law in the name of "religion."

Regarding the first point, William Bunce of the Religions Division maintained the view throughout the Occupation that no new legislation solely concerned with religion or religious organizations was necessary. He was convinced that religious bodies should use the civil code in order to protect them against a resurgence of prewar government control. In the face of persistent opposition by Bunce and others within CI&E, the Education Ministry's officials began to lobby the Religions League to support the introduction of a new law. Recognizing that "public opinion" about matters concerning religious institutions would likely influence SCAP's decisions, the ministry's officials once again drew support from the Religions League, as it had done when the Religious Affairs Section was under threat in 1948. In the autumn of 1949, a delegation of religious leaders requested the division's cooperation in the drafting of a new law.[63] As their views represented "public opinion," Bunce could not ignore them despite his personal reservations. The Religions and Cultural Resources Division approved the drafting of the law in October 1949.

On the second point, Woodard holds that the reason why religious leaders wanted a law drafted before the end of the Occupation was because they would still be free to approve or disapprove the recommendations of the Religions Division. But once the Occupation was over, they would be at the mercy of the political rulers and might have been forced to accept stricter government controls over religious activities.[64] However, the issue of introducing more government controls concerned SCAP officials most, and Bunce was strongly opposed to introducing a new law.

Nevertheless the Japanese authorities were also caught in a bind when it came to groups that abused the privileges available under the Religious Corporations Ordinance. On the one hand, in prewar times their job was to control religion, a role that was removed by SCAP. On the other hand, there were increasing demands for stronger government controls. Fukuda Shigeru's successor as chief of the Religious Affairs Section, Shinohara Yoshio, articulated this complex bind in the *Yomiuri Shinbun* on 22 August 1950: "The Religious Corporations Ordinance deprived us of the right to supervise religions. We have, therefore, no legal grounds to control bogus religions."[65] While Bunce objected to the notion of government "supervision," the abuses perpetrated by some groups were undeniable. This is related to the third issue, the question of controls over "suspect" or "bogus" religions. Some representatives of established religious groups were in favor of government supervision within limits. For example, Reverend Kozaki Michio of the United Church of Japan stated in the Christian newspaper *Kirisutokyō Shinbun* on 1 March 1951:[66]

> As a principle, religion should not be supervised or controlled in view of freedom of faith.... From our point of view, provisions should be made for the qualifications of religious preachers. I think there should be some regulations regarding their character and educational background. Just as the candidates for ministry are examined for their qualifications so all religious bodies should be required by law to set standards for qualifying their preachers.

SCAP refused the first draft of the law proposed by the Education Ministry because it suggested that the government determine which groups had the right to become incorporated under the law on the grounds of their contribution to social welfare. SCAP held: "the social status of religious organizations should not be determined by the Government and it is doubtful that all the religions are necessarily contributing to social welfare. The purpose of the law should be limited to the maintenance of property of religious organizations."[67]

Faced with a draft that SCAP found unacceptable, the Religions and Cultural Resources Division undertook a series of talks with religious leaders, lawyers, and others to gather opinions about the proposed draft. But the opinion of the religious representatives seemed to concentrate on two areas: the protection of tax-exempt status and control of the new religions. Woodard, who was intimately involved in the drafting process and held numerous conferences at the offices of the Religions and Cultural Resources Division, states that because each party had to compromise, the final result was not particularly satisfactory, especially from SCAP's point of view.[68]

Despite Bunce's reservations, the Religious Corporations Law, which was passed into law on 3 April 1951, did not discriminate between religious organizations, nor did it provide specific provisions that would allow government authorities to act against "suspicious religions."[69] And although many representatives of established religions had been keen on some type of controls, others welcomed the restraint of the new law. As Woodard points out, an active and respected Christian leader intimated that he had been opposed to the law because he supposed that it was intended to control "suspicious religions." He said he changed his mind when he learned that the law did "not discriminate between religious organizations, whether large or small, new or old, true or false, good or bad." "I welcome this system," he concluded, "because we shall be free from control by the government that often dared to touch even the inner area of religion."[70] But when the enactment of the new law was reported, rumors spread about the difficulties groups would have in asserting independence once the law was in place. As a result, the numbers of groups registering under the Religious Corporations Ordinance boomed toward the end of the Occupation. During this time, the problems facing established religious groups did not diminish, and the criticism of new religions became more frequent. The cases of Makoto Kyōdan, the tax evasion cases of Sekai Kyūsei Kyō and Reiyūkai, and continuing reports of abuses by various new religions gave the proponents ample ammunition to propose the introduction of controls within the provisions of the law.

NEW RELIGIONS PRESENT A UNITED FRONT

As moves got underway to introduce the Religious Corporations Law, religious groups were encouraged by SCAP's Religions Division to form associations and collective organizations to allow them to have a unified voice and to negotiate more effectively with government offices. Established religious organizations had already formed the Sectarian Shinto Union (Kyōha Shinto Rengōkai), the Japan Buddhist Association, the Japan Christian Association (Nihon Kirisutokyō Rengōkai), and also the Japan Religions League.[71] However, new religions were quite isolated and had no formal association through which they could defend individual members.[72] What the new religions did share was a hostility that was articulated in print media reports.

Around mid-1950, plans to establish an organization specifically designed for new religions began to formulate. Some sources suggest that Woodard, acting in his capacity as the head of Special Projects and Religions Research within the Religions Division, actually initiated the proposal by bringing it up with the leader of PL Kyōdan.[73] However, a Religions Division report states that on 20 August 1950, a visitor to the division's office reported that Okada Mokichi, the leader of Sekai Kyūseikyō, had originally proposed the forming of such an alliance.[74] Okada was apparently inspired to propose the formation of such a group because of the "constant needling that postwar religious organizations have been receiving at the hands of the press." The writer of the SCAP report took a somewhat sarcastic tone, stating Okada's idea that if certain new religions banded together, "they could present a united front to their hecklers, and lumping together would somehow cause an air of sanctity to materialize the organizations that individually have received a rough going over by the papers and have taken the treatment lying down."[75]

Following after Jikōson and Kitamura Sayo, these founders and leaders sustained significant press criticism. But rather than deal with the issues they faced individually, they were attempting to present a united front. In Okada's view, not all new religions would be acceptable, "for applications to enter the Union would be subject to close scrutiny to eliminate those that are superstitious or abnormal in nature." By making such a declaration barring "superstitious or abnormal groups," Okada was no doubt hoping that the negative press attention he and his colleagues had attracted would be staved off.[76] This group was always intended to be exclusive. The writer of the report stated that "it is expected that before the associate members finally get around to taking the roll, they will have received the rough side of the tongue from one of their own; that magnificent unregenerated lady evangelist, Madame Sayo Kitamura."[77] Tenshō Kōtai Jingū Kyō never joined the association, and there are no indications in the SCAP records that show it was ever invited.

Conclusion

IN THIS BOOK I have discussed the multiple ways in which new religions, media and media workers, and various authorities—including government bureaucrats, police, psychologists, and other scholars—interacted, focusing specifically on two cases during the immediate postwar period. In order to make sense of media representations of new religions, I have insisted on taking a historical approach. This is because media, in reporting on new religions, often rely on stories related to groups of the past.

Focusing on Jiu and Tenshō Kōtai Jingū Kyō, I have argued that the print media of the Occupation and immediate postwar period portrayed the leaders and founders of these groups as being partly molded in the images of dominant media narratives of leaders of new religions of the past. These narratives promoted in print media generally held that the new religions promoted suspect and dangerous doctrines and that they engaged in socially abhorrent practices, including fraud, illicit sex, or healing techniques that defied accepted medical standards. Leaders and founders of new religions were presented predominantly as individuals who were usually mentally unstable, and their followers as uneducated people easily duped by superstitions or seriously lacking judgment because they had allowed themselves to be cheated by clever shysters. The narratives were repeated and adjusted in articles of major newspapers, magazines, and books.

Crucial to these representations were the interactions between the groups and the media. Jikōson and Kitamura Sayo were charismatic leaders who commanded the loyalty of their supporters and followers, and drew attention to themselves through their millennial predictions and actions designed to promote their respective causes. Although they did not develop their own media technologies in the same way as Ōmoto's Deguchi Onisaburō did, they nevertheless established their own "celebrity cultures" within their own relatively small circles of influence. The external media and their products, that is, media not related to or produced and vetted by the groups themselves, attempted to subvert their influence and represent them as notorious "celebrity gods"—people who were allegedly living gods, but whose lives were infused with the basest of human qualities.

Some people who are described as celebrities these days do not necessarily want to be in the public eye all the time. Faced with a messy divorce, a business deal gone bad, or unwelcome revelations from their past, they may try to avoid the media attention they normally appear to crave. Jikōson's case was similar in that she attempted to play a public relations game with the press using a genuine celebrity, Futabayama. Some, for example, relish media attention and will thrust themselves in situations they hope will gain them maximum exposure. Although she was hurt by negative press criticism, Kitamura Sayo was an example of this. Not all celebrities have the same reactions to media attention, and this applies to leaders of new religions as well.

The situation concerning media representation of new religions has changed radically since that period. As Ian Reader has argued, Aum Shinrikyō established a new paradigm for the relationship between new religions, the authorities, the media, and society.[1] Postwar Japanese society, which became committed to democracy and freedom of religion through the Occupation, has been forced to come to terms with a number of difficult issues in relation to religion, and particularly religious groups that appear to be "irrational" or out of step with modern society. In the immediate postwar period, the media continued with its self-constructed role as watchdog and public guardian at a time when the traditional guardian, the government, became restricted by legal boundaries.

Before 1995 and the sarin gas attack in Tokyo involving Aum, cases of new religions that were seen as problematic social movements that stood opposed to normative behaviors and institutions appeared periodically. Nakano Tsuyoshi has argued that when the groups connected to the Union (Federation) of New Religious Organizations of Japan were accepted into the Japan Religions League (Nihon Shūkyō Renmei) in 1952, new religious organizations acquired citizenship, at least in form, in the Japanese religious world.[2] Comprised of groups whose leaders were also reported negatively in the press, this organization marked a significant step toward their maturity within society. This step toward legitimization did not keep these organizations immune from scandals that involved media reporting. The new religion Risshō Kōseikai became embroiled in what was known as the "Yomiuri affair" in the mid 1950s. After an unfavorable radio broadcast on the group, the *Yomiuri Shinbun* launched a significant attack on the group which eventually led to involvement by the Ministry of Education and the Ministry of Justice. Up until the Aum affair, a number of new religions, including Risshō Kōseikai , developed educational institutions, became actively involved in politics and community activities, and were studied extensively by scholars.

Morioka Kiyomi argues that the Risshō Kōseikai case demonstrates that the authorities in the postwar period were more careful than in the past about actively interfering in the affairs of any religious group. Morioka claims that the mass media tended to spearhead attacks on groups, and from there the government would move in to impose controls, and "were supported by an intelligentsia with little patience for the freedom of belief when this principle is applied to the new religions."[3] Morioka's perspective is important because it does raise the issue of media-generated campaigns that characterized cases like Renmonkyō. It also indicates the reticence of the authorities, which has been called a "taboo," to get too closely involved in affairs of religious groups. This became an important discussion point in the wake of the Aum incident. Takagi Hiroo claimed that government authorities had become loath to investigate religious groups in the postwar period because they might be accused of official interference. However, the role of media does need to be considered in more detail, given the vast changes that have occurred. Since the Occupation and immediate postwar periods, the Aum Shinrikyō incident and its aftermath have arguably had the most significant effect on Japan's religious landscape.

In considering journalists and representations of new religions in the immediate postwar period, Murakami Naoyuki holds that Ōya Sōichi and other journalists attempted to present a version of "how civil society should be," and religion (and new religions in particular) became the media's "necessary scapegoats." Murakami's broader argument is that one role of the media during this period was as arbiters of social meaning and value, with Ōya Sōichi representing the standard which other media workers strove to achieve at the time. Ōya's writings on new religions are aimed at providing a cure or answer to the fundamental moral concerns he saw affecting postwar society.

As noted in Chapter 7, Murakami labels Ōya the "founder of Japan's mass media religion" and asserts that the "hatred" for religion that journalists in the modern period displayed results from their blind obedience to the "secular religion of the media." Although criticizing Ōya is essentially a taboo subject within journalism today, Murakami argues that this is an important issue that needs addressing.[4] Irrespective of the validity of this argument, it cannot be transferred to the contemporary situation without some adjustments. Although it is true that there were dominant narratives about new religions that were presented in print media of many varieties during that period, the idea of a "hatred" for religion in the aftermath of the Aum incident is questionable.

Journalist Nishide Takeshi offers some valuable perspectives regarding media and religion in the postwar period up to and including the Aum incident. Nishide worked for Kyōdō News Service—which supplies domestic and international information for Japanese newspapers, radio, and television—during the Aum incident. In acknowledging that newspapers like the *Yomiuri Shinbun* did launch attacks on new religions in the immediate postwar period, he believes that this reflects the change between "modern" Japan (from the Meiji period until 1945) and "democratic" Japan. While media in the modern period was characterized by active efforts to influence how society should function—which may be viewed in terms of the "watchdog" and "servant" dichotomy—media in the postwar democracy necessarily had to adjust to new circumstances. While the role of "servant" to government and other authorities was ostensibly removed with the change to democracy, some elements of the media continue to watch over society.

Nishide argues that the reporting of religion is characterized by a lack of education on religious issues by journalists. At the time of writing, there are virtually no reporters who identify themselves as being religion specialists. There is one religious press club in Japan based in Kyoto which has one representative from the major media companies who stay for one year before being transferred to another desk. This club generally reports on festivals connected with temples and about the conflicts between the Nishi Honganji and Higashi Honganji temple complexes of the Jōdo Shinshū sect. He argues that in general people working in the mass media have no knowledge of religion, and they do not have the inclination to check out religious groups. The easiest way for journalists to deal with religion, he holds, is to avoid reporting about religion at all. He states that "the tendency within the media in postwar Japan is to act as if religion does not exist."[5]

Nishide's comments echo those of former *Nihon Keizai Shinbun* reporter Kawakami Tsuneo, who indicates that religion is generally covered by nonspecialist journalists working in the newspaper sections covering society (*shakaibu*) or art and science (*gakugeibu*). Kawakami argues that new religions became the subject of journalistic attacks in the immediate postwar period because the media was influenced by rationalism and modernization, which was characterized by the notion that "superstitions" promoted by new religions held back Japan's progress. He holds that major newspapers presented exposés on new religions until around the mid-1950s, which was when weekly magazines began to appear. These publications, together with monthly magazines, generally focus on scandals and rumors concerning new religions, and have been a staple part of their realm since that time. Significantly, large newspapers rely on money from advertising and subscriptions; reporting scandals will not generate income for these publications whereas they will for weekly and monthly magazines.[6]

The comments of these former journalists are important when considering the Aum incident. After the gas attack, multiple aspects of the Aum case were reported obsessively in the print and broadcast media. As the investigations continued, shocking revelations of kidnapping, drugging, torture, poisoning, and murder of apostates unfolded. The press were on hand to record the murder of one of Aum Shinrikyō's top leaders, Murai Hideo, in April 1995, and also the arrest of Asahara Shōkō in May. Although the intensity of the reporting had subsided by mid-June, Aum Shinrikyō-related stories continued to appear at the end of the year. The public naturally demanded protection from further attacks and strongly supported any action by the authorities to protect them from such dangerous religious groups. Thus the government felt compelled to act and immediately tried to implement various legal changes.

Within the context of a "taboo" on government authorities investigating suspicious activities by religious groups, Maki Tarō, former editor of the weekly magazine *Sandē Mainichi*, claimed that it was not only the authorities but also the media that feared being accused of persecuting religious groups.[7] Kōfuku no Kagaku's strident criticisms of the Kōdansha publishing company contributed to this. However, both Nishide and Kawakami argue that most media organizations treat religious stories very carefully. In stressing the lack of understanding about religion in general, Kawakami holds that media organizations subscribe to the principle of "no incident, no story." In Nishide's rendering, there is not so much a taboo that exists but rather a gap between religious groups' doctrines and the media's "secularist, neutral stance." Given this, the model of media as acting in a "watchdog" or "servant" capacity does not apply to the contemporary situation. While it could be applied to the Renmonkyō and Ōmoto cases, it has less explanatory value when considering cases in the postwar period.

These perspectives suggest that the notion that a collective "hatred" exists within media toward religion cannot be sustained. What is more feasible is that the general lack of education in Japanese society in the postwar period about the role of religions in society is reflected in media organizations that are required to report on religious issues when they appear. The media, which supplies images and words that can influence the authorities and the public, assumes an educational role in cases where their knowledge is limited.

The shocking events of 1995 and the images of Aum Shinrikyō were so deeply engrained in the public consciousness that when the press reported on other religious groups that displayed unusual behavior, the image of Aum and Asahara as a crazed guru in the public consciousness played a major part.

Aum's impact was also evident in an incident in May 2003 involving a hitherto little-known group known as Pana Wave. Pana Wave was a millennial group whose founder predicted that after her own death, environmental disasters would occur and be followed by global destruction. The organization claimed to be the "scientific arm" of Chino Shōhō, a small religious group founded by Chino Yūko. Chino had been associated with the new religion GLA. When Chino became ill in the early 1990s, the group established Pana Wave Laboratory in order to conduct research into electromagnetic radiation, which the members felt was the cause of her illness. Members began to wander around western Japan in search of a location that was free from electromagnetic radiation. They wore white clothing, drove white vehicles, and swathed their camping sites in white cloth.

The story of Pana Wave broke a week after prosecutors argued for imposing the death penalty on Asahara. Media attention was triggered by a series of articles in the weekly magazine *Shūkan Bunshun*. On April 25 the magazine labeled some facilities owned by Pana Wave "satyams," a Sanskrit word for truth that Aum Shinrikyō had used to identify its places of worship and the laboratories where members produced the gas that was used in the subway attack. But the story also added the claim that Pana Wave members launched an aborted attempt in March 2003 to kidnap a nonhuman celebrity, a stray seal nicknamed Tama-chan.

Tama-chan first appeared in Tokyo's heavily polluted Tama River during August 2002, and became very popular among schoolchildren and others who fell for its "cuteness." The news media followed the story whenever Tama-chan surfaced occasionally, and the seal also became a cause célèbre for environmentalists. Pana Wave members released an announcement in early May that they believed by rescuing Tama-chan global destruction could be averted, and Pana Wave's leader later claimed that "saving" Tama-chan was essential in their quest to save the earth. Other media organizations quickly picked up the story, and on 1 May the chief of the National Police Agency (NPA), Satō Hide-hiko, announced that the group looked strange and resembled Aum in its early days. He did not go into specifics and provided no evidence. Thereupon the Pana Wave story saturated the news for two weeks as Japanese and international media organizations gathered en masse at the itinerant group's temporary parking site.

Intense coverage of the group's movements followed, stirring up public fears and memories of the gas attack in Tokyo eight years earlier.[8] On 14 May, some three hundred police investigators swooped down on twelve Pana Wave facilities located around the country as well as on the seventeen white vehicles that made up the cavalcade. After collecting around four hundred pieces of evidence, the police charged the group with possessing three falsely registered vehicles. Once this investigation was over, the story of Pana Wave quickly disappeared from the media.

In the Pana Wave case, Nishide Takeshi notes, large newspapers and other major media organs were careful not to report about the religious aspects or beliefs of Pana Wave in a positive or negative manner. In other words, they maintained a "secularist, neutral" stance, which is a far cry from media positions in previous eras.

Amid the overheated stories about the potential dangers of groups that "resembled Aum in its early days," a dissenting voice came from within the media's own ranks. Egawa Shōko, the crusading, independent journalist who wrote extensively about Aum, spoke out in the major newspaper *Asahi Shinbun* on 10 May against the media, comparing them to paparazzi who chased after the latest celebrities. She also criticized the NPA chief's "impressionistic meanderings" connecting Pana Wave to Aum which, she claimed, were way off the mark. She wrote that if the authorities were serious about looking at a group that "resembled Aum in its early days" they should concentrate their energies on investigating Aum's latest incarnation, Aleph. She reminded readers that Aum Shinrikyō in its early days certainly looked strange with Asahara's followers dancing around in elephant masks and singing unusual songs, but the truly fearful thing about Aum Shinrikyō was that it kept its dangerous aspects cleverly hidden from view through manipulation of the media and the law. In contrast, she held, Pana Wave's use of the media smacked of amateurism, and its attempt to appropriate the image of Tama-chan for public relations was naïve and ham-fisted. Egawa's appeal in a major newspaper to the media in general is significant because of her extensive experience dealing with Aum Shinrikyō. Nevertheless, her voice was barely audible among the media narratives that loudly condemned groups "like Aum."

In the case of Aum's Asahara Shōkō, the media representations of him as an insane leader with an insatiable desire to control the world are borne out in the low levels of trust in "religion" the Japanese people continue to hold. The complex interweaving of religious groups and media, combined with the actions of authorities and a general lack of education about religion, reveals a significant dilemma for Japan that began with the Occupation and still remains unresolved: how to maintain a commitment to democracy and freedom of religion at the same time as upholding those principles for religious groups that flaunt social conventions (or commit serious crimes, as in the case of Aum). Another equally complex issue for concerned observers is how to read, absorb, and analyze the media in such cases, given the general lack of background and interest many journalists have concerning religious issues and the media's propensity to search for past stories in order to explain leaders of new religions. While media literacy skills are not generally part of scholars' toolkits, the recognition of how media can shape religion and how, in turn, religion can shape media is a crucial issue that continues to have significance.

Notes

Details of SCAP records are listed in the bibliography.

INTRODUCTION

1. The piece was published a year later in his book *Shūkyō o nonoshiru* [Scolding religion] Ōya Sōichi, *Ōya Sōichi zenshū*, vol. 4, 21–25.

2. For example, questions arise over the precise point that a new religion becomes "established" and, indeed, who has the authority to determine this. Furthermore, it is questionable whether "old" new religions such as Tenrikyō, which developed in the mid-nineteenth century, can be equated with newer groups, such as Sōka Gakkai, Risshō Kōseikai , or Sekai Kyūsei Kyō. These are groups that have significant histories themselves. While these may be vexing questions for scholars, at bottom the very categories that are used may be seen as downright offensive to people who belong to groups that some might label "new religions." When I visited Tenshō Kōtai Jingū Kyō's headquarters in Tabuse, Yamaguchi prefecture, on 16 December 1998, two informants, who requested anonymity, balked at the term "new religions" in relation to their group because they insisted that while the group was new compared to other religions, the founder's teachings were universal and not her invention.

3. Hayashi Makoto, "Religion in the Modern Period," 214.

4. Inoue Nobutaka, "Masukomi to shinshūkyō" in *Shinshūkyō jiten*, 516–18. For an example of print media criticism of a new religion in the Meiji period see Takeda Dōshō, "The Fall of Renmonkyō"; see also Oku Takenori, *Renmonkyō suibō shi* and *Sukyandaru no Meiji*, 43–80; and Inoue Nobutaka, *Shinshūkyō no kaidoku*, 53–81. For arguments about the mostly negative print media criticism of new religions in the immediate postwar period, see Kishimoto Hideo, *Sengo no shūkyō to shakai*, 212, and Morioka Kiyomi, "Attacks on the New Religions." For an opinion about press criticism of new religions from the perspective of a SCAP Religions Division official, see SCAP #20. Helen Hardacre provides a brief discussion on new religions and Japanese media in "After Aum."

5. *Jakyō* was recently used by the Chinese government to denounce Falun Gong. See John Wong & William T. Liu, *The Mystery of China's Falun Gong*, 31. See also Danny Schechter, *Falun Gong's Challenge to China*.

6. SCAP, meaning the Supreme Commander for the Allied Powers, also referred to General Douglas MacArthur, the commander-in-chief of the Occupation force.

7. H. Neill McFarland, *The Rush Hour of the Gods*. McFarland cites Inui Takashi (237), whose book *Nihon wa kurutteru* includes a chapter by Saki Akio entitled "Rush Hour of the Gods." The frequently cited image of religions mushrooming like "bamboo shoots after the rain" must have resonated with the spirit of the times

because people spoke of living a "bamboo-shoot existence" (*take no ko seikatsu,* selling one's clothes to earn a living) during the Occupation.

8. Chris Rojek, *Celebrity*, 18.

9. Tenshō Kōtai Jingū Kyō, *Seisho* vol. 1.

10. Catherine Wessinger, *How the Millennium Comes Violently*, 2.

11. Michael Barkun, *Disaster and the Millennium*, 1.

12. Among Yasumaru's works are *Nihon no kindaika to minshū shisō, Deguchi Nao,* and *Bunmeika no keiken.*

13. Inoue Nobutaka, *Japanese College Students' Attitudes Towards Religion,* 20.

14. Hardacre, "Aum Shinrikyō and the Japanese Media," 171–74.

15. Stuart A. Wright, "Media Coverage of Unconventional Religion," 101.

16. Hardacre, "Aum Shinrikyō and the Japanese Media," 184–85.

17. Ian Reader, *Religious Violence in Contemporary Japan.*

Beat (Kitano) Takeshi, one of Japan's foremost media personalities, is a comedian, actor, and director whose films are widely known in the West. Aum was not the only new religious movement in which he displayed some interest. In the 1980s, he appeared in two feature-length films for television based on two widely criticized groups in Japan, Iesu no Hakobune (Yagi, *Iesu no hakobune*) and Jehovah's Witnesses (Yagi, *Settoku*). Kitano still appears on television programs that discuss supernatural phenomenon, although he is not associated with any particular religious group or philosophy publicly.

18. This group, founded in 1986, changed its official English name from "The Institute for Research in Human Happiness" to "Happy Science" in 2008.

19. Watanabe Manabu, "Reactions to the Aum Affair," 37–38.

20. Personal interview, 27 January 2010, Tokyo.

21. Reader, *Religious Violence in Contemporary Japan,* 34.

22. Stewart M. Hoover, "Introduction," in *Practicing Religion in the Age of the Media,* 1.

23. William Gamson and Gadi Wolfsfeld, "Movements and Media as Interacting Systems," 115.

24. Ibid., 116–17.

25. Thanks to Erica Baffelli for pointing this out.

26. Trevor Astley, "The Transformation of a Recent Japanese New Religion," 371.

27. Shimazono Susumu, "Kyōso to shūkyōteki shidōsha sūhai no kenkyū kadai," in *Kyōso to sono shūhen,* 27.

28. Nancy K. Stalker, *Prophet Motive,* 12–13.

29. Ibid., 3.

30. Shimazono, "Kyōso to shūkyōteki shidōsha," 27.

31. Daniel J. Boorstin, *The Image,* 57.

32. Graeme Turner *Understanding Celebrity*, 5.

33. Graeme Turner, Frances Bonner, and P. David Marshall. *Fame Games*, 11.

34. Marshall, *Celebrity and Power*, 71.

35. Turner, *Understanding Celebrity*, 10.

36. Richard Schickel, *Intimate Strangers*.

37. Neal Gabler, *Winchell*.

38. Leo Braudy, *The Frenzy of Renown*.

39. Tom Payne, *Fame*.

40. Rojek, *Celebrity*, 16.

41. Ibid., 10.

42. Max Weber, "The Nature of Charismatic Authority and its Routinization," 49.

43. Marshall, "Introduction to part one" in *The Celebrity Culture Reader*, 19.

44. Rojek, *Celebrity*.

45. John Frow. "Is Elvis a God?"; Rojek, *Celebrity*, 51–99.

46. Stephen Prothero, *American Jesus*, 108–120.

47. Malcolm Boyd, *Christ and Celebrity Gods*, 17.

48. Ibid., 11.

49. "Why do we have celebrity gods?", *USA Today*, Faith and Reason section <http://content.usatoday.com/communities/religion/post/2009/06/68492944/1> (26 June 2009); accessed 26 July 2009).

50. "Celebrity gods: The religion of stardom", ReligionLink, <http://www.religionlink.com/tip_100105.php>; accessed 27 January 2011.

51. Stalker, *Prophet Motive*, chapter four ("Exhibitionist Tendencies: Visual Technologies of Proselytization").

I RENMONKYŌ AND THE MEIJI PRESS

1. James Huffman, *Creating a Public*.

2. Janine Sawada, *Practical Pursuits*, 236.

3. Maria Hsia Chang, *Falun Gong*, 43–46. These terms are still used by the Chinese government. *Jakyō* has appeared on the Chinese embassy's Japanese website to describe the Falun Gong movement ("Jakyō 'Hōrinkō' no kigai [The harm of Falun Gong; undated page] <http://www.china-embassy.or.jp/jpn/zt/xjflg/> (accessed 23 July 2009), while the group has been labeled an "evil cult" on the English-language website of the Chinese embassy in Israel ("Sheer lies from an evil cult" <http://il.chineseembassy.org/eng/sggg/t252750.htm> (accessed 23 July 2009).

4. James Ketelaar, *Of Heretics and Martyrs*, 42.

5. The issue of what constitutes "religion" (*shūkyō*) in the Japanese context has been the subject of recent academic discussion, with important questions being

raised over the transferring of Western-based notions of religion as opposed to how actual practices were perceived. Jason Ānanda Josephson, citing Shimazono Susumu and Isomae Jun'ichi, states that "in the pre-Meiji period Buddhism was largely understood as something one did, not something one believed. It was only under the influence of the Western concept of religion that Buddhism became a commitment to a series of propositions rather than rituals." Jason Ānanda Josephson, "When Buddhism Became a 'Religion'," 148.

6. Ketelaar, *Of Heretics and Martyrs*, 50–51. In 1880, article 426 of the Penal Code threatened criminal prosecution to those who mislead people and profit from the use of spells.

7. Hardacre, *Shintō and the State*, 64.

8. Sheldon Garon, *Molding Japanese Minds*, 63.

9. Article 28: Japanese subjects shall, within limits not prejudicial to peace and order, and not antagonistic to their duties as subjects enjoy freedom of religious belief.

10. Article 3: The Emperor is sacred and inviolable.

Article 4: The Emperor is the head of the Empire, combining in Himself the rights of sovereignty, and exercises them, according to the provisions of the present Constitutions.

11. Incidently, in 1897 Uchimura joined *Yorozu Chōhō*, which had become Japan's largest newspaper and played a major role in Renmonkyō's downfall. His career in journalism did not last long though, when he resigned in 1903 due to conflicts over his pacifist views and those of the publisher in the lead up to the Russo-Japanese War (1904–1905).

12. For more on Inoue and his work, see Josephson 2006.

13. Yasumaru, *Bunmeika no keiken*, 338–39.

14. Garon, *Molding Japanese Minds*, 81.

15. Hardacre, *Shintō and the State*, 51.

16. Ibid., 53.

17. Ibid., 82.

18. Ibid., 58.

19. Takeda, "The Fall of Renmonkyō," 33–39.

20. Ibid., 27.

21. Ibid., 34.

22. Ibid., 26–28.

23. There are three different accounts of how many churches Renmonkyō held by 1894. Taiseikyō records show the number as thirty-four, *Yorozu Chōhō* newspaper counted thirty-seven, while a descendant of Shimamura claimed there were ninety-two churches. Whatever the correct figure is, it is clear that the group achieved remarkable growth in a very short time (Ibid., 29).

24. Huffman, *Creating a Public*, 2–9.

25. Satō Takumi, *Gendai media shi*, 86–87.

26. Huffman, *Creating a Public*, 8.

27. Ibid., 374–75.

28. Susan Pharr, "Introduction," 6–7 and 11–12.

29. Huffman, *Creating a Public*, 371.

30. John Pierson, *Tokutomi Sohō, 1863–1957*, 265.

31. Richard Mitchell, *Censorship in Imperial Japan*, 43.

32. Huffman, *Creating a Public*, 375–76.

33. Sawada, *Practical Pursuits*, 246.

34. Tamaki Akira, *Goshippu to shūbun*, 104.

35. Benedict Anderson, *Imagined Communities*, 6–7.

36. Ibid., 37.

37. Huffman, *Creating a Public*, 194.

38. Yamamoto Taketoshi, *Shinbun kisha no tanjō*, 186.

39. Oku, *Renmonkyō suibō shi*, 113.

40. Huffman, *Creating a Public*, 212.

41. Ibid., 371.

42. Yamamoto, *Shinbun kisha no tanjō*, 196.

43. Huffman, *Creating a Public*, 194.

44. Takeda, "The Fall of Renmonkyō," 39–40.

45. Ibid., 42.

46. Ibid.

47. Oku, *Sukyandaru no Meiji*, 172.

48. Ibid., 165.

49. Ibid., 157–58.

50. Takeda, "The Fall of Renmonkyō," 39–40; see also Oku, *Renmonkyō suibō shi*, 114–15.

51. Ibid., 44.

52. Ibid., 43; Sawada, *Practical Pursuits*, 253–54.

53. Itō Yōjirō, *Inshi jūichi kyōkai*, cited in Oku, *Sukyandaru no Meiji*, 144. Oku states that despite its title, the book dealt with twenty new religions of the period.

54. Takeda, "The Fall of Renmonkyō," 45.

55. Takeda indicates that the *Kaishin Shinbun*'s position on Renmonkyō and its subsequent backdown was one of the factors that contributed to the paper's demise a few years later ("The Fall of Renmonkyō," 44).

56. Oku, *Sukyandaru no Meiji*, 129–30.

57. Inoue, *Shinshūkyō no kaidoku*, 103.

58. Takeda, "The Fall of Renmonkyō," 47–48.

59. Sawada, *Practical Pursuits*, 258.

60. Ibid., 102–43

61. Takeda, "The Fall of Renmonkyō," 26.

62. Ibid., 51.

63. Murakami Shigeyoshi, *Japanese Religion in the Modern Century*, 51.

64. Hayashi Makoto, "Religion in the Modern Period," 208–12.

2 DEGUCHI ONISABURŌ AS A PREWAR MODEL

1. Ōya, *Ōya Sōichi zenshū*, 10. Although the material concerning the prewar period was originally published in 1931 the publication source is not mentioned in this volume, which is a collection of his writings on religion throughout his career.

2. Garon, *Molding Japanese Minds*, 64.

3. Ibid., 63.

4. Ibid., 66.

5. Yasumaru, *Nihon no kindaika to minshū shisō*; *Deguchi Nao*. Miyata Noboru, *Shūmatsukan no minzokugaku*.

6. Stalker, *Prophet Motive*, 43.

7. Inoue, *Shinshūkyō no kaidoku*, 108.

8. For details on Asano, see Hardacre, "Asano Wasaburō."

9. Stalker, *Prophet Motive*, 87.

10. Ibid., 59.

11. Ibid., 80.

12. Ibid., 97.

13. Inoue, *Shinshūkyō no kaidoku*, 109.

14. Stalker, *Prophet Motive*, 98.

15. Ibid.

16. Hardacre, "Asano Wasaburō," 146.

17. The comprehensive Newspaper Law was passed in 1909 and was to remain in place until 1945. Among the various restrictions imposed, judicial power to terminate a paper remained, and Home Ministry bureaucrats were authorized to ban specific journal editions and seize all copies without having to prosecute the offending publisher. Among the law's principle tenets were lists of forbidden subjects including the publication of material subversive of public order or manners and morals. If a publication broke this rule, the Home Minister could terminate publication. See Gregory J. Kasza, *The State and the Mass Media in Japan*, 15–19.

18. Inoue, *Shinshūkyō no kaidoku*, 128.

19. Ibid., 129.

20. Richard Young, "From Gokyō-dōgen to Bankyō-dōkon," 273.

21. Ibid.

22. Stephan Feuchtwang, "Spiritual Recovery," 67–71.

23. Inoue, *Shinshūkyō no kaidoku*, 111.

24. Tsushima Michihito, "Emperor and World Renewal," 80–81.

25. Garon, *Molding Japanese Minds*, 74.

26. Tsushima, "Emperor and World Renewal," 81.

27. The former Tenri Honmichi leaders began their religious activities again after the surrender. They became the subject of a police investigation reminiscent of prewar years in 1949. The Special Investigation Bureau (Tokubetsu shinsa kyoku) of the Office of the Attorney General was involved in the investigation of this group. Although SCAP's Religions Division and the Government Section attempted to verify numerous claims from new religions about police investigations, apparently they could not stop the illegal investigations. The group became simply known as Honmichi. See Woodard, *The Allied Occupation of Japan*, 182, note 1.

28. Garon, *Molding Japanese Minds*, 68–69.

29. Ibid., 77.

30. Sato Tatsuya, "Rises and Falls of Clinical Psychology in Japan," 137.

31. Inoue, *Shinshūkyō no kaidoku*, 120–21.

32. This term was basically synonymous with "pseudo religions," the term preferred by the government bureaucracy (ibid., 121).

33. Garon, *Molding Japanese Minds*, 79.

34. The leaders of Hito no Michi and Seichō no Ie were also labeled in this fashion by Nakamura.

35. Inoue, *Shinshūkyō no kaidoku*, 128.

36. Garon, *Molding Japanese Minds*, 80.

37. Inoue, *Shinshūkyō no kaidoku*, 131.

38. Ōkuma Hideo, *Hadaka no Ōya Sōichi*, 223.

39. Ōya, *Ōya Sōichi zenshū*, 312.

40. Ibid., 3.

41. "Newly arisen religions" was a term that was used occasionally in the press in the prewar period. It was picked up again during the Occupation period.

42. Ōya, *Ōya Sōichi zenshū*, 42–43.

43. Ibid., 41–42.

44. Ibid., 43.

45. He published a series of articles on the experience. This collection is entitled "Deguchi Onisaburō *hōmon nikki*" (Diary of a visit to Deguchi Onisaburō). Ōya, *Ōya Sōichi zenshū*, 117–46.

46. Cited in Ōkuma, *Hadaka no Ōya Sōichi*, 226–30.

47. Stalker, *Prophet Motive*, 178.

48. Morioka, "Attacks on the New Religions," 309.

49. Kawamoto Saburō, "Ōya Sōichi," 259.

50. Matsuura Sōzō, "Ōya Sōichi," 137.

51. Inoue, *Shinshūkyō no kaidoku*, 130–31.

52. Cited in Garon, *Molding Japanese Minds*, 79.

53. Sakamoto Koremaru. "Shūkyō dantaihō no zengo," 484.

3 THE BIRTH OF TWO CELEBRITY GODS

1. Tsushima Michihito, "Haisen to yonaoshi 1," 343.

2. SCAP #1.

3. SCAP #2. The date of the interview is not recorded.

4. Carmen Blacker, *The Catalpa Bow*, 129.

5. Ellen Schattschneider, *Immortal Wishes*, 31.

6. Blacker, *The Catalpa Bow*, 204.

7. When I interviewed Katsuki on two occasions (in Yokohama in June 1998 and February 1999), he was in his mid-90s and led a small group of people who considered Nagaoka (whom they called Jikōson) to be a great leader and a living god. They believed Katsuki himself was an *ikigami*.

8. Personal interview, Fukuoka, 6 August 2009.

9. Tsushima, "Haisen to yonaoshi 1," 343.

10. Before he left Ōmoto, Ōshima was Deguchi Onisaburō's secretary, and he later became the president of Tōyō University. Ōta led the "Chrysanthemum Society" (Kikkakai), a spiritual research group that splintered from Ōmoto in 1930 yet continued to receive funding from the organization. Tsushima "Haisen to yonaoshi 1," 340.

11. Go Seigen, *Go Seigen kaisō roku*.

12. Tian Zhuangzhuang, dir., *Go Seigen*. This film tells Go's story from his perspective, and although the details in some parts of the film are at variance with other recorded sources, it clearly shows his ultimate disillusionment with Jiu in the late 1940s.

13. Go, *Go Seigen kaisō roku*, 101.

14. Tsushima "Haisen to yonaoshi 1," 339. Securing mineral resources was of vital concern to the nation because it was trying to consolidate its military capabilities after years of conflict on the Chinese mainland.

15. Ibid.

16. An example of Kōdō Daikyō's activities was an attempt to gather funds in order to establish mining and smelting facilities in a mountain in Nagano prefecture. Go, *Go Seigen kaisō roku*, 103.

17. Tsushima "Haisen to yonaoshi 1," 340–41.

18. One explanation of the name "Jiu" was offered to a SCAP official by members of Jiu during an interview. They stated that *Ji* 璽 meant "emperor's seal," which is a symbol of the throne, and *u* 宇 referred to "house" in this context. Jiu therefore can be read to mean palace or imperial shrine. See SCAP 1.

19. Tsushima, "Haisen to yonaoshi 1," 340–41.

20. Ibid., 342.

21. SCAP I.

22. Murakami Shigeyoshi, *Shūkyō no Shōwa shi*, 83.

23. Tsushima "Haisen to yonaoshi I," 345–46.

24. Monbu Daijin Kanbō Shūmuka, "Jikōson shisatsu hōkoku."

25. Tsushima, "Haisen to yonaoshi I," 344.

26. Personal interview, Katsuki Tokujirō, 28 February 1999, Yokohama.

27. Personal interview, Yamada Senta, 6 August 2009, Fukuoka.

28. Personal interview, Katsuki Tokujirō, 28 February 1999, Yokohama.

29. Tsushima, "Haisen to yonaoshi I," 347–48.

30. Katsuki, "Jiu to Futabayama," 13 (my page numbering).

31. Tsushima, "Haisen to yonaoshi I," 345–46.

32. SCAP's Religions Division translated *tenji shōmyō* (天璽照妙) as "The Celestial Jewel Shines Mysteriously." See SCAP I. According to Yamada Senta, the character *ji* 璽 within the context of the prayer indicates the precious nature of the universe that can shine a light on all humanity (telephone interview, 11 February 2010).

33. Personal interview, Katsuki Tokujirō, 28 February 1999, Yokohama.

34. Tsushima, "Haisen to yonaoshi I," 349.

35. Ibid., 347.

36. Go, *Go Seigen kaisō roku*, 128.

37. Tsushima, "Haisen to yonaoshi I," 349–50.

38. Ibid., 348.

39. Ibid., 352. Jikōson's status among her followers was confirmed by Yamada Senta, who told me of his experience with her.

40. Personal interview, Katsuki Tokujirō, 28 February 1999, Yokohama.

41. Go, *Go Seigen kaisō roku*, 119. Fifty years later, in an article in the *Asahi Shinbun* (27 September 1998), Go appeared to maintain the same view, commenting that he had fallen completely under Jikōson's spell during the time he was associated with the group. The film *Go Seigen* (Tian, dir.) similarly depicts the situation in this manner, which is not surprising given that Go cooperated closely with the director.

42. SCAP I.

43. Katsuki Tokujirō, "Jiu to Futabayama," 28.

44. Personal interview, Yamada Senta, 25 January 2010, Fukuoka.

45. Tsushima, "Haisen to yonaoshi I," 353.

46. He was detained for a longer period than Jikōson at that time as well. Yet no evidence was released by the police on either occasion relating to Katsuki's guilt.

47. Paragraph 1-j of SCAPIN 448 ("The Shinto Directive"): "The use in official writings of the terms 'Greater East Asia War' (Dai Toa Sonso [*sic*]), 'The Whole

World under One Roof" (Hakko Ichi-u), and all other terms whose connotation in Japanese is inextricably connected with State Shinto, militarism, and ultranationalism is prohibited and will cease immediately." SCAP-A, 468.

48. Personal interview, Yamada Senta, 8 August 2009, Yufuin, Kyushu.

49. Tsushima, "Haisen to yonaoshi 1," 352.

50. *Seisho* is a homonym of the Bible (*Seisho* 聖書).

51. Tenshō Kōtai Jingū Kyō, *Seisho* vol. 1, 5.

52. Blacker, *The Catalpa Bow*, 134.

53. Tenshō Kōtai Jingū Kyō, *Seisho* vol. 1, 11–16.

54. Ibid., 20–24.

55. Ibid., 35–36.

56. Ibid., 38–42. The translations of *shinkō* and *gasshō* and the other terms used by Kitamura are taken from Tenshō Kōtai Jingū Kyō's official English publications, *Divine Manifestation* and *The Prophet of Tabuse*.

57. According to Kitamura, *na* is "name," *myō* is "wonderful," and both *hō* and *kyō* mean "sutra." *Na-myō-hō-renge-kyō* means that "a humble woman connects both man and God with the heavenly sutra." Kitamura Sayo, "Tenshō Kōtai Jingū Kyō," 37. Ono Yasuhiro explains that, for Kitamura, *na-mu* (南無) of the Nichiren tradition meant that "the South was lost"—in other words the Japanese army had failed in its southern invasion—and that the teaching of *myōhō-renge-kyō* (妙法連結経) would appear in the time of world renewal. Ono Yasuhiro, "Tenshō Kōtai Jingū Kyō," 174.

58. Stalker, *Prophet Motive*, 54–55.

59. John Dower mistakenly labeled the group "Amaterasu Kōtai Jingūkyō" in *Embracing Defeat*, 307.

60. SCAP 2. The writer of this report argues that Kitamura incorporated ideas from Tenrikyō doctrine, such as using the term "muddy sea" (*doro umi*) in her prophecies. The report also notes similarities between Kitamura's concept of the six worldly desires and the eight misbehaviors (*yatsu no kokoro chigae*) of Tenrikyō doctrine.

61. Tenshō Kōtai Jingū Kyō, *The Prophet of Tabuse*, 25–26. See Tenshō Kōtai Jingū Kyō, *Seisho* vol. 1, 61.

62. Dower, *Embracing Defeat*, 303–304.

63. Nishiyama Shigeru and Fujii Takeshi, "The Propagation and Spread of Tenshō Kōtai Jingū Kyō," 141.

64. Tenshō Kōtai Jingū Kyō, *Seisho* vol. 1, 63.

65. Blacker, *The Catalpa Bow*, 135.

66. Takezawa Shōichirō, "Kyōdō tai no keisei to karisuma no keishō," 9.

67. Sometimes the *Seisho* account details people who stay well clear of Kitamura and others who appear desperate to hear her teachings, no matter how uncomfortable they are for the listener.

68. Tenshō Kōtai Jingū Kyō, *The Prophet of Tabuse*, 39–46.

69. Tenshō Kōtai Jingū Kyō, *Seisho* vol. 1, 144; Tenshō Kōtai Jingū Kyō, *The Prophet of Tabuse*, 68.

70. Kitamura, "Tenshō Kōtai Jingū Kyō," 41. Kishi wrote a glowing appraisal in a magazine called *Fēsu* (Face) in April 1965 ("Gendaijin ni fukaketsuna shinri o toku" [Teaching indispensible truths for people of today]). He cited his release from prison after three years of incarceration, just as she had predicted. However, not all her predictions were quite so accurate. She told him that he would be remembered as being a great reformer of Japan, which is not the case.

71. Dan Kurzman, *Kishi and Japan*, 222–23.

72. This information was provided by three followers (who requested anonymity) during a personal interview conducted on 15 December 1998 at the headquarters of Tenshō Kōtai Jingū Kyō in Tabuse, Yamaguchi.

73. Kitamura, "Tenshō Kōtai Jingū Kyō," 41.

4 BUREAUCRACY, RELIGION, AND THE PRESS UNDER THE OCCUPATION

1. Dower (*Embracing Defeat*, 73) points out that the term "Allied Occupation" is a misnomer because the United States alone determined basic policy and exercised decisive command over all aspects of the Occupation.

2. Two years later SCAP's Religions Division (whose Japanese name, Shūkyōka, is not to be confused with the pre-1945 government agency of the same name) merged with the Arts and Monuments Division to form the Religions and Cultural Resources Division (henceforth, the Religions Division).

3. Woodard, *The Allied Occupation of Japan*, 9–10.

4. Dower, *Embracing Defeat*, 27.

5. Wilton Dillon, personal interview, 27 September 1999, Washington DC. Dr. Dillon, who was at that time Senior Scholar Emeritus with the Smithsonian Institution, worked as a press officer for SCAP and knew Nichols personally.

6. A collection of Woodard's materials, including correspondence, manuscripts, Allied Occupation documents, research files, film, and audiotapes, is held in the University of Oregon Libraries.

7. Ibid., xv.

8. Wilhelmus H. M. Creemers, "*The Allied Occupation of Japan 1945–1952 and Japanese Religions* by William P. Woodard," 311.

9. Woodard, *The Allied Occupation of Japan*, xiii.

10. Nakano Tsuyoshi, "America no tai-Nichi shūkyō taisaku no keisei," 27.

11. The magazine *Taiyō* published a discussion chaired by Woodard that included the leaders of Sekai Kyūsei Kyō, Risshō Kōseikai , and PL Kyōdan. These organizations were all involved in discussions with Woodard concerning the development of the Religious Corporations Law in 1950 and 1951.

12. Woodard, *The Allied Occupation of Japan*, 28.

13. Religious services were conducted in accordance with notices issued by the Education Ministry that demanded that priests and practitioners "pray for the

protection of the *kami* and the buddhas and the consolidation of the home front in order to achieve a decisive victory." Ibid., 179.

14. This law provided state recognition for certain religious organizations, but it also gave the state authority to interfere with religious affairs. The Indoctrination Bureau (Kyōgaku kyoku) within the ministry was responsible for the "supervision and guidance" of religious organizations through its Religions Section (Shūkyōka, later Shūmuka). "Supervision and guidance," according to SCAP's interpretation, meant that the religious bodies that were officially recognized under the Religious Organizations Law were subject to government control in their operations.

15. Wilton Dillon, personal interview, 27 September 1999, Washington DC.

16. *Shūmu jihō*, "Zadankai," 2.

17. Woodard, *The Allied Occupation of Japan*, 197.

18. Ibid., 282.

19. Fukuda Shigeru, "Kenshō: GHQ no shūkyō seisaku," 1–2.

20. SCAP-C.

21. Ibid., 95–97.

22. Woodard, *The Allied Occupation of Japan*, xii.

23. Fukuda, "Kenshō," 2.

24. Woodard, *The Allied Occupation of Japan*, xvii.

25. Ibid., 179.

26. Woodard, *The Allied Occupation of Japan*, 183.

27. Ibid.

28. Shinshūren Chōsa Shitsu, eds. *Sengo shūkyō kaisō roku*, 77–78.

29. Woodard, *The Allied Occupation of Japan*, 183–84.

30. Ibid., 313.

31. Ibid., 83.

32. Ibid., 83–84.

33. Ibid., 89.

34. SCAP-C, 126.

35. SCAP-B.

36. Union of the New Religious Organizations in Japan, "Reminiscences of Religion in Postwar Japan," (June 1965), 126.

37. SCAP-C, 126.

38. The Religious Corporations Ordinance of 1945 remained in effect until the promulgation of the Religious Corporations Law (Shūkyō Hōjin Hō) on 3 April 1951.

39. Woodard, *The Allied Occupation of Japan*, 91.

40. Joseph M. Kitagawa, *On Understanding Japanese Religion*, 283.

41. Woodard, *The Allied Occupation of Japan*, 91.

42. Ibid., 43.

43. SCAP #26.

44. Ibid.

45. Cited in Shinshūren Chōsa Shitsu, *Sengo shūkyō kaisō roku*, 78.

46. Fukuda, "Kenshō," 21.

47. Woodard, *The Allied Occupation of Japan*, 282.

48. Fukuda, "Kenshō," 16.

49. SCAP #27.

50. Union of the New Religious Organizations in Japan, "Reminiscences of Religion," (June 1965), 200–201.

51. Fukuda, "Kenshō," 17.

52. Takagi Hiroo, *Shinkō shūkyō*, 1–3.

53. Article located in SCAP #23. This article was translated by SCAP's Allied Translator and Interpreter Service.

54. Fukuda, "Kenshō," 13 and 23.

55. Woodard, *The Allied Occupation of Japan*, 210.

56. Shinshūren Chōsa Shitsu, *Sengo shūkyō kaisō roku*, 45–46.

57. Ibid., 46–48.

58. Ibid.

59. Allan Burnett Cole and Nakanishi Naomichi, eds. *Japanese Opinion Polls*, 537.

60. Woodard, *The Allied Occupation of Japan*, 209.

61. Takagi, "Sengo ni okeru shinkōshūkyō no dōkō," 1–2.

62. McFarland, *The Rush Hour of the Gods*, 39–70.

63. SCAP #18. Denshinkyō's other deities are not cited in the source.

64. SCAP #18.

65. SCAP #28.

66. SCAP-B, 39–40.

67. Matsuura Sōzō, "Ōya Sōichi," 139.

68. Ibid., 138–41.

69. Berkov, "The Press in Postwar Japan," 162.

70. Dower, 413.

71. Ibid., 407.

72. Etō Jun, *Tozasareta gengo kūkan*, 132.

73. Robert Spaulding, "CCD Censorship of Japan's Daily Press," 3.

74. SCAP-D, 123.

75. Ibid.

76. Ibid., 105–106.

77. For example, D.T. Suzuki, who became famous in the West as a promoter of Zen Buddhism, wrote in the *Asahi Shinbun* that readers should be wary of those

Buddhist leaders who claimed to support postwar democracy but had actually supported militarists during the war (Dower, *Embracing Defeat*, 240). It is ironic that Suzuki made this comment in the light of evidence that he has been accused of promoting militant Buddhist nationalism (see, for example, Robert Sharf, "The Zen of Japanese Nationalism").

78. Woodard, *The Allied Occupation of Japan*, 235–37.

79. *Nippon Times*, 14 February 1947.

80. SCAP #10.

81. SCAP-B, 39.

82. SCAP-C, 129.

83. SCAP #15.

5 JIKŌSON AND JIU: BATTLING WITH CELEBRITY

1. Dower, *Embracing Defeat*, 308–309.

2. Ibid. 303.

3. Katsuki, "Jiu to Futabayama," 8.

4. Reader, *Religious Violence in Contemporary Japan*, 64.

5. Tsushima, "Haisen to yonaoshi I," 354.

6. Go, *Go Seigen kaisō roku*, 127–28.

7. Tsushima, "Haisen to yonaoshi I," 351.

8. Ibid., 357.

9. Ibid., 357–58.

10. Benjamin Dorman and Ian Reader, "Editors' Introduction," 7–8.

11. SCAP #1.

12. One disturbed individual handed a letter to SCAP's Religions Division (undated) calling MacArthur a "living savior" and praising his "exalted and godlike benevolence." This man had left his wife and young child to fend for themselves in the street and dropped off a letter written in his own blood exhorting the general to join him in his self-proclaimed mission. The report reads, in part: "[the man] signed himself Spiritual King of the East, and the Second Christ of the Last Ages. He was persuaded [by CIE staff member WMC Kerr] to change these titles to Servant of Christ, and to return home and try to change his own surroundings before starting on the task of converting the world."

In another report located in the same file and dated 30 July 1948, Mr. Kongo Kawakami of the "World Religious Association" brought in a copy of the New Testament to the Religions Division and explained to two staff members that "everything points to the starting of Paradise next year. In view of this, he wished to accomplish the amalgamation of Shinto with Catholicism, and a few more religions added for good measure. He would then hope to get the better of communism by peaceful means, but if necessary force would be employed. He wished to have Gen. MacArthur as chief advisor for the association." He sought official approval, which was, not surprisingly, denied, yet he was told that if it were a religious project he had "perfect freedom to proceed with it. He is apparently unbalanced, so no definite advice was given to him except to beware of the error made so frequently in tying up the Book of Revelation with the conditions of one particular day." SCAP #3.

13. Tsushima, "Haisen to yonaoshi 1," 361.

14. Ibid., 358–59.

15. Katsuki, "Jiu to Futabayama," 22.

16. Tsushima, "Haisen to yonaoshi 1," 359–60.

17. Shimada, "Media to no kakawari," 253.

18. Tsushima, "Haisen to yonaoshi 1,"360.

19. Ibid.

20. For enlightening insights into the extraordinary phenomena of MacArthur worship, see the letters to him in Sodei Rinjirō's *Dear General MacArthur*.

21. Katsuki Tokujirō, personal interview, 28 February 1999, Yokohama.

22. SCAP #1.

23. Go, *Go Seigen kaisō roku*, 132–33.

24. Ibid., 133; Katsuki, "Jiu to Futabayama," 22–24.

25. SCAP #6.

26. Katsuki Tokujirō, personal interview, 28 February 1999, Yokohama.

27. SCAP #23.

28. SCAP #6.

29. Katsuki, "Jiu to Futabayama," 25–27.

30. Woodard, *The Allied Occupation of Japan*, 181–82.

31. Tsushima, "Haisen to yonaoshi 1," 361–62. See also Katsuki, "Jiu to Futabayama," 23.

32. Tsushima, "Haisen to yonaoshi 1," 359.

33. Katsuki, "Jiu to Futabayama," 22. He does not provide any details of the publications or the writers.

34. As mentioned in chapter 4, the Religions Division often used Japanese scholars other than Kishimoto Hideo to assist in their research. These included Hiyane Antei and Watanabe Baiyū.

35. SCAP #10. William C. Kerr wrote in the report, "He has charts and a poem embodying the contents of the prophecy. His story was listened to in main outline, and then he was referred to Research, Lt. Comdr. Woodard."

36. SCAP #4.

37. Although the researchers requested an interview with Jikōson, Go initially refused to allow them to meet her. Instead, he "rattled on and ignored [their] questions, and spoke of how Confucianism, Buddhism, Mohamedanism, and Christianity seem to be different, but in reality the object of worship is the same. This truth is at present revealed in Saint Jikō [Jikōson]." Ibid.

38. Tsushima Michihito, "Haisen to yonaoshi 2," 155.

39. SCAP #6.

40. SCAP #4.

41. SCAP #7.

42. SCAP #5.

43. SCAP #6.

The police continued to inform the Religions Division about their surveillance activities, and on 7 December 1946, a letter from the Chief of the Criminal Section of the Metropolitan Police Board addressed to William K. Bunce, the chief of the Religions Division, informing him that Jikōson was a "suspicious woman who has a habit of writing letters to SCAP [referring to MacArthur]." He also told the division that Jiu had just moved from Suginami to a village in Ishikawa prefecture near Kanazawa. Meanwhile, the Religions Division received other letters related to the case, including one urging SCAP to investigate Jikōson and her followers.

44. Ishii, *Kyojin no shōzō*, 36–37. This book is a biography of Futabayama and another famous wrestler, Rikidōzan. It contains recollections of Futabayama's involvement in Jiu by Fujii Tsuneo, an *Asahi Shinbun* journalist who was close to the wrestler.

45. Katsuki, "Jiu to Futabayama," 60.

46. Katsuki Tokujirō, personal interview, 28 February 1999, Yokohama.

47. Ishii, *Kyojin no shōzō*, 37–38.

48. Katsuki, "Jiu to Futabayama," 59–60.

49. Ibid., 26–28. Tsushima, "Haisen to yonaoshi 1," 363–64.

50. According to Katsuki, they negotiated an agreement with their former landlord but the police heard about their plans to relocate. The police then contacted Jiu's former landlord and told him of the trouble they had caused for them. He then reneged on his agreement with Katsuki to allow the group to return. Katsuki, "Jiu to Futabayama," 26–27.

51. Allen Guttmann and Lee Thompson, *Japanese Sports*, 145.

52. Ishii, 119–20.

53. Ibid., 10–11.

54. Membership to this association is limited to former wrestlers who have achieved a certain rank. Only members are allowed to train new sumo wrestlers. They receive a salary and are expected to assist in the running of the association.

55. In general, Japanese newspapers contain two departments that may deal with religion: the society section (*shakaibu*), which handles crimes and social problems, and the art and science section (*gakugeibu*), which deals with "culture." The relevant department will deal with the case depending on the type of story. Japan's press club system was established in 1890 in order to push for media access to parliament and have press conferences. Nevertheless, it has evolved into what Laurie Freeman (2000, 4) calls "information cartels," in which selected members are allowed access to certain information from state agencies and major corporations.

56. Ishii, *Kyojin no shōzō*, 12–18.

57. Cited in ibid., 32–39.

58. Katsuki, "Jiu to Futabayama," 1–7.

59. Ibid., 31–34.

60. Cited in Ishii, *Kyojin no shōzō*, 11.

61. Go gives no indication that he joined through Katsuki's urging. See Go, *Go Seigen kaisō roku*, 100–105, 114–19.

62. Cited in Ishii, 38–39.

63. Katsuki, "Jiu to Futabayama," 27.

64. Tsushima, "Haisen to yonaoshi 1," 363.

65. Katsuki, "Jiu to Futabayama," 34–36.

66.Tsushima, "Haisen to yonaoshi 1," 364; Katsuki, "Jiu to Futabayama," 8.

67. Katsuki, "Jiu to Futabayama," 37–40.

68. Ibid., 40–42.

69. Ibid., 58.

70. Ibid., 26–27.

71. Cited in Tsushima, "Haisen to yonaoshi 1," 364.

72. Go, *Go Seigen kaisō roku*, 144.

73. SCAP #4.

74. Tsushima, "Haisen to yonaoshi 1," 365.

75. SCAP #8.

76. SCAP #9.

77. SCAP #5.

78. Tsushima, "Haisen to yonaoshi 1," 369. See also Akimoto's report to the CIC commander; Akimoto Haruo, "Mōsōsha 'Jikōson' to sono ichidan ni kansuru chōsa hōkoku."

79. Cited in Tsushima, "Haisen to yonaoshi 1," 369; see also Akimoto, "Mōsōsha 'Jikōson'."

80. Katsuki, "Jiu to Futabayama," 47.

81. Ibid., 22–24.

82. Cited in Ishii 1980, 97–99.

83. Katsuki Tokujirō, personal interview, 28 February 1999, Yokohama.

84. Ishii, *Kyojin no shōzō*, 138–39.

85. Tsushima, "Haisen to yonaoshi 1," 367.

86. Myōgan Gaijirō, "Jikōson, Futabayama kenkyo jiken no supai," 79; Tsushima, "Haisen to yonaoshi 1," 367.

87. Tsushima, "Haisen to yonaoshi 1," 365–66.

88. Even publications dedicated to promoting Futabayama's legend as a "superstar" mention this aspect of his life. See, for example, the pamphlet edited by Kikaku Henshū Hanuman, *Sūpāsutā densetsu*, 39.

89. Katsuki, "Jiu to Futabayama," 72–75.

90. Tsushima, "Haisen to yonaoshi I," 367.

91. Katsuki, "Jiu to Futabayama," 47–49.

92. Katsuki (ibid., 88–100) describes how he attempted to contact Futabayama by letter. He also sent messages from Jikōson using different people including Wakasaki, who had failed in this the first time around, to pass them on. However Futabayama never replied to any of the letters and the messengers all failed in their various bids to reach him. Nevertheless, Katsuki recalled Futabayama with fondness (personal interview, 28 February 1999, Yokohama). Yamada Senta also made numerous attempts to contact Futabayama, but these were in vain (personal interview, 7 August 2009, Fukuoka). Futabayama went on to become general director of the Sumo Association in 1957.

93. Tsushima, "Haisen to yonaoshi I," 367–68; Katsuki Tokujirō, personal interview, 28 February 1999, Yokohama.

94. Tsushima, "Haisen to yonaoshi I," 369.

95. SCAP #10.

96. The Religions Division requested a report on the case from the Japanese police. Although this report did eventually find its way through to the division, it had to pass through a number of bureaucratic hoops. Any report produced by the police bureau of the Japanese Home Ministry had to be submitted first to the Public Safety Division. Colonel Pulliam, the chief of the Public Safety Division, learned of the request by the Religions Division and immediately instructed the Home Ministry to prepare a report. Apparently the Home Ministry misunderstood his instructions and withheld the report from the Religions Division. Pulliam's swift reaction to the Religions Division request suggests his division was clearly sensitive to the nature of the request and the implications of police involvement in religious activities. SCAP #10.

97. SCAP-C 1948, 139.

98. SCAP #9.

99. Ōishi Shūten, "A Review Article," 64.

100. Myōgan 1957. See also Tsushima, "Haisen to yonaoshi I," 367; Murakami, *Japanese Religion in the Modern Century*, 87.

101. Murakami, *Japanese Religion in the Modern Century*, 87.

102. Tsushima, "Haisen to yonaoshi I," 367.

103. Go, *Go Seigen kaisō roku*, 145.

104. Katsuki has emphatically denied these claims (personal interview 28 February 1999, Yokohama).

105. Thanks go to Ian Reader for pointing out the significance of *ucchari* in this context.

106. Rojek, *Celebrity*, 88.

107. Tsushima, "Haisen to yonaoshi I," 365.

108. Report contained in SCAP #11.

109. Woodard, *The Allied Occupation of Japan*, 209.

110. Katsuki, "Jiu to Futabayama," 87.

111. Ibid., 36.

112. Ibid., 36–37. Jiu's post-Kanazawa movements are covered in Tsushima 2000.

113. Tsushima, "Haisen to yonaoshi: Jiu no sennen ōkoku shisō to undō 2," 153–55.

114. Katsuki, "Jiu to Futabayama," 8–17; Katsuki Tokujirō, personal interview, 28 February 1999, Yokohama.

115. Katsuki Tokujirō made this clear to me in an interview held on 28 February 1999 in Yokohama.

6 KITAMURA SAYO: CELEBRITY IN THE MAGGOT WORLD

1. Tenshō Kōtai Jingū Kyō, *The Prophet of Tabuse*, 57–61.

2. This information was provided by three followers (who requested anonymity) during an interview conducted on 15 December 1998 at the headquarters of Tenshō Kōtai Jingū Kyō in Tabuse, Yamaguchi.

3. Tenshō Kōtai Jingū Kyō, *The Prophet of Tabuse*, 64–66.

4. Ibid., 69.

5. Ibid., 72–75.

6. SCAP #13.

7. Tenshō Kōtai Jingū Kyō, *Seisho* I, 169–82. It is possible that these two priests may have had some concerns because of the similarity between the chant advocated by Kitamura, *na-myō-hō-renge-kyō*, and that associated with schools of Nichiren, *namu-myōhō-renge-kyō*.

8. This information appears in an undated study conducted by the Religious Affairs Section of the Ministry of Education that is in the SCAP records. SCAP #2.

9. SCAP #15.

10. Sodei, *Dear General MacArthur*, 88; Dower, *Embracing Defeat*, 305–306.

11. SCAP #13.

12. Tenshō Kōtai Jingū Kyō, *Seisho* I, 190–92.

13. Ibid.

14. Although *Sengo shūkyō kaisō roku* (Shinshūren Chōsa Shitsu, ed., 64) states that the group was reported in national newspapers as the "dancing religion" after this first trip to Tokyo, national reporting actually began some months after this initial trip.

15. Seichō no Ie began in 1930. Taniguchi was originally a member of Ōmoto but left after the first persecution in 1921. His group promoted nationalistic aims during the war and was not targeted by the authorities.

16. Tenshō Kōtai Jingū Kyō, *The Prophet of Tabuse*, 91–94.

17. Tenshō Kōtai Jingū Kyō, *Seisho* I, 222.

18. Ibid., 223–24.

19. Ibid., 242–44.

20. Ibid., 247–71. This section outlines details of the trial.

21. Ibid., 266–69.

22. Ibid., 274.

23. Ibid., 325–26.

24. SCAP #13.

25. Tenshō Kōtai Jingū Kyō, *Seisho* I, 421–22.

26. Three adherents interviewed at the group's headquarters on 15 December 1998 were not willing to provide estimates of the number of adherents, citing "Ōgamisama's dislike for such records."

27. See, for example, SCAP #14.

28. SCAP #13.

29. SCAP #16.

30. SCAP #18.

31. Woodard, *The Allied Occupation of Japan*, 1973, x.

32. SCAP #21.

33. A number of these are contained in SCAP #15.

34. Wilton Dillon, personal interview, 27 September 1999, Washington DC.

35. SCAP #15.

36. SCAP #17.

37. SCAP #22.

38. Regarding the Religions Division's efforts in dealing with MacArthur's blatant promotion of Christianity over other faiths during the Occupation, see Woodard, *The Allied Occupation of Japan*, 241–48.

39. SCAP #14.

The CLO was an institutional link between the Japanese government and SCAP that "played a crucial role in translating SCAP policies into action and assuring that Occupation reforms proceeded smoothly." Takemae, *The Allied Occupation of Japan*, 113.

40. SCAP #12.

41. See note 57 within Chapter 3 for an explanation of this phrase.

42. SCAP #15.

Watanabe's name first appears in a Religions Division report filed on 2 September 1947: "He claims to be the first religions expert employed by the Education Ministry. He belongs to the Soto Zen sect.... Officials [even at the Education Ministry] do not understand religion. [He argued that] there is a long-felt need for an organ with which to publicize and interpret the regulations as they are issued." Watanabe contributed a number of articles to *Shūkyō jihō* (Religious News).

43. SCAP #15.

44. SCAP #13.

45. On a visit to the headquarters in Tabuse in December 1998, I stayed overnight in a guesthouse and was not required to pay for food or accommodation. A number of participants in the ceremonies I attended told me that no financial requirements had been placed on them at any time.

46. SCAP #15.

47. Ibid.

48. "Protests from townspeople against the dancing religion: Cries against "maggot beggars" blaring through a microphone" ("Odoru shūkyō e machi no kōgi: 'Uji mushi domo yo' no maiku hōsō ni himei"). Incidentally, the article states that the group was at that time claiming a membership of 600,000, but no other verification is mentioned.

49. SCAP #13.

50. Woodard, *The Allied Occupation of Japan*, 181–82.

51. SCAP #18.

52. According to Dower, the concept of *zange* was "placed at the center of public debate on August 28, the day the first advance contingent of Americans arrived at the Atsugi air base" (*Embracing Defeat*, 496). The government promoted an official version of repentance, while Tanabe Hajime, a highly influential philosopher, wrote a manuscript on the subject, albeit one that was nationalistic and used "old religious teachings for new ideological purposes (497–502).

53. Tenshō Kōtai Jingū Kyō, *Seisho* 1, 435–36.

54. SCAP #18.

55. Ibid.

56. This particular conference is not mentioned in *Seisho*.

57. SCAP #18.

58. Ibid.

59. Tenshō Kōtai Jingū Kyō, *Seisho* 1, 442.

60. SCAP #13. This meeting is not recorded in *Seisho*.

61. SCAP #12. The following list is a sampling of the newspapers that published reports on the "dancing religion": *Nishi Nippon Shinbun* (5 and 22 February 1947); *Chūgoku Shinbun* (19 April and 18 July 1947); *Kyūshū Taimuzu* (20 January 1948); *Mainichi Shinbun* (20 April 1947, 4 August 1948) its English-language version *Mainichi* (28 September 1948); *Yomiuri Shinbun* (29 September 1948); *Asahi Shinbun* (9 and 27 September 1948; 10 October 1948); the English language *Nippon Times* (25 September 1948); *Tōkyō Minpō* (27 September 1948); *Tōkyō Taimuzu* (29 November 1948 and 21 January 1949); *Shin Kyūshū* (3 March 1949); *Tōkyō Shinbun* (29 March 1949); *Nagasaki Minpō* (19 July 1949); *Kyūshū Taimuzu* (29 December 1949). This list is far from exhaustive, yet it does demonstrate that the "dancing religion" was reported in the major newspapers and their subsidiaries, and in local newspapers, often at times when Kitamura and her retinue traveled to those areas.

62. Fujii Takeshi, "Tenshō Kōtai Jingū Kyō," 541.

63. Tenshō Kōtai Jingū Kyō, *Seisho* I, 410.

64. Ibid., 415–17.

65. According to a survey of new religions by the Ministry of Education's Religious Affairs Section, the film was produced in March 1946 (SCAP #2). This date is incorrect because Kitamura and Tenshō Kōtai Jingū Kyō had not been publicized to any great degree by other national media outlets at that stage.

66. Fujii, "Tenshō Kōtai Jingū Kyō," 541–42.

67. SCAP #15. Both articles translated by SCAP's Allied Translator and Interpreter Service.

68. Tenshō Kōtai Jingū Kyō, *Seisho* I, 411.

69. SCAP #13.

70. Fujii, "Tenshō Kōtai Jingū Kyō," 542.

71. Tenshō Kōtai Jingū Kyō, *Seisho* I, 403.

72. Ibid., 403–404.

73. SCAP #15.

74. Ōkuma, *Hadaka no Ōya Sōichi*, 320–21.

75. Matsuura, "Ōya Sōichi," 119–22.

76. Dower, *Embracing Defeat*, 234.

77. Matsuura, "Ōya Sōichi," 138.

78. The Greater East Asia Co-Prosperity Sphere was a wartime slogan that encapsulated the vision of a new Asia concocted by Japan's war planners. The new Asia would be economically and politically independent of Western powers yet be controlled and defended by Japan.

79. Cited in Matsuura, "Ōya Sōichi," 139–40.

80. Ibid.

81. Ibid., 139.

82. Ibid.

83. Kannonkyō was another name for Sekai Kyūseikyō; PL Kyōdan was a postwar offshoot of Hito no Michi.

84. Cited in Ōya, *Ōya Sōichi zenshū*, 296–303.

85. Ibid., 307–308.

86. Tenshō Kōtai Jingū Kyō, "Ōgamisama: Ōya Sōichi ni go-seppō," 11.

87. This dialogue was part of an extensive series of interviews that were later put into book form called *Montō yūyō* ("Meaningful Dialogues").

88. Tenshō Kōtai Jingū Kyō, *Seisho* I, 335–36.

89. Katsuki Tokujirō, personal interview 28 February 1998, Yokohama; Tenshō Kōtai Jingū Kyō members' interview, 15 December 1998, Tabuse.

90. Tokugawa Musei, "Hara ni kamisama ga yadoru odoru kyōso: Kitamura Sayo," 202.

91. Ibid., 216.

92. Ibid., 217–18.

93. Ōkuma, *Hadaka no Ōya Sōichi*, 322.

94. Ibid., 323.

95. Tenshō Kōtai Jingū Kyō, "Ōgamisama," 12.

96. Ōkuma, *Hadaka no Ōya Sōichi*, 323–24.

97. Ibid., 325.

98. Tenshō Kōtai Jingū Kyō, "Ōgamisama," 11.

99. Ōkuma, *Hadaka no Ōya Sōichi*, 325.

100. Fujii, "Tenshō Kōtai Jingū Kyō," 542.

101. Tenshō Kōtai Jingū Kyō members' interview, 15 December 1998, Tabuse.

7 NEW RELIGIONS AND CRITICS IN THE IMMEDIATE POSTWAR PRESS

1. Nakano Tsuyoshi, "Religion and State," 124.

2. SCAP #11.

3. Takagi, "Sengo ni okeru shinkō shūkyō," 4.

4. SCAP #29.

5. Article 12: The freedoms and rights guaranteed to the people by this Constitution shall be maintained by the constant endeavor of the people, who shall refrain from any abuse of these freedoms and rights and shall always be responsible for utilizing them for the public welfare.

6. Woodard, *The Allied Occupation of Japan*, 94.

7. Takagi, "Sengo ni okeru shinkō shūkyō," 5.

8. Minami Hiroshi, "Naze jakyō wa ryūkō suru ka."

9. Inui, *Nihon wa kurutteru*, 142.

10. Ibid., 175.

11. Ibid., 178.

12. Ibid., 181.

13. Ōishi Shūten, "Senryōki to shinshūkyō," 493–94.

14. Ibid.

15. Ōishi, "A Review Article," 59.

16. Ibid., 61.

17. Cited in ibid., 62.

18. Ōishi Shūten, cited in Taki Taizō, *Kamigami tabō*, 2.

19. This was authored by Saki Akio, Inui Takashi, Oguchi Iichi, and Matsushima Eiichi.

20. Kishimoto Hideo, ed., *Sengo no shūkyō to shakai*, 211–22.

21. The director's recollections of meeting with Sōka Gakkai's Toda Jōsei are contained in Yoshida Naoya, *Eizō to wa nan darō ka*, 2–12.

22. Kishimoto, *Sengo no shūkyō to shakai*, 211.

23. Ibid., 212.

24. Ibid., 212.

25. Cited in Taki, 1.

26. Shinshūren Chōsa Shitsu, *Sengo shūkyō kaisō roku*, 70; see also Union of the New Religious Organizations in Japan, "Reminiscences of Religion," (June 1965), 190.

27. Morioka, "Attacks on the New Religions," 282.

28. Both Akimoto's article (for which I have been unable to reconfirm the journal's name) and Akai's statement are contained in SCAP #11. They were translated by SCAP's Allied Translator and Interpreter Service. Although this folder is labeled 21 May 1947, no date or publication source is given for Akai's statement.

29. Morioka, "Attacks on the New Religions," 289.

30. Dower, *Embracing Defeat*, 185.

31. SCAP #24.

32. Ibid.

33. Ōya, *Ōya Sōichi zenshū*, 308.

34. Ōya, "Meiji, Taishō, Shōwa shinkō shūkyō no zensen," 1–3.

35. Ōya, *Ōya Sōichi zenshū*, 37–41. The original publication details are not cited.

36. Ibid., 1–3.

37. Butsuryūkō was a group that based itself on the Nichiren tradition.

38. Ōya, "Meiji, Taishō, Shōwa shinkō shūkyō no zensen," 4.

39. Ibid., 7.

40. The term "professional religionists" is probably meant to indicate representatives from established Buddhist, Christian, and Shinto groups.

41. Ōya, "Meiji, Taishō, Shōwa shinkō shūkyō no zensen," 13. Taniguchi graduated from the arts faculty of Waseda University.

42. Ibid., 17.

43. Ibid., 19.

44. Ibid., 20.

45. Ibid., 22.

46. Ibid., 26.

47. Ibid., 28.

48. Ōkuma, *Hadaka no Ōya Sōichi*.

49. Matsuura, "Ōya Sōichi," 119–22. Matsuura argues that the reason why many different media representatives attended Ōya's funeral on 22 November 1970 was because Ōya was essentially a freelance journalist who never became "Asahi's

Ōya" or "NHK's Ōya." He was connected with the *Mainichi Shinbun* during the prewar era for an extended period. Although he remained unaffiliated to one particular company or organization, he still commanded the respect of his colleagues. Matsuura holds that while there were many valedictory articles lauding "Ōya the Great" after the funeral, there were no negative assessments of his life.

50. Ibid., 125.

51. Cited in Taki, *Kamigami tabō*, 15.

52. Ibid., 16.

53. Ibid.

54. Quoted in Taki, *Kamigami tabō*, 1.

55. Ibid., 4.

56. Sugata Masaaki, *Nihon shūkyō no sengo shi*, 32.

57. Walter Nichols, "Nihon no shinkō shūkyō."

58. SCAP #20.

59. Ibid., 1–2 (my page numbering).

60. Ibid., 1.

61. Ibid., 2–3.

62. Woodard, *The Allied Occupation of Japan*, 93–94.

63. Ibid., 94.

64. Ibid.

65. SCAP #24.

66. Cited in Woodard, *The Allied Occupation of Japan*, 102.

67. Union of the New Religious Organizations in Japan, "Reminiscences of Religion," (September 1966), 257–58.

68. Woodard, *The Allied Occupation of Japan*, 96–97.

69. The preamble of the Religious Corporations Law states that the purpose of the law is "to provide religious organizations with the legal capability" to maintain and use property for their own activities and enable them to engage in profit-making enterprises. There are three regulations that must be followed by bodies applying to become religious corporations: public notification, government certification, and the appointment of legally responsible officers. It differs from the Religious Corporations Ordinance in that prior to registration a group must file a public notice detailing adherents and individuals who are connected to the organization. And the group must obtain a certificate from the proper government office confirming the rules it proposes to follow. As noted in chapter 3, the prewar Religious Corporations Law had been based on government recognition (*kōnin*), the Religious Corporations Ordinance was a system of notification (*todokede seido*), and the Religious Corporations Law is a system of certification (*ninshō seido*).

70. Woodard, *The Allied Occupation of Japan*, 101.

71. Ibid., 180.

72. Union of the New Religious Organizations in Japan, "Reminiscences of Religion," September 1966, 251.

73. Ibid., 250–51; Ōishi, "Senryōki to shinshūkyō," 491.

74. SCAP #33.

75. Ibid.

76. Both the *Yomiuri Shinbun* and the *Mainichi Shinbun* ran highly critical campaigns against Okada, concentrating on his faith-healing claims.

77. SCAP #33.

CONCLUSION

1. Ian Reader, "Consensus Shattered: Japanese Paradigm Shifts and Moral Panic in the post-Aum era."

2. Nakano Tsuyoshi, "Religion and State," 124. The current English name of the Nihon Shūkyō Renmei is the Japanese Association of Religious Organizations.

3. Morioka, "Attacks on the New Religions," 309.

4. Murakami Naoyuki, "Sengo Nihon no shūkyō hōdō o kenshō suru," *Seikyō Shinbun*.

5. Personal interview, 27 January 2010, Tokyo.

6. Personal interview, 27 May 2006, Nagoya.

7. "Tabū hihan osoreruna," *Asahi Shinbun*, 24 January 2004.

8. Benjamin Dorman, "Pana Wave: The New Aum Shinrikyō or another Moral Panic?"

Bibliography

SCAP RECORDS

The SCAP records listed below are all contained in Record Group 331, SCAP (Supreme Commander for the Allied Powers), National Archives II Building, College Park, Maryland, USA. Microform versions were also accessed at the Japanese Political History Materials Room (Kensei shiryō shitsu 憲政資料室), National Diet Library, Tokyo, and the National Library of Australia, Canberra. The first part of the reference indicates the record title, the second the reference number of the folder, followed by the relevant SCAP section. The dates when the reports were made, where available, have also been included.

SCAP #1   Religions Research—Jiu or 'the Mansion Jewel' Interviews with Mr. Go Seigen on September 16 ... and with Jikoson on September 20, 1946; Folder 68—Other Religions Jiu-kyo; Religious Data Research; Special Projects Branch. Religion and Cultural Resources Division. Civil Information and Education Section.

SCAP #2   A Survey of New Religious Sects 1, 12 May 1949; Folder 24—Education to New Religions; Research File and Publications; Arts and Monuments Branch. Religion and Cultural Resources Division. Civil Information and Education Section.

SCAP #3   Cooperation with General MacArthur to Convert the World. [Undated] Microform A08574.

SCAP #4   General Information Concerning Jiu (undated): Buddhist Sector to Other Religions; Folder 68—Other Religions Jiu-kyo. Religious Data Research; Special Projects Branch. Religion and Cultural Resources Division. Civil Information and Education Section.

SCAP #5   A Supplement to the Report on the 'Religious Cult' of Jiu: General Information Concerning Jiu (undated); Buddhist Sector to Other Religions, Folder 68—Other Religions Jiu-kyo; Religious Data Research; Special Projects Branch. Religion and Cultural Resources Division. Civil Information and Education Section.

SCAP #6   Subject: The Rumour about Jikōson's Arrest is Denied, 4 November 1946; Buddhist Sector to Other Religions, Folder 68—Other Religions Jiu-kyo; Religious Data Research; Special Projects Branch. Religion and Cultural Resources Division. Civil Information and Education Section.

SCAP #7   Current Newspapers #2; Folder 15—Religious Magazine and Newspaper Digest 31; Research File and Publications; Arts and Monuments Branch. Religion and Cultural Resources Division. Civil Information and Education Section. [Folder undated. Contains newspaper articles from 1946].

SCAP #8   Subject: Removal of Suspicious Religious Society; Buddhist Sector to Other Religions, Folder 68—Other Religions Jiu-kyo; Religious Data Research; Special Projects Branch. Religion and Cultural Resources Division. Civil Information and Education Section. [Document dated 1946].

SCAP #9   Letter from a Democrat [document dated 1946]; Buddhist Sector to Other Religions, Folder 68—Other Religions Jiu-kyo; Religious Data Research; Special Projects Branch. Religion and Cultural Resources Division. Civil Information and Education Section.

SCAP #10 Conferences—Religions Division, 14 February 1947; Folder 20—Conferences January 1947; Research File and Publications; Arts and Monuments Branch. Religion and Cultural Resources Division. Civil Information and Education Section.

SCAP #11 Publications Analysis, 21 May 1947; Folder 1—Youth to Household Shinto; Research File and Publications; Arts and Monuments Branch. Religion and Cultural Resources Division. Civil Information and Education Section.

SCAP #12 Monthly Reports, Jan. 1949 (Author Unknown); Folder 1—Monthly Summaries; Research File and Publications; Arts and Monuments Branch. Religion and Cultural Resources Division. Civil Information and Education Section.

SCAP #13 Other Religions—Tensho Kotai Jingu Kyo; Folder 25—Shinto Sector; CIE—Analysis and Research Division Research Unit (Religions); Religious Data Research; Special Projects Branch. Religion and Cultural Resources Division. Civil Information and Education Section.

SCAP #14 Conferences—Religions Division; Folder 27—Conference Reports (June 1947); Research File and Publications; Arts and

Monuments Branch. Religion and Cultural Resources Division. Civil Information and Education Section.

SCAP #15 Dancing Religions; Folder 34; CIE—Analysis and Research Division Research Unit (Religions); Religious Data Research; Special Projects Branch. Religion and Cultural Resources Division. Civil Information and Education Section. [Document dated 1948].

SCAP #16 Conferences—Religions Division; Folder 21—Conference Reports (December 1948); Research File and Publications; Arts and Monuments Branch. Religion and Cultural Resources Division. Civil Information and Education Section.

SCAP #17 Letters to Religions and Cultural Resources Division; CIE— Analysis and Research Division Research Unit (Religions) Folder 31; Religious Data Research; Special Projects Branch. Religion and Cultural Resources Division. Civil Information and Education Section.

SCAP #18 Monthly Reports, Apr. 1949 (Author: Kotani, T.); Folder 1—Monthly Summaries; Research File and Publications; Arts and Monuments Branch. Religion and Cultural Resources Division. Civil Information and Education Section.

SCAP #19 Christianity to List of Temples; Folder 17, 1948 Christian Yearbook; Research File and Publications; Arts and Monuments Branch. Religion and Cultural Resources Division. Civil Information and Education Section. [Relevant documents dated 1949].

SCAP #20 Walter Nichols, Report on New Religions, "The New Religions" 29 November 1950; Folder 3—New Religions General Comment; New Religions to Sectarian Shinto; Religious Data Research; Special Projects Branch. Religion and Cultural Resources Division. Civil Information and Education Section.

SCAP #21 (1) Public Meeting of Tensho Kotai Jingukyo ("Dancing Religion") Mrs. Sayo Kitamura. 29 July 1950 Hibiya Hall; (2) Miss Nakajima, Education Ministry—Activities of Mrs. Kitamura, 2 August 1950: Folder 34—Religions Research to Christianity; Religious Data Research; Special Projects Branch. Religion and Cultural Resources Division. Civil Information and Education Section.

SCAP #22 Sermon, Interview with Dr. Bunce, 25 November 1950; Folder 25—Religions Research to Christianity; Religious Data Research; Special Projects Branch. Religion and Cultural

Resources Division. Civil Information and Education Section.

SCAP #23 Japan Review Vol. 1 No. 16, 24 Jan. 1947—7 May 1947; Folder 11; Library Section Subject File 1945–50; Military Intelligence Division. Assistant Chief of Staff, G-2 (Intelligence).

SCAP #24 Newspaper articles; Folder 3—New Religions General Comment; New Religions to Sectarian Shinto; Research File and Publications; Arts and Monuments Branch. Religion and Cultural Resources Division. Civil Information and Education Section. [All articles dated 1950. Translated by SCAP's Allied Translator and Interpreter Service].

SCAP #25 "Detailed Import & Export Statistics to Japan Review Vol. 3"; Japan Review Vol. III Nos. 38–50, 10 Oct 1947—30 Dec 1947; Folder 13; Library Section Subject File 1945–50; G-2 Intelligence Division.

SCAP #26 Conferences—Religions Division; Folder 9—Conference Reports (November 1947); Research File and Publications; Arts and Monuments Branch. Religion and Cultural Resources Division. Civil Information and Education Section.

SCAP #27 Conferences—Religions Division; Folder 15—Conference Reports (June 1948); Research File and Publications; Arts and Monuments Branch. Religion and Cultural Resources Division. Civil Information and Education Section.

SCAP #28 Conferences—Religions Division; Folder 27—Conference Reports (July 1949); Research File and Publications; Arts and Monuments Branch. Religion and Cultural Resources Division. Civil Information and Education Section.

SCAP #29 Conferences—Religions Division; Folder 19—Conference Reports (October 1947); Research File and Publications; Arts and Monuments Branch. Religion and Cultural Resources Division. Civil Information and Education Section.

SCAP #30 Conferences—Religions Division; Folder 17—Conference Reports, (November 1950); Research File and Publications; Arts and Monuments Branch. Religion and Cultural Resources Division. Civil Information and Education Section.

SCAP #31 Conferences—Religions Division; Folder 19—Conference Reports, (January 1951); Research File and Publications; Arts and Monuments Branch. Religion and Cultural Resources Division. Civil Information and Education Section.

SCAP #32 Conferences—Religions Division; Folder 11—Conference Reports, (May 1950); Research File and Publications; Arts and

Monuments Branch. Religion and Cultural Resources Division. Civil Information and Education Section.

SCAP #33   Conferences—Religions Division; Folder 14—Conference Reports, (August 1950); Research File and Publications; Arts and Monuments Branch. Religion and Cultural Resources Division. Civil Information and Education Section.

PUBLISHED SCAP DOCUMENTS

SCAP-A   Supreme Commander for the Allied Powers, Government Section, *Political Reorientation of Japan—September 1945 to September 1948* (Vols. 1&2). Washington DC: US Government Printing Office, 1949.

SCAP-B   Supreme Commander for the Allied Powers, Historical Section, *History of the Non-Military Activities of the Occupation of Japan 1945–51 No. 32 Religion.* Microform mfm 1422, National Library of Australia.

SCAP-C   Supreme Commander for the Allied Powers, Religion and Cultural Resources Division, Civil Information and Education Section. *Religions in Japan,* 1948.

SCAP-D   Supreme Commander for the Allied Powers, Historical Section, *History of the Non-Military Activities of the Occupation of Japan, Tokyo, 1945–51. No. 15 Freedom of the Press (1945 to January 1951).* Microform mfm 1422, National Library of Australia.

OTHER SOURCES

Akimoto Haruo 秋元春夫. Mōsōsha 'Jikōson' to sono ichidan ni kansuru chōsa hōkoku 妄想者「璽光尊」とその一団に関する調査報告, (1947).

_____. "Mōsō no henreki: Jikōson no kenshin kiroku kara" 妄想の遍歴—璽光尊の検診記録から. *Chūō Kōron,* March (1947): 68–74.

Aldous, Christopher. *The Police in Occupation Japan: Control, Corruption and Resistance to Reform.* London: Routledge, 1997.

Anderson, Benedict. *Imagined Communities: Reflections on the Origin and Spread of Nationalism.* Revised edition. London: Verso, 2006. (First published 1983).

Ariyama Teruo 有山輝雄. *Senryōki media-shi kenkyū: Jiyū to tōsei, 1945-nen* 占領期メディア史研究—自由と統制, 1945年. Tokyo: Kashiwa Shobō, 1996.

Astley, Trevor. "The Transformation of a Recent Japanese New Religion: Ōkawa Ryūhō and Kōfuku no Kagaku." *Japanese Journal of Religious Studies* 22/3–4 (1995): 343–80.

Barkun, Michael. *Disaster and the Millennium*. New York: Syracuse University Press, 1986. (First published by Yale University Press, 1974).

Beer, Lawrence W. *Freedom of Expression in Japan: A Study in Comparative Law, Politics, and Society*. New York: Kodansha International, 1984.

Berkov, Robert. "The Press in Postwar Japan." *Far Eastern Survey* 16 (1947), 162–65.

Blacker, Carmen. "Millenarian Aspects of New Religions in Japan." In *Tradition and Modernization in Japanese Culture*, Donald H. Shively, ed., 563–600. Princeton NJ: Princeton University Press, 1971.

———. *The Catalpa Bow: A Study in Shamanistic Practices in Japan*. Richmond, VA: Japan Library, 1999. (First published by George Allen and Unwin, Ltd., 1975).

Boorstin, Daniel J. *The Image: A Guide to Pseudo-Events in America*. New York: Vintage Books, 1992. (First published 1961).

Boyd, Malcolm. *Christ and Celebrity Gods: The Church in Mass Culture*. Greenwich, CN: The Seabury Press, 1958.

Braudy, Leo. *The Frenzy of Renown: Fame and Its History*. New York: Vintage Books, 1997. (Originally published by Oxford University Press, 1986)

Breen, John, and Mark Teeuwen, eds. *Shintō in History: Ways of the Kami*. London: Curzon Press, 2000.

Bunce, William K. *Religions in Japan: Buddhism, Shinto, Christianity*. Rutland, VT: Charles E. Tuttle Co, 1955.

Capra, Frank, and Joris Ivens, dir. *Know Your Enemy: Japan*. Film (63 mins).

Chamberlain, Basil Hall. "The Invention of a New Religion." http://jolly roger.com/xlibrary/TheInventionofCB/TheInventionofCB1 .html.html (accessed 31 July 2010).

Chang, Maria Hsia. *Falun Gong: The End of Days*. New Haven, CN: Yale University Press, 2004.

Clart, Philip. "Moral Mediums: Spirit-Writing and the Cultural Construction of Chinese Spirit-Mediumship." *Ethnologies* 25/1 (2003): 153–190.

Cole, Allan Burnett, and Nakanishi Naomichi, eds. *Japanese Opinion Polls with Socio-Political Significance 1947–1957*. Medford, MA: Tufts University, 1960.

Cooper-Chen, Anne, with Miiko Kodama. *Mass Communications in Japan*. Ames, IO: Iowa State University Press, 1997.

Cowan, Douglas E., and Jeffrey K. Hadden. "God, Guns, and Grist for the Media's Mill: Constructing the Narratives of New Religions and Violence." *Nova Religio* 8/2 (2004): 64–82.

Creemers, Wilhelmus H. M. "*The Allied Occupation of Japan 1945–1952 and Japanese Religions* by William P. Woodard." *Contemporary Religions in Japan* 11, 3/4 (1970): 309–316.

Croteau, David, and William Hoynes. *Media/Society: Industries, Images, and Audiences.* Thousand Oaks, CA: Pine Forge Press, 1997.

Deguchi Kyotarō. *The Great Onisaburo Deguchi.* Kyoto: Oomoto Foundation, 1973.

Dorman, Benjamin. "Aum Alone." *Religion in the News* 4 (2001): 21–22.

____. "SCAP's Scapegoat? The Authorities, New Religions, and a Postwar Taboo." *Japanese Journal of Religious Studies* 31 (2004): 105–140.

____. "Pana Wave: The New Aum Shinrikyō or another Moral Panic?" *Nova Religio* 8 (2005b): 83–103.

____. Representing Ancestor Worship as "Non-Religious": Hosoki Kazuko's Divination in the Post-Aum Era. *Nova Religio* 10 (2007): 32–53.

Dorman, Benjamin, and Ian Reader. "Editors' Introduction: Projections and Representations of Religion in Japanese Media." *Nova Religio* 10 (2007): 5–12.

Dower, John. *Embracing Defeat: Japan in the Wake of World War II.* New York: W. W. Norton & Company, 1999.

Earhart, H. Byron. *The New Religions of Japan: A Bibliography of Western-language Materials.* Tokyo: Sophia University, 1970.

Etō Jun 江藤 淳. *Tozasareta gengo kūkan: Senryōgun no shinbun ken'etsu to sengo Nihon* 閉ざされた言語空間—占領軍の新聞検閲と戦後日本. Tokyo: Bungei Shunjū, 1989.

Feuchtwang, Stephan. "Spiritual recovery: A Spirit-writing Shrine in Shifting Under Japanese Rule." *Bulletin of the Institute of Ethnology, Academia Sinica* 88 (1999): 63–89.

Freeman, Laurie Anne. *Closing the Shop: Information Cartels and Japan's Mass Media.* Princeton, NJ: Princeton University Press, 2000.

Fridell, Wilbur. *Japanese Shrine Mergers 1906–12: State Shinto Moves to the Grassroots.* Tokyo: Sophia University, 1973.

Frow, John. "Is Elvis a God? Cult, Culture, and Questions of Method." *International Journal of Cultural Studies* 1/2 (1998): 197–210.

Fujii Takeshi 藤井健志. "Tenshō Kōtai Jingū Kyō" 天照皇大神宮教. In *Shinshūkyō jiten* 新宗教事典, Inoue Nobutaka et al., eds., 540–43, 1994.

Fujitani, Takashi. "Inventing, Forgetting, Remembering: Toward a Historical Ethnography of the Nation-State." In *Cultural Nationalism in East Asia: Representation and Identity*, Harumi Befu, ed., 77–106. Research Papers and Policy Studies 39. Berkeley, CA: University of California Press, 1993.

Fukuda Shigeru 福田繁. "Kenshō: GHQ no shūkyō seisaku" 検証―GHQの宗教政策. *Shūmu jihō* 79 (1988): 1–24.

Gabler, Neal. *Winchell: Gossip, Power and the Culture of Celebrity*. New York: Vintage Books, 1994.

Gamson, William, and Gadi Wolfsfeld. "Movements and Media as Interacting Systems." *Annals of the American Academy of Political and Social Science* 528 (1993): 114–27.

Garon, Sheldon. *Molding Japanese Minds: The State in Everyday Life*. Princeton, NJ: Princeton University Press, 1997.

Gluck, Carol. *Japan's Modern Myths: Ideology in the Late Meiji Period*. Princeton, NJ: Princeton University Press, 1985.

Go Seigen 呉清源. "Yonaoshi go" 世直し碁. *Chūō Kōron* (October 1948): 35–38.

____. *Go Seigen kaisō roku: Ibun kaiyū* 呉清源回想録―以文会友. Tokyo: Hakusuisha, 1984.

Guttmann, Allen, and Lee Thompson. *Japanese Sports: A History*. Honolulu: University of Hawai'i Press, 2001.

Hall, Stuart, ed. *Representation: Cultural Representations and Signifying Practices*. London: Sage Publications, 1997.

Hardacre, Helen. *Kurozumikyō and the New Religions*. Princeton, NJ: Princeton University Press, 1986.

____. *Shintō and the State 1868–1988*. Princeton, NJ: Princeton University Press, 1989.

____. "Asano Wasaburō and Japanese Spiritualism in early Twentieth-Century Japan." In *Japan's Competing Modernities: Issues in Culture and Democracy, 1900–1930*, Sharon A. Minichiello, ed., 133–53. Honolulu: University of Hawai'i Press, 1998.

____. "The Postwar Development of Studies of Japanese Religions." In *The Postwar Development of Japanese Studies in the United States*, 195–226. Helen Hardacre, ed. Leiden: Brill, 1998.

____. "After Aum: Religion and Civil Society in Japan." In *The State of Civil Society in Japan*, Frank J. Schwartz and Susan J. Pharr, eds., 135–53. Cambridge: Cambridge University Press, 2003.

_____. "State and Religion in Japan." In *Nanzan Guide to Japanese Religions*, Paul Swanson and Clark Chilson, eds., 274–288.

_____. "Aum Shinrikyō and the Japanese Media: The Pied Piper Meets the Lamb of God." *History of Religions* 47/2 (2007): 171–204.

Hayashi Makoto. "Religion in the Modern Period." In *Nanzan Guide to Japanese Religions*, Paul Swanson and Clark Chilson, eds., 202–219.

Hioki Shōichi 日置昌一. "Jikōson to Makkāsā gensui no monogatari" 璽光尊とマッカーサー元帥の物語. *Bungei Shunjū* (October 1952): 182–93.

Hirano Naoko 平野直子. "Shinbun, zasshi kiji ni okeru 'shinshūkyō' gensetsu no hassei to tenkai" 新聞・雑誌記事における(新宗教)言説の発生と展開. *Shakaigaku nenpō* 47 (2006): 85–99.

Hoover, Stewart M. "Introduction: The Cultural Construction of Religion in the Media Age." In *Practicing Religion in the Age of the Media: Explorations in Media, Religion, and Culture*, Stewart M. Hoover and Lynn Schofield Clark, eds., 1–6. New York: Columbia University Press, 2002.

Huffman James L. *Creating a Public: People and Press in Meiji Japan.* Honolulu: University of Hawai'i Press, 1997.

Ikado Fujio. "Trends and Problems of New Religions: Religion in Urban Society." *Journal of Asian and African Studies* 3 (1968): 101–117.

Ikegami Yoshimi. "Local Newspaper Coverage of Folk Shamans in Aomori Prefecture." In *Folk Beliefs in Modern Japan*, ed. Inoue Nobutaka, trans. Norman Havens, 9–91. Tokyo: Institute for Japanese Culture and Classics, Kokugakuin University, 1994.

Inoue Nobutaka 井上順孝. "Masukomi to shinshūkyō" マスコミと新宗教. In *Shinshūkyō jiten* 新宗教事典, Inoue Nobutaka et al., 516–59. Tokyo: Kōbundō, 1994.

_____. *Shinshūkyō no kaidoku* 新宗教の解読. Tokyo: Chikuma Gakugei Bunko, 1996.

_____. *Japanese College Students' Attitudes Towards Religion: An Analysis of Questionnaire Surveys from 1992 to 2001.* Tokyo: Kokugakuin University, 2003.

Inoue Nobutaka, ed. *New Religions: Contemporary Papers in Japanese Religion 2*. Tokyo: Kokugakuin University, 1991.

Inoue Nobutaka et al., eds. *Shinshūkyō jiten* 新宗教事典. Tokyo: Kōbundō, 1994. (Reduced-size edition)

Inui Takashi 乾孝. *Nihon wa kurutteru: Sengo ijōshinri no bunseki* 日本は狂ってる―戦後異常心理の分析. Tokyo: Dōkōsha Isobe Shobō, 1953.

Ishii Daizō 石井代蔵. *Kyojin no shōzō: Futabayama to Rikidōzan* 巨人の肖像―双葉山と力道山. Tokyo: Kōdansha, 1980.

Josephson, Jason Ānanda. "When Buddhism Became a 'Religion': Religion and Superstition in the Writings of Inoue Enryō." *Japanese Journal of Religious Studies* 33/1 (2006): 143–68.

Kaminogō Toshiaki 上之郷利昭. *Kyōso tanjō* 教祖誕生. Tokyo: Shinchōsha, 1987.

Kangaku Ryō 勸學 寮, ed. *Shinkō shūkyō kaisetsu* 新興宗教解説. Kyoto: Hyakkaen, 1952.

Kasza, Gregory J. *The State and the Mass Media in Japan 1918–1945.* Berkeley: University of California Press, 1988.

Katsuki Tokujirō 勝木德次朗. Jiu to Futabayama no kankei (1–3) 璽宇と双葉山の関係. Unpublished manuscript, 1970.

Kawamoto Saburō 川本三郎. "Ōya Sōichi" 大宅壯一. In *Koramu de hihan suru* コラムで批判する, 245–69. Tokyo: Kōdansha, 1985.

Ketelaar, James E. *Of Heretics and Martyrs in Meiji Japan: Buddhism and its Persecution.* Princeton, NJ: Princeton University Press, 1993.

Kikaku Henshū Hanuman 企画編集ハヌマン, ed. *Supāsutā densetsu: Shōwa no daiyokozuna, Futabayama Sadaji to Usa* スーパースター伝説―昭和の大横綱、双葉山定次と宇佐. Usa, Ōita Prefecture: Sanwa Bunko, 2003.

Kishi Nobusuke 岸 信介. "Gendaijin ni fukaketsuna shinri o toku" 現代人に不可欠な真理を説く. *Fēsu* (April 1965): 32.

Kishimoto Hideo 岸本英夫, ed. *Sengo no shūkyō to shakai* 戦後の宗教と社会. Tokyo: Keiseisha, 1976.

Kitagawa, Joseph M. *On Understanding Japanese Religion.* Princeton, NJ: Princeton University Press, 1987.

———. *Religion in Japanese History.* New York: Columbia University Press, 1990.

Kitamura Sayo. "Tenshō Kōtai Jingū-Kyō (1)." *Contemporary Religions of Japan* 2/3 (1961): 26–42.

Kurihara Akira. "The Emperor System as Japanese National Religion: The Emperor System Module in Everyday Consciousness." *Japanese Journal of Religious Studies* 17/2–3 (1990): 315–40.

Kokusai Shūkyō Kenkyūjo 国際宗教研究所, ed. *Gendai shūkyō, tokushū: Media ga umidasu kamigami* 現代宗教「特集」、メディアが生み出す神々. Tokyo: Akiyama Shoten, 2008.

Kurzman, Dan. *Kishi and Japan: The Search for the Sun.* New York: Ivan Obolensky, Inc., 1960.

Marshall, David P. *Celebrity and Power: Fame in Contemporary Culture.* Minneapolis/London: University of Minnesota Press, 1997.

———. "Introduction to part one." In *The Celebrity Culture Reader*, ed. David P. Marshall, 19–20. New York: Routledge, 2006.

Masunaga Reihō 増永霊鳳. "Shinkō shūkyō no dōkō to sono hihan" 新興宗教の動向とその批判. In *Shinkō shūkyō no kaibō* 新興宗教の解剖, Nakanō Kyōtoku 中濃教篤, ed., 11–29. Tokyo: Tōsei Shuppansha, 1954.

Matsuura Sōzō 松浦総三. "Ōya Sōichi: Ippon no pen o buki ni Shōwa no sesō o nadegirishite jūō mujin" 大宅壮一: 一本のペンを武器に昭和の世相をナデ斬りして縦横無尽. In *Jinbutsu Shōwa shi 4: Masu komi no kishu* 人物昭和史―マスコミの旗手, 119–54. Tokyo: Chikuma Shobō, 1978.

McCloud, Sean. *Making the American Religious Fringe: Subversives and Journalists, 1955–1993.* Chapel Hill, NC: University of North Carolina Press, 2004.

McFarland, H. Neill. "The New Religions of Japan." *Contemporary Religions of Japan* 1/2: 35–47; 1/3: 30–39; 1/4 (1960): 57–69.

____. *The Rush Hour of the Gods: A Study of the New Religious Movements in Japan.* New York: Harper Colophon, 1970. (First published 1967).

Minami Hiroshi 南博. "Naze jakyō wa ryūkō suru ka" なぜ邪教は流行するか. *Mainichi jōhō,* January 1950.

Mitchell, Richard H. *Censorship in Imperial Japan.* Princeton, NJ: Princeton University Press, 1983.

Miyata Noboru 宮田登. *Shūmatsukan no minzokugaku* 終末観の民俗学. Tokyo: Chikuma Gakugei Bunko, 1998.

Miyazaki Fumiko. "The Formation of Emperor Worship in the New Religions: The Case of Fujidō." *Japanese Journal of Religious Studies* 17/2–3 (1990): 281–314.

Miyoshi Tōru 三好徹. "Sengo jinbutsu shi: Kitamura Sayo" 戦後人物史―北村サヨ. *Ōru Yomimono* (undated): 240–54.

Monbu Daijin Kanbō Shūmuka 文部大臣官房宗務課. "Jikōson shisatsu hōkoku" 璽光尊視察報告. *Monbudaijin kanbō shūmuka tokubetsu chōsa shiryō* 1, 1950.

Mori Hidehito 森秀人. "Sengo shūkyōjin retsu den: Jiu, Jikōson" 戦後宗教人列伝―璽宇、璽光尊. *Shinpyō,* September 1978: 23–46.

Morioka Kiyomi. "Attacks on the New Religions: Risshō Kōseikai and the 'Yomiuri affair'." *Japanese Journal of Religious Studies* 21/2–3 (1994): 281–310.

Morris-Suzuki, Tessa. "Europe in the Making of Japanese Values." *European Review* 6/1 (1998): 63–74.

Mullins, Mark R. "Ideology and Utopianism in Wartime Japan: An Essay on the Subversiveness of Christian Eschatology." *Japanese Journal of Religious Studies* 21/2–3 (1994): 261–80.

Murakami Naoyuki 村上直之. *Kindai jānarizumu no tanjō: Igirisu hanzai hōdō no shakaishi kara* 近代ジャーナリズムの誕生―イギリス犯罪報道の社会史から. Tokyo: Iwanami Shoten, 1995.

———. "Gendai jānarizumu to shūkyō zōo" 現代ジャーナリズムと宗教憎悪. *Seikyō Shinbun* 14 February 1998.

———. "Sengo Nihon no shūkyō hōdō o kenshō suru" 戦後日本の宗教報道を検証する. *Seikyō Shinbun* 13 March 1999.

———. "Genzekyō toshite no masu media" 現世教としてのマスメディア. In *Nijūisseiki no Nihon to shūkyō* 21世紀の日本と宗教. Tokyo: Daisan Bunmeisha, 2000.

———. "Taidan: *Goshippu to shūbun* o megutte" 対談―『ゴシップと醜聞』をめぐって [Dialogue with Tamaki Akira]. <http://murakaminaoyuki. blog7.fc2.com/blog-date-200105.html>; dated 5 May 2001. Accessed 29 July 2009.

———. "Taidan: Shūkyō hōdō no shakai gaku o megutte" 対談―宗教報道の社会学を巡って [Dialogue with Nomura Kazuo 野村一夫]. < http:// murakaminaoyuki.blog7.fc2.com/blog-date-200005.html>; dated 30 May 2000.

Murakami Shigeyoshi 村上重良. *Kindai minshū shūkyōshi no kenkyū* 近代民衆宗教史の研究. Kyoto: Hōzōkan, 1958.

———. "Shinkō shūkyō to kisei shūkyō" 新興宗教と既成宗教. In *Gendai Nihon shūkyō hihan* 現代日本宗教批判, Yanagida Kenjūrō 柳田謙十郎 and Saki Akio 佐木秋夫, eds., 105–24. Tokyo: Sōbunsha, 1967.

———. *Japanese Religion in the Modern Century*. H. Byron Earhart, trans. Tokyo: University of Tokyo Press, 1980.

———. *Shūkyō no Shōwa shi* 宗教の昭和史. Tokyo: Sanrei Shobō, 1985.

Myōgan Gaijirō 明翫外次郎. "Jikōson, Futabayama kenkyo jiken no supai" 璽光尊／双葉山検挙事件のスパイ. *Bungei Shunjū*, April 1957: 78–85.

Nakamura Naofumi 中村直文. *Yasukuni: Shirarezaru senryōka no kōbō* 靖国―知られざる占領下の攻防. Tokyo: NHK Shuppan, 2007.

Nakano Tsuyoshi 中野毅. "America no tai-Nichi shūkyō seisaku no keisei" アメリカの対日宗教政策の形成. In *Senryō to Nihon shūkyō* 占領と日本宗教, Ikado Fujio 井門富二夫, ed., 27–72. Tokyo: Miraisha, 1993.

———. "Religion and State." In *Religion in Japanese Culture: Where Living Traditions Meet a Changing World*, Tamaru Noriyoshi and David Reid, eds., 115–36. New York: Kodansha International, 1996.

Nakatani, Yoji. "The Birth of Criminology in Japan." In *Criminals and their Scientists: The History of Criminology in International Perspective*, Peter Becker and Richard F. Wetzell, eds., 281–98. New York: Cambridge University Press, 2006.

Nichols, Walter. "Nihon no shinkō shūkyō" 日本の新興宗教. *Shūkyō kōron* 20/8 (1950): 2–7.

Nishiyama Shigeru and Fujii Takeshi. "The Propagation and Spread of Tenshō Kōtai Jingū Kyō within Japanese-American Society on Hawaii Island." In *New Religions: Contemporary Papers in Japanese Religion* 2, Inoue Nobutaka, ed., Norman Havens, trans., 125–61. Tokyo: Kokugakuin University, 1991.

Nomura Kazuo 野村一夫. "Nijū kijun o hoshu suru masu komi no mondaisei: Uchi to soto o kubetsu suru media no kyōdōtai ishiki" 二重基準を保守するマスコミの問題性―ウチとソトを区別するメディアの共同体意識. *Seikyō Shinbun* 22 February 2000.

____. "Ichimai iwa no soshiki" to iu gensō: 'Shinjiru hitobito' to no deai no nai media" "一枚岩の組織"という幻想―「信じる人びと」との出会いのないメディア. *Seikyō Shinbun* 28 March 2000.

____. "Sukyandaru no sōzō to dentō no saisōzō: Kokumin kokka ga hitsuyō toshita shinshūkyō to iu 'tasha'" スキャンダルの創造と伝統の再創造―国民国家が必要とした新宗教という〈他者〉. *Seikyō Shinbun* 26 April 2000.

____. "'Kamigami no rasshu awā' toshite hajimatta sengo: Engekironteki ni monogatari o kōchiku suru media" 「神々のラッシュアワー」として始まった戦後―演劇論的に物語を構築するメディア. *Seikyō Shinbun* 23 May 2000.

____. "Minzoku shūkyō toshite no kenkōshugi: Masukomi ga shusai suru shintai kanri 'shinkō'" 民俗宗教としての健康主義―マスコミが主宰する身体管理"信仰". *Seikyō Shinbun* 27 June 2000.

O'Brien, David M. *To Dream of Dreams: Religious Freedom and Constitutional Politics in Postwar Japan.* Honolulu: University of Hawai'i Press, 1996.

Ōishi Shūten 大石秀典. Review of *Nihon no Shinkō Shūkyō* ("The Newly Established Religions of Japan") by Hiroo Takagi." *Contemporary Religions in Japan* 1 & 2 (1960): 59–63.

____. "A Review Article: The New Religious Sects of Japan." *Contemporary Religions in Japan* 5/1 (1964): 45–80.

____. "Senryōki to shinshūkyō" 占領期と新宗教. In *Senryō to Nihon shūkyō* 占領と日本宗教, Ikado Fujio, ed., 471–95. Tokyo: Miraisha, 1993.

Oku Takenori 奥 武則. *Renmonkyō suibō shi* 蓮門教衰亡史. Tokyo: Gendai Kikakushitsu, 1988.

____. *Sukyandaru no Meiji: Kokumin o tsukuru tame no ressun* スキャンダルの明治―国民を創るためのレッスン. Tokyo: Chikuma Shinsho, 1997.

Ōkuma Hideo 大隈秀夫. *Hadaka no Ōya Sōichi: Masukomi no teiō* 裸の大宅壮一―マスコミの帝王. Tokyo: Sanseidō, 1996.

Ono Yasuhiro 小野泰博. "Tenshō Kōtai Jingū Kyō: Odoru shūkyō to dozokusei" 天照皇大神宮教—踊る宗教と土俗性. In *Shinshūkyō no sekai* 5 新宗教の世界 5, Shimizu Masato 清水雅人 ed., 168–201. Tokyo: Daizō Shuppan, 1978.

Ōya Sōichi 大宅壮一. "Meiji, Taishō, Shōwa shinkō shūkyō no zensen" 明治、大正、昭和の新興宗教の前線. In *Shinkō shūkyō* 新興宗教, Nakanishi Kiyoshi 中西潔. ed., 1–23. Tokyo: Gīpusha, 1950.

——. *Ōya Sōichi zenshū* 4 大宅壮一全集 4. Tokyo: Sōyōsha, 1975.

Panauēbu to Tama-chan o Kangaeru Kai パナウェーブとタマちゃんを考える会. *Panauēbu Shiroshōzoku no nazo to ronri* パナウェーブ白装束の謎と論理. Tokyo: Kosumikku Intānashonaru, 2003.

Payne, Tom. *Fame: What the Classics Tell Us about Our Cult of Celebrity.* New York: Picador, 2010.

Pharr, Susan. "Introduction: Media and Politics in Japan: Historical and Contemporary Perspectives." In *Media and Politics in Japan*, Susan Pharr and Ellis Krauss, eds., 3–17. Honolulu: University of Hawai'i Press, 1996.

Pierson, John. *Tokutomi Sohō, 1863–1957: A Journalist for Modern Japan.* Princeton, NJ: Princeton University Press, 1980.

Prothero, Stephen. *American Jesus: How the Son of God Became a National Icon.* New York: Farrar, Straus and Giroux, 2003.

Reader, Ian. *Religious Violence in Contemporary Japan: The Case of Aum Shinrikyō.* Nordic Institute of Asian Studies Monograph Series, No. 82. Richmond, VA: Curzon Press, 2000.

——. "Scholarship, Aum Shinrikyō and Integrity." *Nova Religio* 3/2 (2000): 368–82.

——. "Consensus Shattered: Japanese Paradigm Shifts and Moral Panic in the Post-Aum Era." *Nova Religio* 4/2 (2001): 225–34.

——. "Positively Promoting Pilgrimage: Media Representations of Pilgrimage in Japan." *Nova Religio* 10/3 (2007): 13–31.

Reader, Ian, and George J. Tanabe. *Practically Religious: Worldly Benefits and the Common Religion of Japan.* Honolulu: University of Hawai'i Press, 1998.

Rojek, Chris. *Celebrity.* London: Reaktion Books, 2001.

Said, Edward W. *Covering Islam: How the Media and the Experts Determine How We See the Rest of the World.* New York: Vintage Books, 1997.

Sakamoto Koremaru 阪本是丸. "Shūkyō dantaihō no zengo" 宗教団体法の前後. In *Shinshūkyō jiten* 新宗教事典, Inoue Nobutaka et al., 477–84. Tokyo: Kōbundō, 1994.(Reduced-size edition).

Sanada Takaaki. "After Prophecy Fails: a Reappraisal of a Japanese Case." *Japanese Journal of Religious Studies* 6/ 1–2 (1979): 217–37.

Saki Akio 佐木秋夫, Inui Takashi 乾 孝, Oguchi Iichi 小口偉一, Matsushima Eiichi 松島栄一. *Kyōso: Shomin no kamigami* 教祖―庶民の神々. Tokyo: Aoki Shoten, 1955.

Satō Takumi 佐藤卓己. *Gendai media shi* 現代メディア史. Tokyo: Iwanami Shoten, 1998.

Sato Tatsuya. "Rises and Falls of Clinical Psychology in Japan: A Perspective on the Status of Japanese Clinical Psychology." *Ritsumeikan ningen kagaku kenkyū* 13 (2007): 133–44.

Sawada, Janine Tasca. *Practical Pursuits: Religion, Politics, and Personal Cultivation in Nineteenth-Century Japan.* Honolulu: University of Hawai'i Press, 2004.

Schattschneider, Ellen. *Immortal Wishes: Labor and Transcendence on a Japanese Sacred Mountain.* Durham, NC: Duke University Press, 2003.

Schechter, Danny. *Falun Gong's Challenge to China: Spiritual Practice or "Evil Cult."* New York: Akashic Books, 2001.

Schickel, Richard. *Intimate Strangers: The Culture of Celebrity in America.* Chicago: Ivan R. Dee, Publisher, 2000. (First published 1985).

Schiffer, Wilhelm. "New Religions in Postwar Japan." *Monumenta Nipponica* 11 (1955): 1–14.

Sharf, Robert. "The Zen of Japanese Nationalism." *History of Religions* 33/1 (1993): 1–43.

Shimada Hiromi 島田裕巳. "Media to no kakawari" メディアとの関わり. In *Shinshūkyō jidai* 5 新宗教時代 5, Shimazono Susumu et al., eds., 211–59. Tokyo: Daizō Shuppansha, 1996.

———. "Shinshūkyō hihan no rekishiteki hensen: Tenrikyō, Sōka Gakkai, Oumu Shinrikyō o jirei ni" 新宗教批判の歴史的変遷―天理教、創価学会、オウム真理教を事例に. *Shūkyō Kenkyū* 357 (2008): 71–94.

Shimazono Susumu 島薗 進 "Kyōso to shūkyōteki shidōsha: Sūhai no kenkyū kadai" 教祖と宗教的指導者―崇拝の研究課題. In *Kyōso to sono shūhen* 教祖とその周辺, Shūkyō shakaigaku kenkyūkai 宗教社会学研究会, eds., 11–35. Tokyo: Yūzankaku Shuppan, 1987.

Shinshūren Chōsa Shitsu 新宗連調査室, eds. *Sengo shūkyō kaisō roku* 戦後宗教回想録. Tokyo: PL Kyōdan, 1963.

Shūkyō Shakaigaku Kenkyūkai Henshū Iinkai 宗教社会学研究会編集委員会, ed. *Kyōso to sono shūhen* 教祖とその周辺. Tokyo: Yūzankaku, 1987.

Shūmu jihō 宗務時報. "Zadankai: Shūsen chokugo no shūmu gyōsei" 座談会―終戦直後の宗務行政. Vol. 65 (1984): 1–36.

Sodei Rinjirō. *Dear General MacArthur: Letters from the Japanese during the American Occupation.* Lanham, MD: Rowman & Littlefield Publishers, Inc., 2006.

Spaulding, Robert M. "CCD Censorship of Japan's Daily Press." In *The Occupation of Japan: Arts and Culture. The Proceedings of the Sixth Symposium.* Thomas Burkman, ed., 1–16. Norfolk, VA: The General Douglas MacArthur Foundation, MacArthur Square, 1984.

Stalker, Nancy K. *Prophet Motive: Deguchi Onisaburō, Oomoto, and the Rise of New Religions in Imperial Japan.* Honolulu: University of Hawai'i Press, 2008.

Sugata Masaaki 菅田正昭. *Nihon shūkyō no sengo shi* 日本宗教の戦後史. Tokyo: Sankōsha, 1996.

Swanson, Paul L., and Clark Chilson, eds. *Nanzan Guide to Japanese Religions.* Honolulu: University of Hawai'i Press, 2006.

Taiyō 太陽. "Zadankai: Kyōso sama wa jō kigen" 座談会—教祖様は上きげん. No. 15 (September 1964): 145–48.

Takagi Hiroo 高木宏夫. "Sengo ni okeru shinkō shūkyō no dōkō" 戦後における新興宗教の動向. *Shūmu jihō* 宗務時報 9 (1957): 1–13.

____. *Shinkō shūkyō: Taishū shisō undō no rekishi to ronri* 新興宗教—大衆思想運動の歴史と論理. Tokyo: Iwanami Shinsho, 1959.

Takeda Dōshō. "The Fall of Renmonkyō, and its Place in the History of Meiji-period Religions." In *New Religions: Contemporary Papers in Japanese Religion* 2, Inoue Nobutaka, ed., Norman Havens, trans., 25–57. Tokyo: Kokugakuin University, 1991.

Takemae Eiji. *The Allied Occupation of Japan.* New York: Continuum, 2002.

Takezawa Shōichirō 竹沢尚一郎. "Kyōdō tai no keisei to karisuma no keishō: Tenshō Kōtai Jingū Kyō" 共同体の形成とカリスマの継承—天照皇大神宮教. In *Nishi Nihon no shin shūkyō undō no hikaku kenkyū* 1 西日本の新宗教運動の比較研究 1. Sakai Nobuo 坂井信生, ed., 5–33. Kyūshū Daigaku Bungakubu Shūkyōgaku Kenkyūshitsu, 1993.

Taki Taizō 滝泰三. *Kamigami tabō: Shinshūkyō kyōso retsuden* 神々多忙—新宗教教祖列伝. Tokyo: Shin'yūkan Shinbunsha, 1956.

Tamaki Akira 玉木明 *Goshippu to shūbun: Sanmen kiji no kenkyū* ゴシップと醜聞—三面記事の研究. Tokyo: Yōsensha, 2001.

Tenshō Kōtai Jingū Kyō. *The Prophet of Tabuse.* Tabuse-machi, Yamaguchi: Tenshō Kōtai Jingū Kyō, 1954.

____. "Ōgamisama: Ōya Sōichi ni go-seppō" 大神様—大宅壮一にご説法. *Wabun Tensei* 和文天声 31 (1956): 10–14.

_____. *Seisho* 生書 1&2. Tabuse-machi, Yamaguchi Prefecture: Tenshō Kōtai Jingū Kyō, 1970.

_____. *Divine Manifestation: Ogamisama's Life and Teaching*. Tabuse-machi, Yamaguchi Prefecture: Tenshō Kōtai Jingū Kyō, 1970.

_____. *Ōgamisama* 大神様. Promotional videotape, Tenshō Kōtai Jingū Kyō, dir., 1970.

Terebi Asahi テレビ朝日. *Asa made nama terebi: Gekiron! Shūkyō to wakamono* 朝まで生テレビ―激論! 宗教と若者. Television program, Asahi Television, broadcast 28 September 1991.

Thomsen, Harry. *The New Religions of Japan*. Tokyo: Charles E. Tuttle Co., 1963.

Tian Zhuangzhuang 田壮壮, dir. *Go Seigen: Kiwami no kifu* 呉清源―極みの棋譜 (English title: *The Go Master*), 2006.

Tipton, Elise. *The Japanese Police State: Tokko in Interwar Japan*. Sydney: Allen & Unwin, 1990.

Tokugawa Musei 徳川夢声. "Hara ni kamisama ga yadoru odoru kyōso: Kitamura Sayo" 肚に神様が宿る踊る教祖―北村さよ. In *Tokugawa Musei no mondō yūyō* 徳川夢声の問答有用, 199–217. Asahi Bunko. Tokyo, 1986. (originally published in *Shūkan Asahi* 1956.3.11, Mondō Yūyō 256)

Tsujimura Shinobu. "Religious Issues in Japan: Religion in a Consumer Society—In the Shadow of Spirituality." *Bulletin of the Nanzan Institute for Religion and Culture* 32 (2008): 40–54.

Tsushima Michihito 対馬路人. "Emperor and World Renewal in the New Religions: The Case of Shinsei Ryūjinkai." In *New Religions: Contemporary Papers in Japanese Religion* 2, Inoue Nobutaka, ed., Norman Havens, trans., 58–92. Tokyo: Kokugakuin University, 1991.

_____. "Haisen to yonaoshi: Jiu no sennen ōkoku shisō to undō 1" 敗戦と世直し―聖字の千年王国思想と運動 1. *Kansei Gakuin Daigaku shakaigakubu kiyō* 63 (1991): 337–71.

_____. "Haisen to yonaoshi: Jiu no sennen ōkoku shisō to undō 2" 敗戦と世直し―聖字の千年王国思想と運動 2. *Kansei Gakuin Daigaku shakaigakubu kiyō* 87 (2000): 153–65.

Turner, Graeme. *Understanding Celebrity*. London: SAGE Publications, 2004.

Turner, Graeme, Frances Bonner, and P. David Marshall. *Fame Games: The Production of Celebrity in Australia*. Melbourne: Cambridge University Press, 2000.

Umehara Masaki 梅原正紀. "Jiu: Aru tennō shugi sha no higeki" 璽宇—あ る天皇主義者の悲劇. In *Shinshūkyō no sekai* 新宗教の世界 4, 147–86. Tokyo: Daizō Shuppansha, 1978.

Union of the New Religious Organizations in Japan, Research Office, ed. "Reminiscences of Religion in Postwar Japan" in *Contemporary Religions of Japan* 6/2 (June 1965): 111–203; 6/3 (September 1965): 295–314; 6/4 (December 1965): 382–402; 7/1 (March 1966): 51–79; 7/2 (June 1966): 166–87; 7/3 (September 1966): 217–73. [This is an English translation of Shinshūren Chōsa Shitsu (eds.) above].

Van Driel, Barend, and James T. Richardson. "Print Media Coverage of New Religious Movements: A Longitudinal Study." *Journal of Communication* 38 (1988): 37–61.

Watanabe Manabu. "Reactions to the Aum Affair: The Rise of the 'Anti-cult' Movement in Japan." *Bulletin of the Nanzan Institute for Religion and Culture* 21 (1997): 32–48.

Weber, Max. "The Nature of Charismatic Authority and its Routiniza-tion." In *On Charisma and Institution Building*, S. N. Eisenstadt, ed. Chicago, IL: University of Chicago Press, 1968.

Wessinger, Catherine. *How the Millenium Comes Violently: From Jones-town to Heaven's Gate*. New York: Seven Bridges Press, 2000.

Wong, John, and William T. Lui. *The Mystery of China's Falun Gong: Its Rise and Its Sociological Implications*. Singapore: World Scientific Press & Singapore University Press, 1999.

Woodard, William P. *The Allied Occupation of Japan 1945–1952 and Japa-nese Religions*. Leiden: E. J. Brill, 1972.

Wright, Stuart A. "Media Coverage of Unconventional Religion: Any 'Good News' for Minority Faiths?" *Review of Religious Research* 39/2 (1997): 101–115.

Yagi Yasuo 八木康夫, prod. *Iesu no hakobune* イエスの方舟. TBS, 1985.

_____. *Settoku: Ehoba no shōnin to yūketsukyohi jiken* 説得—エホバの証人と輸血拒否事件. TBS, 1993.

Yamaguchi Hiroshi 山口広, Nakamura Shūji 中村周而, Hirata Hiroshi 平田広志, and Kitō Masaki 紀藤正樹. *Karuto shūkyō no toraburu tai-saku: Nihon to ōbei no jitsujō to torikumi* カルト宗教のトラブル対策—日本と欧米の実情と取り組み. Tokyo: Kyōiku Shiryō Shuppankai, 2000.

Yamamoto Taketoshi 山本武利. *Shinbun kisha no tanjō: Nihon no media o tsukutta hitobito* 新聞記者の誕生—日本のメディアを作った人々. Tokyo: Shin'yōsha, 1991.

_____. *Senryōki media bunseki* 占領期メディア分析. Tokyo: Rissei Daigaku Shuppan Kyoku, 1996.

Yasumaru Yoshio 安丸良夫. *Nihon no kindaika to minshū shisō* 日本の近代化と民衆思想. Tokyo: Aoki Shoten, 1982. (First published 1974).

———. *Deguchi Nao* 出口なお. Tokyo: Asahi Shinbunsha, 1987. (First published 1977).

———. *Bunmeika no keiken: Kindai tenkanki no Nihon* 文明化の経験—近代転換期の日本. Tokyo: Iwanami Shoten, 2007.

Yoshida Naoya 吉田直哉. *Eizō to wa nan darō ka: Terebi seisakusha no chōsen* 映像とは何だろうか—テレビ制作者の挑戦. Tokyo: Iwanami Shoten, 2003.

Yoshioka Yoshitoyo 吉岡義豊. *Gendai Chūgoku no sho shūkyō: Minshū shūkyō no keifu* 現代中国の諸宗教—民衆宗教の系譜. Ajia Bukkyōshi Chūgoku, ed. Tokyo: Kōsei Shuppan, 1974.

Young Richard F. "From Gokyō-dōgen to Bankyō-dōkon: A study in the self-universalization of Ōmoto." *Japanese Journal of Religious Studies* 15/4 (1988): 263–86.

Index

Page numbers in bold type refer to images.